Chika.

~~Moole~~

22/09/2009

STUDIES IN HIGHER EDUCATION

Edited by
Philip G. Altbach
Monan Professor of Higher Education
Lynch School of Education, Boston College

A ROUTLEDGE SERIES

STUDIES IN HIGHER EDUCATION

PHILIP G. ALTBACH, *General Editor*

Democratizing Higher Education Policy

Constraints of Reform in Post-Apartheid South Africa

Molatlhegi Trevor Chika Sehoole

Routledge
New York & London

Published in 2005 by
Routledge
Taylor & Francis Group
270 Madison Avenue
New York, NY 10016

Published in Great Britain by
Routledge
Taylor & Francis Group
2 Park Square
Milton Park, Abingdon
Oxon OX14 4RN

© 2005 by Taylor & Francis Group, LLC
Routledge is an imprint of Taylor & Francis Group.

Transferred to Digital Printing 2008

International Standard Book Number-10: 0-415-97445-3 (Hardcover)
International Standard Book Number-13: 978-0-415-97445-5 (Hardcover)
Library of Congress Card Number 2005005709

Library of Congress Cataloging-In-Publication Data

Sehoole, Molatlhegi Trevor Chika.
    Democratizing higher education policy : constraints of reform in
post-apartheid South Africa / Molatlhegi Trevor Chika Sehoole.-- 1st ed.
      p. cm. -- (Studies in higher education)
    Includes bibliographical references and index.
    ISBN 0-415-97445-3
    1. Higher education and state--South Africa. 2. Educational
change--South Africa. 3. Democracy--South Africa. I. Title.
    II. Series: Studies in higher education, dissertation series.

LC180.S6S45 2005
378.68--dc22
                                                                2005005709

Taylor & Francis
Taylor & Francis Group

LONDON AND NEW YORK
Taylor & Francis Group
is the Academic Division of T&F Informa plc.

Visit the Taylor & Francis Web site at
http://www.taylorandfrancis.com

and the Routledge Web site at
http://www.routledge-ny.com

*This book is dedicated to my son, "Doctor" Masego Sehoole,
whose fond memories kept me going and
sane during the writing process.*

Contents

Acronyms

ANC	African National Congress
AUT	Advisory Council on Universities and Technikons
AZAPO	Azanian People's Organisation
BTF	Broad Transformation Forums
CEPD	Centre for Education Policy Development
CHE	Council on Higher Education
CHEPS	Centre for Higher Education Policy Studies
CHET	Centre for Higher Education Transformation
CNE	Christian National Education
CODESA	Convention for a Democratic South Africa
COSATU	Congress of South African Trade Unions
COTEP	Committee on Teacher Education Policy
CTM	Committee for Tutorial Matters
CTP	Committee of Technikon Principals
CUMSA	Curriculum Model for Education in South Africa
CUP	Committee of University Principals
DEP	Department of Economic Policy
DET	Department of Education and Training
DNE	Department of National Education
DOE	Department of Education
EPU	Education Policy Unit
ERS	Education Renewal Strategy
FETT	Further Education Task Team
GEAR	Growth, Employment and Redistribution
GNU	Government of National Unity
HAIs	Historically Advantaged Institutions
HBUs	Historically Black Universities
HDIs	Historically Disadvantaged Institutions
HEC	Higher Education Council

HEF	Higher Education Forum
HETT	Higher Education Task Team
HSRC	Human Sciences Research Council
HWIs	Historically White Institutions
HWUs	Historically White Universities
IFP	Inkatha Freedom Party
IPET	Implementation Plan for Education and Training
MDM	Mass Democratic Movement
MEC	Member of Executive Council
MERG	Macroeconomic Research Group
MTEF	Medium Term Expenditure Framework
NCHE	National Commission on Higher Education
NECC	National Education Coordinating Committee
NEDLAC	National Economic Development and Labour Council
NEPI	National Education Policy Investigation
NGO	Non-Government Organization
NP	National Party
NQF	National Qualifications Framework
NRF	National Research Foundation
NSFAS	National Student Financial Aid Scheme
NTC	National Transformation Commission
NUSAS	National Union of South African Students
NWG	National Working Group
PAC	Pan-Africanist Congress
PASO	Pan-Africanist Students Organisation
RDP	Reconstruction and Development Programme
RTI	Research Triangle Institute
SABC	South African Broadcasting Corporation
SACP	South African Communist Party
SADTU	South African Democratic Teachers' Union
SANCO	South African National Civics Organisation
SANSCO	South African National Student Congress
SAQA	South African Qualifications Authority
SASCO	South African Students' Congress
SAUVCA	South African Universities Vice-Chancellors Association
SMT	Strategic Management Team
SRC	Student Representative Council
TBVC	Transkei, Bophuthatswana, Venda and Ciskei
UDUSA	Union of Democratic University Staff Associations

UNESCO	United Nations Educational, Scientific and Cultural Organization
USAID	United States Agency for International Development
USIS	United States Information Services

Foreword

This is an excellent book marked by the clarity of its narrative and the strength of its argument. The book presents a strong narrative about the ways in which post-apartheid educational authorities in South Africa sought to develop a more democratic educational alternative out of the ruins of the inherently unjust apartheid system. It opens with an account of apartheid's higher educational policy culture, both in historical terms and in terms of the manner in which it was experienced by the author. This personal account helps to situate the policy challenges, dilemmas and hard choices faced by the reformers. Indeed, the idea of dilemmas presents itself as a pivotal notion in the analysis of the wide ranging empirical data reported in the book, with a diverse set of theoretical resources based on recent policy literature. So for example, the book shows some of the dilemmas encountered in attempts to tame the apartheid bureaucracy and get it to embrace democratic aspirations, only to find the established bureaucratic culture to be much robust, stubborn and intransigent. Similarly, the compact developed between the ANC and the National Party in 1994 created a set of political conditions in which democratic reforms proved extremely difficult to implement. Forces of globalization from outside the country and the impact of the neo-liberal macro-economic policy that was adopted by the new government also served to dilute reforms and slow down the pace of change. In the end, a policy culture emerged in South Africa in which administrative reforms were constantly resisted and democratic aspirations sometimes compromised. In my assessment, Sehoole tells this narrative with a great deal of passion and commitment to the causes of democracy, in a language that is remarkable for its clarity and accessibility. I have no doubt that this book will be widely read not only in South Africa but also by any one interested in the fate of democratic reforms in higher education in the age of seemingly unstoppable corporatization and marketization of universities everywhere.

Fazal Rizvi
Professor of Educational Policy Studies
College of Education at the University of Illinois-Urbana Champaign

Acknowledgments

This book, first conceptualized in 1997 as a research project, has taken five years to complete. It was initially submitted to the University of the Witwatersrand in fulfillment of the requirements for the Doctor of Philosophy degree in 2002. Its translation into this book format was done as part of my post-doctoral fellowship at the University of Illinois at Urbana-Champaign. I first want to thank the Center for African Studies and the College of Education at the University of Illinois at Urbana-Champaign for providing me with a conducive space and the intellectual environment to carry out this work. I particularly want to thank Professor Fazal Rizvi for his intellectual leadership and mentorship in helping me to translate the dissertation into this book format. Thanks to Professor Michael Cross for doing the final reading of the manuscript and his input in finalizing this book. I want to also thank Professor Phil Altbach for his confidence in my intellectual work and recommending this book for publication.

The Rockefeller Foundation and the National Research Foundation (NRF) provided funding for my stay at the University of Illinois. A word of gratitude also to the Faculty of Education at the University of Pretoria for granting me leave that enabled me to take up this fellowship in the US.

Sections of Chapter Five have previously been published in South African Journal of Education (23:2), and I am grateful to the editors for granting permission for their inclusion in this manuscript.

Chapter One
Introduction

On the 10th May 1994, the world witnessed something that a decade before had been unthinkable: a first black president for South Africa. Nelson Rolihlahla Mandela was sworn in at the Union Buildings grounds in Pretoria, the capital city. Shortly after the new President had concluded his inaugural address, with the words that had put an end to apartheid still reverberating on the horizons of Pretoria, that "never, never, and never again shall it be that this beautiful land will again experience the oppression of one by another and suffer the indignity of being the skunk of the world," that the gathering lifted their eyes in awe as a spectacular array of South African jets, helicopters and troop carriers roared in perfect formation over the Union Buildings. This was not only a display of pinpoint precision and military force, but also a demonstration of the military's loyalty to democracy, to a new government that had been freely and fairly elected. Finally, a chevron of Impala jets left a trail of black, red, green, blue and gold, the colors of the new South African flag.[1] With that, a curtain was drawn on formal apartheid, and a new era of a non-racial, free and democratic South Africa was ushered in.

Ten years later, the same event was repeated at the same venue when South Africa celebrated its ten years of democracy, and as President Thabo Mbeki was inaugurated for his second term of office. This time, unlike in 1994 when the ruling party, the African National Congress (ANC), had won 62.6 percent of the votes, it now secured 69.7 percent of the votes. This was not only a vote of confidence in the ruling party, but also in the progress that had been made to cement democracy since 1994.

The formal end of apartheid was not followed by a smooth transition to democracy. It turned out to be a long and rocky road that was characterized by resistance to change, and by tensions between the bureaucratic past and democratic future in the establishment of the new state and bureaucracy, as well as by subversion and attempts to undermine the new agenda of government. On the other hand, the formal end of apartheid paved the way for a new era of reconstruction and transformation of the apartheid system in line with the vision of the new government. It came to be referred to as triple transition, which entailed firstly, government's creation of new democratic structures, secondly, the dismantling of old apartheid structures and reconstructing and integrating them into new ones, and thirdly, changes in the economic model from a state to a market led one. At the time, however, it was not clear that it was going to be market led. With a ruling party that had fought the apartheid system for over four decades, and had come into power on a negotiated pact underpinned by compromises, the task of reconstruction and transformation was not to be easy.

One of the areas that were targeted by the new government was education, the system renowned for its racial inequalities. The urgency of tackling the problems of higher education was demonstrated by the government's appointment of the National Commission on Higher Education (NCHE), ten months after it came to office. The task of the Commission was to conduct research on the higher education sector and make recommendations on how it could be transformed. This was the beginning of a long struggle that exposed the complexities of effecting and managing change by the new government. Strikes, walkouts, demonstrations, conferences, and hostage-taking came to characterize the process—one for which the country was not prepared. The work of the NCHE, that started in 1995 and was completed in 1996, contributed to the development of a new higher education policy and legislation that was formally adopted with the passing of the *Higher Education Act* in December 1997. The process of the development of higher education policy and legislation, which has been flaunted as a model for other countries in transition to follow, is what this book is about.

The question that is posed in this book, is why, despite good intentions to democratize higher education and redress the inequities of the past, there has been little or slow progress in achieving these ideals? The book argues that the policy process that was initially aimed at being democratized through the application of the principles of participation, consultation and representation, became bureaucratized as the new government faced the challenges of governance, power and control. The realities of the negotiated pact that underpinned the Government of National Unity (GNU), as well as the challenges of transition from apartheid to a democratic social order within an increasingly global environment, became more influential in shaping the policy process and its outcome than the intended democratic principles. This resulted in a tension between democratic aspirations and bureaucratic processes, as the old and the new wrestled for the soul and agenda of the new government.

Legally, the new government found itself constrained as a consequence of the negotiated pact that underpinned the transition from the apartheid social order to a new democratic dispensation. In order not to disrupt the transfer of power from the old to the new dispensation, the legal tenets of apartheid became the basis of the new government in its first few years until these could be replaced. These included, among others, the apartheid Public Service Commission, which became the basis of employment for new personnel under the new government in its first few years, and the continued existence and operation of the old apartheid education departments until they were replaced by the new ones. Of significance was what became known as the "sunset clause," which guaranteed jobs for all the civil servants for the first five years of the new dispensation. These resulted in the new government's constraints in implementing its transformation agenda.

The new government did not remain passive in the face of this pact. Innovations were introduced, such as the establishment of Strategic Management Teams (SMTs), which allowed the new government ministers to employ new people in support of transformation. This resulted in the coexistence of the old and new bureaucracy within the newly created Department of Education (DOE). Using Weber's theory of bureaucracy, the book shows the tensions that ensued from bureaucratic actions and decision-making that were guided by the objectives of efficiency, calculability and predictability on the one hand, and the quest for democratization of decision-making in the operation of the new DOE. The book further pursues the debate of the efficacy of relying on the use of the old bureaucrats in the new social order. Arguments for and against this practice are analyzed. Despite some of the arguments made against reliance on the old bureaucracy, the value of the use of the old bureaucracy in ensuring continuity between the old and the new dispensation is explored. However, this was not easy and tensions, irritations and struggles came to characterize this practice during this period.

South Africa's transition to democracy in the mid 1990s took place in the context of a rapidly globalizing world that was influenced by neo-liberal policies. With the collapse of socialism in the late 1980s, economic policy debates globally were increasingly geared towards the celebration of the "triumph" of capitalism combined with assertions for the rolling back of the state. These developments also characterized debates on macro-economic policies of the new South African state, as different forces wrestled for the soul of the African National Congress's (ANC) economic policy. On assuming power, there was more inclination towards redistributive policies as reflected in the Reconstruction and Development Programme (RDP); however the governmentalization of the RDP saw shifts from these redistribution policies to neo-liberal policies as expressed through the Growth Equity and Redistribution (GEAR) strategy that was adopted by government in 1996. This resulted in the rise and prominence of the Department of Finance in the formulation of policies for different departments with more inclination to fiscal austerity and recession of redistribution policies. These shifts, compromises and tradeoffs should be understood in the context of the emerging embryonic state that faced pressures and competing demands both locally and globally.

The adoption of neo-liberal macro-economic policies had implications for the nature of the state that was to implement these policies. While on the one hand it had to respond to pressures to develop globally relevant policies, the new state also faced the imperative of keeping the balance of pursuing a transformation agenda underpinned by social justice, democracy and equity. In particular, the policy process and outcomes had to reflect the balance that had to be maintained. Debates within the ruling party concerning the nature of the state favored an evolution of what was regarded as a strong state able to lead and deliver on the transformation agenda of government. However, given the competing demands made on the state, the new government evinced features of a weak democracy, which Adler and Webster explain as a form of government that is "strong enough to govern effectively, but weak enough not to be able to govern against important interests."[2]

Following three years of inability to provide leadership in the transformation of the higher education sector as a result of a vacuum of policy and legislation in higher education, the government ensured that it empowered itself through legislation to lead transformation. This was done through legislation that vested power in the Minister of Education, the Department of Education, and institutional councils. The debates and tensions that characterized this outcome are explored in terms of the evolution of governance policy starting from the work of the National Commission on Higher Education to the adoption of the Higher Education Act. The process of policy development during this period was characterized by an initial outsourcing of the policy development as a result of the imperative of mobilizing the public behind the new policy; meanwhile the new government was building capacity and dealing with the new challenges of restructuring the old education system. At the same time there were challenges associated with the establishment of new structures, procedures, systems and institutional cultures or norms. Providing leadership in this state of instability and flux was not something that came easily. It required a certain level of expertise, political leadership and vision that constituted policy literacy, which came to be acquired as government gained experience and confidence in office. The acquisition of experience of government, which came simultaneously with the recession in the impact of the transitional pact that underpinned the Government of National Unity, saw the ascendancy of the government in taking control of policy development in higher education following the work of the Commission. This resulted in a relatively strong education state empowered to lead the transformation agenda.

This book is organized around three themes. The first theme, covered in Chapters Two and Three, deals with the origins of apartheid policies and practices and how these were challenged and resisted, leading to the development of alternatives. Chapter Two addresses the tenets of apartheid education and practices, arguing that what was conceived initially as an instrument of division, became the basis of resistance and the demise of apartheid education. Chapter Three focuses on the development of alternative policies to apartheid education by the liberation movement. The quest for alternatives saw a plethora of policy developments and initiatives both within and outside of government, which led to the production of policy documents that laid the basis for the development of post-apartheid higher education policy. As a result, the new post-apartheid government inherited a rich legacy of policy development tradition that assisted it in laying the foundation for the development of new policies. This was different from what was the case for many post-colonial states, which had to start from scratch in developing new policies.

The second theme concentrates on the nature of the new post-apartheid state, and this is covered in Chapters Four and Five. Chapter Four analyzes the impact of the negotiated pact and the emerging neo-liberal economic agenda on the new state, showing the constraints the new government faced. This resulted in government's making shifts in its macro-economic policies towards more neo-liberal and market-based policies. This had consequences for subsequent education policies. Chapter Five analyzes the impact of the negotiated pact in the establishment of the new Department of Education and operation of the bureaucracy. In what is characterized as tension between bureaucratic past and democratic future, the chapter shows the challenges of the co-existence of the old and new bureaucracy in the new order. The merits and demerits of this, especially in relation to ensuring continuity, are analyzed.

The third theme focuses on the policy process and its outcomes, which are explored in Chapters Six, Seven and Eight. Chapter Six explores the policy process taking place outside of the state through the NCHE, which became a theater in which stakeholder politics and interests came to be played out. In what is referred to as change commissioned, the chapter demonstrates the impact of GNU arrangement and sufficient consensus principle in the appointment, mode of operation and outcomes of the Commission's work. The NCHE produced a framework of transformation report, which laid the basis for the new government to develop policy and legislation. Chapter Seven explores the movement of policy from outside into the state, which entailed the government's response to the NCHE report through the *Green Paper,* the formal adoption of higher education policy through the *White Paper,* and the development of formal governance structures for transformation through the adoption of the *Higher Education Act.* The chapter illustrates how the government tried to overcome the constraints of its first three years in office without formal policy, by vesting powers in the Department of Education and relevant structures which the state could influence in order to spearhead transformation.

Chapter Eight reflects on the policy process and challenges of transformation which the new government faced, arguing that in addition to the constraints of the negotiated pact, the impact of the global and neo-liberal policies, and the dynamics of the establishment of the new bureaucracy, there was also a lack of policy literacy that was required for both the state and bureaucracy to work together in facing the challenges of transformation and change to ensure the desired outcomes. Given the importance attributed to policy literacy, the question is posed as to who was qualified to provide this policy literacy. It is argued that given the context in which the policy process was new to everyone, there was no agency or organization qualified to provide this policy literacy. As a result, the process turned out to be an experience of learning by doing for all involved.

The book tells a story, drawing from the author's background in working with the progressive movement in South Africa. This facilitated access to key government officials for interview purposes, a methodology that combines the voices of the old and the new bureaucrats, the stakeholders and the author's analysis. The period of this study, namely 1997–2001, which cuts across the first and second terms of the ANC government, constitutes some of the interesting periods of democratization in South Africa. The book provides the voices and perspectives of the key policy makers within the education bureaucracy during the Mandela administration (1994–1999), and immediately thereafter, with some of the key actors now outside of government, and new players having emerged. In particular, the period of the GNU, from 1994 to 1996, with all its partners participating in government, was one of the distinctive features of the transition period in South Africa. Interviews were conducted with officials with fresh memories of the challenges entailed in restructuring the education system. The challenges of transition and transformation were succinctly captured by one of the former apartheid bureaucrats who characterized them as "changing the wheels while the car is moving." After the second national elections in 1999, interviews were conducted with the new senior government officials and former officials who had by then retired from service in government. The latter were crucial in that they were at the center of driving the change process and putting in place the new policy and legislative process. As a result, the Mandela administration is renowned for having put in place new policies, while the Mbeki administration of the post-1999 period is characterized by focusing on implementation of policies. While the latter is of interest, this book is concerned with the process of policy development of the first five years of democracy, namely the 1994–1999 period.

This study was motivated by my participation in the various policy development initiatives in education between the period 1990 and 1994, and during the immediate post-1994 era. During this period, emphasis was put on ensuring that the development of policy incorporated the principles of participation, consultation and representation. This was in part related to the goal of redressing the legacy of apartheid, where policy development was a monopoly of apartheid politicians and excluded the black majority. The initial concern was to investigate the impact of the application of these principles on the policy process and its outcomes. However, the fieldwork broadened my understanding and interpretation of the role of these principles, as I discovered new issues that seemed to have determined the policy process and its outcomes. These issues included the nature of the state overseeing the process, the context of the transition within which the process unfolded and which was shaped by the Interim Constitution and macro-economic policies, different policy actors involved, the policy documents that were produced and the meaning and significance attached to them. The issues were discovered in the field as well as shaped by the field. Thus, rather than imposing them on the study, they emerged naturally. It was like discovering the other side of transition.

South Africa's transition from apartheid to democracy was based on a compromise: the GNU could be likened to an arranged marriage where new partners were to live under the same roof for the first time. If the new South Africa could be regarded as a house, the formal structures put in place would be viewed as walls, and the interior as furniture and people living within these walls. What this book does is to take the reader inside the house, to the education living room or bedroom, to get a sense of what life inside this house was like, what the house rules were, how they were developed, the compromises and adjustments that had to be made. It needs to be noted that the arranged marriage was such that one of the partners was living in the house already, having relinquished full ownership and power, and it therefore fell to the new partner to set the rules and take leadership. Relinquishing power is not easy. The tensions that ensued from this arrangement sometimes led to strikes, walkouts in protest, and marginalization. This is described in the book in terms of the tension between the bureaucratic past and democratic future, leading to one of the partners staging a walkout from the house, and beginning to engage the remaining partner from outside. The walkout provided a breather for the remaining new partner, and this allowed space for acceleration of rule setting. However, in walking out, the old partner ensured that structures for bureaucratic accountability had been put in place and that some of the elements of the old order remained intact. Thus, the book takes the reader through the negotiations of the pact, the terms of agreement, how these were implemented and the ensuing tensions, the breakdown of the pact, and the post-pact arrangement. These episodes are presented using a combination of voices of actors, written documents, and insights from personal experience as both an outsider and insider to this process.

The insider perspective stems from my participation in the policy process in the pre- and post-1994 period. As a practitioner, I had assumed a certain level of knowledge and expertise of the policy process and content. I had also been a beneficiary of the application of the principles of participation and representation, given my racial and disadvantaged background. This was also work on issues and processes which I was passionate about. I had objectives which I had shared with some actors in government, having to deal with individuals they had once opposed. The outsider perspective stems from remaining outside formal government employment when many former colleagues were appointed in the new bureaucracy. What became apparent was that the study became of interest to many of the officials of the Department, since it addressed issues they were grappling with on a daily basis. I came as a researcher, from an institution which was "credible" in terms of its scholarly work, and as a former colleague and comrade, and the focus of the study on contemporary issues made my interviewees willing to talk about their experiences. Given the level of tensions and challenges that these entailed, the interview sessions came to be used in some instances as ventilation sessions. Former apartheid bureaucrats did not want to be associated with the past and so became cooperative. Generally the bureaucracy (new layer) showed interest but raised challenges. Some of them were interested in this research since they believed it could assist them in the reconstruction of higher education. Therefore many spoke with a sense of sincerity but also with an element of trying to move from rhetoric to reality. For some of the former comrades, there was a new sense of sobriety, and they thus indicated issues that worked and did not work in running the bureaucracy. This particularly referred to the kinds of skills required in policy management. The research therefore also posed the challenge of managing the complexities of loyalty within a newly established bureaucracy. This related to this policy project against the background of mistrust and betrayal which characterized the apartheid era. That I was black, with an activist background, minimized the impact or made this concern irrelevant. There was a sense of loyalty and integrity.

I therefore had to manage the distance between myself as researcher in interviews with former colleagues. Through interviews, I was able to gain access to the challenges entailed in the constitution of a new identity in the new bureaucracy, how the old and new were reconstituted, and how, as a researcher, I had to interface with these fluid identities. The book also relies on the active voices of the actors involved, whereby old voices had to move to the background and new voices had to take center stage. As a researcher, I had to adopt a subtle way of accessing these voices and attaching meaning to them. It was indeed a privilege to conduct this research during this period of transition while there was still a thin layer around state formation, so actors were able to speak not from an established institutional memory or framework, but from their individual perspectives as they saw the process unfolding. The book captures insights that were informed by a particular historical moment never to be repeated again in the history of this country. This also constitutes the strength and contribution of this book.

Chapter Two

Struggling Apartheid Education

STRUGGLING APARTHEID EDUCATION

This chapter provides a description and analysis of the history of apartheid education with specific focus on higher education. The purpose is to provide a context and understanding of the kind of system the new government was faced with when it came to power and the policy context of this system. The description and analysis will be in relation to the ideology, philosophy, policy-making processes and their effects on the intended beneficiaries. It will argue that even though the introduction of apartheid education in higher education in 1959 was aimed at producing a docile civil service to serve the apartheid's Bantustan system, it produced the opposite effects in these institutions as they became centers of resistance to the apartheid system.

THE LEGAL, IDEOLOGICAL AND RACIAL BASES OF APARTHEID EDUCATION

The history of apartheid education can be traced to the victory of the National Party over the United Party in 1948. Though segregation in education had been practiced prior to 1948, what the apartheid policy did was to formalize, institutionalize and promote it with the backing of the legal system and all the other state apparatuses at the disposal of the government. Immediately upon obtaining power, the apartheid government moved swiftly to institutionalize racial segregation. In 1949 the *Prohibition of Mixed Marriages Act* was passed, prohibiting all future marriages between whites and members of other racial groups. This was followed by the *Population Registration Act* of 1950, which was designed to racially categorize the South African population, and by stiffening penalties for violations of the Immorality Act, which made extramarital intercourse a more serious offense if committed across racial lines. Under the *Population Registration Act* South African society was divided into four races, namely, White, Indian, Colored and African,[1] which also determined the hierarchy of supremacy and benefits under apartheid, with whites at the top and Africans at the bottom of the ladder. The *Group Areas Act* of 1950 proclaimed residential and business areas for various racial groups. The *Group Areas Act* initiated the era of forced removals, where Black communities were violently relocated because white landowners either did not want Black living next to them or simply wanted their land.

Alongside the development of the legal and institutional settings for the operation of apartheid, was the development and enunciation of the philosophical base for the operation of this machinery. Education became a strategic sector for the implementation and promotion of the apartheid philosophy, since most South African children would go through it to some extent. To this effect, the ruling party developed and adopted Christian National Education (CNE) as an education philosophy, which, according to Ashley, has been the educational expression of apartheid, of the Afrikaner National government's belief in the need for racial segregation.[2] The idea of Christian National Education was first introduced to South Africa in the 1870s as part of an effort to apply Calvinist teachings to all areas of life. This followed the examples set in the Netherlands earlier in the century. CNE received its formal modern codification in 1948, when it was published as a policy statement for the government.[3] Although it started as a policy meant for white Afrikaner children, it has had far-reaching consequences for the education of all children in South Africa. According to articles 14 and 15 of the policy, black education was the responsibility of "white South Africa" or more specifically of "the Boer nation as the senior white trustee of the 'native' who is in the state of 'cultural infancy.'" The notion of racial superiority was essential to the function of an ideology like CNE. In his critique of CNE, Ashley points out that there consistently have been two central features in its development, the first being that all education should be based on the Christian Gospel, and the second that mankind was divided into nations and that education should reflect these national differences.[4] The religious basis of this ideology was central to the development of adherents of apartheid among whites since they saw the support and practice of apartheid as part of their faith and of doing God's will. As such, opposition to apartheid would be seen as opposition to God's will. At the higher education level the CNE came to be promoted through the development of what was known as Fundamental Pedagogics as a theory of education. This was mainly taught in Afrikaans-language universities, such as at the University of South Africa and University of Pretoria, and was taught in education faculties of the black universities as faculty in the latter was drawn mainly from Afrikaans institutions.[5] Even though CNE was passed as policy in 1948 initially aimed at the education of white Afrikaner children, it was extended to a national policy through the passing of the *National Education Act* of 1967.

In line with this policy in 1953, five years after coming to power, the National Party government passed the infamous *Bantu Education Act,* which sought to put the apartheid stamp on African education. The passing of the Act was preceded by a *Report of the Commission on Native Education* under the chairmanship of Dr W.W.M. Eiselen. The Commission's terms of reference reflected government's policy of racial segregation and the influence of CNE further set the tone of what was to follow. The terms of reference included among others:

> The formulation of the principles and aims of education for Natives as an independent race, in which their past and present, their inherent racial qualities, their distinctive characteristics and aptitude, and their needs under ever-changing conditions are taken into consideration.[6]

The recommendation of the Commission led to the passing of the *Bantu Education Act* in 1953. The Act transferred control of African education from the Department of Education to the much-loathed Native Affairs Department. Under the Act, African primary and secondary schools that were operated by the Church and mission bodies were given a choice of either turning over their schools to the government or receiving gradually diminished subsidies. Either the government took over education for Africans or there would be no education for Africans. This measure allowed government to close any educational programs which did not support its aims. The government's insistence on taking control of all African education should be understood in the light of the power and influence government would then have over the curriculum, code of conduct, rules and regulations, and conditions of employment, which all came with the control of African education. African teachers were not permitted to criticize the government or any government authority. Dr Hendrik Verwoerd, one of the apartheid ideologues at the time, explained that education "must train and teach people in accordance with their opportunities in life," and further that "there is no place for the Bantu in the European community above the level of certain forms of labour."[7] Briefly, Africans were supposed to be trained for menial work, leaving them in a position of perpetual subordination to the whites. As Mandela puts it, it was an intellectual *baaskap* [bossiness], a way of institutionalizing inferiority.[8] This view was not only expressed in words, but the allocation of resources, appointment to jobs, and remuneration at work, ensured that Black people were social-ized into inferior positions.

One of the aims of Bantu Education was to facilitate the reproduction of relations of production in a docile form, so that these relations would appear natural and based on common sense. Stressing the cultural differ-ences between white and black, and the development of a separate black community, in which black aspirations could be realized, the Bantu Education system would thus be able to prepare Blacks to accept differ-ences as part of the unchallenged order. To this effect, Christie and Collins in 1984 pointed out that the reproduction of labor would take place as a two-fold process, on the one hand involving the reproduction of attitudes and values appropriate to the social relations of production, and willing-ness to participate in capitalist exchange relations; and on the other hand, reproduction of appropriate skills. Drawing from the Eiselen Commission report, they show how the Commission made an explicit link between schooling and work. Along with religious knowledge, hygiene, and literacy in a black and at least one white language, it sets out the following func-tions of schooling:

> Social patterns and values which make a man a good member of his community, a good parent and a useful member of his society. (He should, for example, possess such qualities as punctuality, initiative, self-confidence, sense of duty, sociability, manneriness, neatness, relia-bility, power to concentrate, etc.).[9]

Explicit references to education and social reproduction are also contained in the following excerpts from parliamentary speeches by prominent Nationalist politicians prior to Bantu Education:

> As has been correctly stated here, education is the key to the creation of the proper power relationship between European and non-European in South Africa. . . . Put native education on a sound basis and half the racial questions are solved. . . .

And:

> We should not give the natives an academic education, as some of you are prone to do. If we do this we shall later be burdened with a number of academically trained Europeans and non-Europeans, and who is going to do the manual labour in this country. . . . We should so conduct

our schools that the native who attends those schools will know that to a great extent he must be a labourer in the country.[10] .

The apartheid system was well thought of, and its architects ensured that whatever policies and laws were passed, or institutions created, there would be structures and resources created or available to support such initiatives. Although the 1953 Bantu Education Act was intended to apply to all levels of education for blacks, it did not have an immediate impact on higher education until the passing of the *Extension of University Education Act* of 1959, which was largely based on an attempt to separate the youth of South Africa at the level of higher education on the basis of race, just as was already the case at primary and secondary school levels. The *Extension of University Education Act* coincided with the passing of the Separate Development Act of 1959. While the latter further balkanized black people into different ethnic groups, where each group was given "national" status and was supposed to be assisted in developing its own culture, the former put in place a long-term plan for each of these ethnic groups to have its own university or higher education institution.

The *Separate Development Act* divided black people into ten ethnic groups, which according to the CNE philosophy, were different from one another. That gave rise to what came to be known as Bantustans, four of which, namely Transkei, Bophuthatswana, Venda and Ciskei, were granted "independent status" by 1981 and the other six, namely Zululand, Lebowa, Qwaqwa, Kangwane, Kwa-Ndebele and Gazankulu were given self-governing status. The Colored and Indian people had their own administrative structures, which in 1983 were co-opted into apartheid parliament, as junior partners in what came to be known as the tri-cameral parliament system. The arrangement gave Coloreds and Indians some "vote," but they were to operate in separate chambers from the white parliament. The *Extension of University Education Act* of 1959 gave rise to five black university colleges: University College of the North based in Sovenga for the Basotho, vha-Vhenda and vhaTsonga; the University of Zululand for the Zulu-speaking people; and the transfer of the University of Fort Hare into the Department of Bantu Education to provide higher education for Xhosa- speaking people; the University College of Durban (later called Durban- Westville) for Indians; and the University College of the Western Cape for Colored people.

Between 1976 and 1983 the state created numerous new higher education institutions leading to the expansion of higher education for blacks in the country. In 1976, the Medical University of Southern Africa

(MEDUNSA) was established, aimed at providing medical training for black students. In 1982, VISTA University opened, operating with a number of satellite campuses around black urban townships but with its administrative offices based in Pretoria. Badat identifies the significance of MEDUNSA and VISTA as the fact that they were urban-based campuses and signaled acceptance by the state of a permanent urban African population in the "white" areas. They could also be seen as part of the state strategy to enforce a divide between urban African residents and rural and Bantustan African residents.[11] Between 1977 and 1983 universities were established in "independent" homelands, namely the universities of Transkei (1977), Bophuthatswana (1979), Venda (1983), and Qwaqwa (1983). The latter was not granted "independent" status. All of these developed their own civil and administrative structures which made apartheid one of the most bureaucratized and decentralized systems in existence.

In their analysis of the *Extension of University Education Act* of 1959, Christie and Collins rightly point out that this Act was aimed at extending state control over those blacks who proceeded to tertiary institutions, thus forming the black elite, and who were to be trained in institutions in which the state could control both the administrative structures as well as the curriculum. State control over schooling meant that schooling and black universities could be used to support other state policies, and in particular the Bantustan or homeland policy. The Bantustan or homeland policy was an important part of the government's separate development policy and its accompanying ideology. The 1959 *Promotion of Bantu Self- Government Act* provided for the establishment of separate black governments in the geographically fragmented Bantustans, under the influence and control of the apartheid government. Tied in with the National Party's stress on the extension of migrant labor, the Bantustan policy reduced the number of permanently settled blacks in urban areas, and provided an alternative basis for the supply and control of black labor. Both politically and economically, Bantustans provided focus for black aspirations for educational development and upward career options outside of the common framework, and this would contribute to continued domination by whites. In the Bantustans a combination of tribal with bureaucratic authority structures would help to retribalize Blacks, and thus further fragment black consciousness.[12] The success of the Bantustan policy depended on the existence of a black elite and a developed bureaucracy in the Bantustans, which would both support these structures ideologically and also provide the means of their operation. Bantu education at school and university levels was to contribute to the Bantustan policy in both ways.

The policy of white supremacy was further extended to universities in terms of how they were conceived, the purposes they were to serve and the role of the State in the process. According to the Commission that led to the passing of the 1959 Act that introduced apartheid in universities, the non-Europeans were "underdeveloped racial groups" (par. 25) without the "requisite sense of responsibility, organizing ability and expert knowledge" (par 23). It was therefore imperative that "the State take them by the hand and give them the necessary guidance and financial assistance" (par. 29).[13] Verwoerd asserted that the state as a guardian was establishing the separate institutions because the respective communities could not be expected to do so; the "White guardian" had to help their development along the "right lines" until the black communities were ready to "acquire full control."[14] This projection of blacks as inferior, and the guardianship role whites were supposed to play, was central to the promotion of the apartheid ideology of white supremacy. It permeated the way work was organized, the way the country was run, and the whole social fabric of society.

The fear of the black majority rule and domination seems to have been at the root of the apartheid policies in general and educational practices in particular. This could be deduced from the statements and motivation made by supporters of the *Extension of University Education Act* of 1959. Prime Minister Verwoerd warned at the time that:

> All forms of social integration could flow from integration at the university level. Then South Africa was inexorably doomed to become a mixed society, a mixed policy, a mixed community in which the masses [would] be dominant and these masses would be non-whites. [15]

Culture and self-determination arguments were also used to justify their actions. The Minister of Education at the time, J.J. Serfontein, in supporting the Bill, argued that the government wanted to make provisions for black students in separate institutions which could "develop towards independence on their own basis." Blacks should be allowed to develop in what was peculiarly their own. They needed to be bearers of their own culture to stimulate the culture among their "national group."[16] However, underlying this approach was the principle of white guardianship in that the "white" state was to help and guide blacks to self determination.

The guardianship role which the State was to play over black people was translated into white Afrikaner guardianship over black people and played itself out in practices in black universities. Nkomo observes that the University Pretoria [where the author is now a faculty member] made a recommendation to the Commission that a university in the Northern

Transvaal be established, stressing "the national heritage for the Bantu [blacks] but which will be Afrikaans in orientation."[17] This submission reflects the contradictions inherent in the purposes for the establishment of these institutions. While they were meant to contribute to the development of cultures of the different ethnic groups for which they were established, the Afrikaans element was to be made part of the package. Contradictory as it may sound, it was, however, put into practice in the following ways: While they were based in rural black areas, and served exclusively black students, university governance, administrative and teaching staff were mainly white and Afrikaner as will be shown. As a result, the institutions became white and Afrikaner in staffing composition and culture, and black in student composition and culture, providing the sources of tension, conflicts and struggle that characterized life in these institutions.

GOVERNANCE

One of the main features of apartheid education was the way in which legislation was used to structure and enforce certain governance arrangements and practices that were supposed to be an extension of official government policy. Universities were not spared in this case, despite the universal tenets of academic freedom underpinning their operations. There was a symbiotic relationship between government policy of introducing apartheid in education and how these institutions were governed.

What the nationalist government did was to ensure that its apartheid policies were implemented and reflected in every state institution including universities, even if it meant compromising the ethos of academic freedom and autonomy. In this respect, the Holloway Commission, whose recommendations led to the passing of the *Extension of University Education Act,* in laying the bases for the intrusion which the state would make on the running of the universities in South Africa, argued that:

> The measure of autonomy conferred on universities, by the State can also be modified by the State, and modifications have in fact been effected at various times. No organization established by the State for the fulfillment of particular social functions may prescribe to the state the course of action which the latter should take in the treatment of the social problems with which it may have to deal. . . . If the State should deem it necessary to prescribe a particular policy regarding relations between European and non-European, the validity of its dictates would not end in the portals of a university. [18]

This principle gave the state absolute powers to adopt policies and take actions in line with the apartheid policy of government. Flowing from this principle, was the powers vested in the state to determine through legislation whom universities could admit, whom to teach and what to teach, which are some of the tenets of academic freedom. Autonomy and academic freedom were only permissible in so far as they were not in conflict with the State's intentions.

Another effect of the *Extension of University Education Act* of 1959 was on the right of universities to appoint staff. Although the white institutions were generally affected by these restrictions, such as the prohibition of the right to admit black students and who was allowed to teach, their effects were exceedingly draconian on the newly created black university colleges. Nkomo points to evidence of termination of staff and faculty who disagreed with the government's position of apartheid in universities. In other words, non-disagreement with government policy was an unwritten policy that would disqualify one from a job in government. For example, in 1959, referring to the dismissal of a number of administrators and faculty at Fort Hare, the Minister of Education is reported to have said: "I disposed of their services because I will not permit a penny of any funds which I have control over to be paid to any persons who are known to be destroying the Government's policy of apartheid."[19] This statement suggests not only the powers the Minister had to dismiss staff who showed "dissent," but also the curtailment of freedom of expression among staff. Meyer observes that many African academics became "intellectually captive or simply cowed down by the power structure" and perceived "their task in the same limited terms as the typical white instructor."[20] Even though there could be an element of truth in this statement, this however did not apply to all black academics as there were those who refused to support the status quo and found themselves either dismissed, imprisoned or forced into exile outside the country.

Internal governance within each of the black university colleges was placed under the administrative control of an all-White Council, which was appointed by the State President and answerable for its actions to the white Minister of Education. All the new posts and promotions required the approval of the Minister. There was further an all-Black Advisory Council which was appointed by the State President for each of the black institutions. Provision was further made for the academic control of each institution by an all-White senate, assisted by an all-Black Advisory Senate. The declared policy of government was that ultimately the Blacks would take over control of their university institutions.[21]

The planning, introduction and coordination of governance arrangements at the black universities were systematic and ensured the Afrikaner orientation through an entrenched peculiar structural and organizational arrangement, and by the deliberate appointment of individuals who identified with Afrikaner nationalism to staff and faculty positions in black university colleges. As Nkomo observed, a strict regimen in terms of regulations was imposed. Transformed into Ideological State Apparatuses, these institutions followed the model of the larger society in their racially determined hierarchical arrangements. They determined the "proper place" for each ethnic group and sought to instill a consciousness that corresponded with the arrangements of the social order. This was, as Nkomo rightly points out, the official culture of institutional ethos that prevailed at the time of inception of the black university colleges under the Department of Bantu Education in 1960.[22] The system of governance evolved over time with black universities having been granted autonomy in 1970, but still with the administrative and academic control vested in predominantly white Councils and Senates. As it will be shown later, this arrangement became a source of conflict and resistance in these institutions.

A significant restructuring in higher education governance at systemic level was effected in 1983 with the adoption of a new Constitution which established education as "own affairs." This means that it was directed by the elected representatives comprising the separate Houses of Assembly (for Whites) Representatives (for Coloreds) and Delegates (for Indians). The education for Africans was to remain a separate portfolio with a white minister in charge, as had been the case in the past.[23] The apartheid structure of own affairs divisions and homeland government arrangements was superimposed on the three sub-sectors of higher education. The National Commission on Higher Education (NCHE) report summarizes the governance arrangements under apartheid until 1994 as follows:

- Co-ordination of the higher education system was the responsibility of the Department of National Education; rather than being a line department in the sense of having other education departments or other individual higher education institutions reporting to it, it was to monitor and set financial and academic norms and standards. Given the ideological distinctions of apartheid policy between general affairs and own affairs, it could not deal with anything other than the general issues of norms and standards.

- Three Departments of Education carried separate responsibilities for universities, technikons and colleges catering for Whites, Coloreds and Indians respectively.
- One Department of Education and Training (DET) was responsible for some universities, some technikons and some colleges for Africans.
- Six Departments of Education were responsible for some technikons and some colleges in the six self-governing territories (Bantustans).
- Four Departments of Education were responsible for universities, technikons and colleges of education in the "independent" states of Transkei, Bophuthatswana, Venda and Ciskei.[24]

As the Commission noted, these divisions resulted in a gross fragmentation of the higher education system. A consequence was that the effectiveness and efficiency of the system suffered badly through a lack of coordination, common goals and systematic planning. No clear strategy of the elements such as the size and shape of the system, social and economic needs, overall funds available, growth rates and the elimination of unnecessary wasteful duplication was provided.[25]

The various purposes for which higher education institutions were created led to the different relationships with the state. For example, the black institutions exhibited more of a state control governance model. Control by legislation was backed up by central government administrative and executive powers with respect to the composition of management, administrative and academic structures, access, student affairs, and funding, as well as the appointments in some cases, of all senior members of staff. In contrast, white institutions contained elements of a weak state-supervision, particularly in terms of growth and funding. Weak supervision was gradually supplemented with the irregular state interference, especially as the agendas of the government and higher education diverged. Thus South Africa experienced all three models of higher education-government relations: state control, state supervision and state interference.[26]

CURRICULUM COMPOSITION

Apartheid architects ensured that there was nothing in the social, political and educational spheres that did not promote apartheid policy. If possible, the air that was breathed in South Africa was also to reflect and promote apartheid. The way the curriculum was organized, the kind of courses approved for different racial groups, who taught these courses and how they were taught, were to ensure promotion of white racial superiority and socialization of black people into the types of roles they were to fulfill within the South African society.

With reference to the courses that were taught, historically black universities were restricted to offer social science, administration, law, commerce, science and theology. Initially only the University of Fort Hare offered a course in agriculture. These courses were mainly linked to the civil service which blacks were supposed to provide in the Bantustans catering for respective ethnic groups. Nkomo asserts that the orientation of these courses, especially in Law, was aimed at addressing the administrative-judicial structure and political economic needs of the Bantustans. Gottschalk adds that they were designed to inculcate "order, obedience, industriousness . . . qualities which imperial rulers desire instilled in their subject race."[27] On the other hand, white universities had in addition to the courses offered in black universities, offered courses in architecture, engineering, medicine, dentistry, which were never allowed to be offered in black universities. While those offered in black universities were not expensive, those offered in white universities were generally more expensive given the expensive facilities they required.

This was particularly the case with respect to laboratory equipment and library facilities which were better catered for in white universities than in black universities. The teaching of science in black universities was not geared to the production of scientists, which was the case for white universities, but was mainly geared to the training of secondary school teachers. These different kinds of orientations for the teaching of these courses for different races led to the unequal funding of similar programs at different institutions. Given the quality of training that white students received as a result of the quality of resources made available to them, they became producers of most of the research that was done in the country and monopolized all the high-level jobs in science and technology, without competition from other racial groups. This contributed to reinforcing the myth of white superiority. Furthermore, none of the black universities had the faculties of engineering (or mining), while most white universities had well-developed engineering programs as a matter of principle. For example, the Department of Education, Arts, and Science annual report of 1966 listed twelve different engineering departments available at five of the nine white residential universities.[28]

The preferential access whites had to higher education and to specialized fields in science and technology, also created a situation where they had no competition in terms of appointments in these fields in universities in

South Africa. However, it was not only their appointments in historically black universities that was problematic and contradictory in terms of the Separate Development policy, but the racial prejudices displayed in the teaching and learning environment which was even more controversial and led to constant clashes between lecturers and students. Because of their belief in white superiority and their biases against black students, statements such as "black students not having enough intelligence to major in Maths and Science" were often attributed to some white lecturers. This was combined with sexist utterances such as "women who were doing Maths and Science were wasting their time." Such racist and sexist statements were further confirmed in practice by the high number of black students who did not succeed in passing these courses, often becoming a source of conflict in these institutions. Students would respond to such discriminatory utterances and practices by calling for the dismissal of such lecturers, which the university authorities would be unwilling to do. Students would then resort to boycotts of academic activities which would sometimes be prolonged with authorities and students locking horns in trying to find solutions to these issues.

Another curriculum aspect worth mentioning relates to the quality of white staff members that were appointed at these institutions. Given that most of the appointees were drawn from the supporters of government, most of the white staff members appointed at the black institutions were mainly Afrikaans-speaking and had English as their second language. A perusal of the calendars of these institutions since their inception shows the overwhelming majority of them were graduates of Afrikaans universities. The challenge they faced was that the language of instruction in black universities was English and the majority of these lecturers had received most of their education, including university education, through the medium of Afrikaans. Their lack of confidence in the speaking of English, and the grammatical errors they committed, undermined the image of white supremacy that was supposed to be portrayed through the system. The hegemony of the use of English in education, and the significance of its mastery in terms of creating long-lasting impressions upon the audience or clients, predates the globalization era we now live in. Thus, the incompetence in English displayed by some white lecturers made them a laughing stock and the basis of ridicule among black students. Phrases such as "remember me to give you your assignments," instead of "remind me to give you your assignments," which were attributed to some lecturers, were often laughed about among students and became part of the campus lingo [language].

Sometimes students used their victimization experience to characterize the practices of their lecturers. For instance, in students' mass meetings to discuss their grievances against lecturers who were believed to be racist and victimizing their students by failing them, it was common language to hear those lecturers referred to as "sterile" and "unable to produce," and therefore seen as unfit to teach and called upon to resign. The call for their resignation would always lead to battles between the university authorities and students, usually leading to class boycotts which would also lead to security police being called to campus. For example, in 1984/5, a call for the dismissal of a Mathematics lecturer at the University of North who was accused of racism and failing students was not accepted by the university authorities. In order to influence the decision-making, a night before the Council sat to decide the fate of the lecturer concerned, a Science building was petrol-bombed. This was an apparent attempt to exert pressure on the Council in its decision-making. The lecturer was later dismissed. Again, a Roman-Dutch Law lecturer who was also accused of failing students became a target of students demonstrations and fell victim to being burned with acid during student demonstration in front of his class. This led to white lecturers leaving the university on that day and threatening not to come back to campus unless their security was assured. The black Vice-Chancellor who at the time was also exposed to pressure from the student community on the one side, and the white lecturers on the other, and had grown impatient with the attitude of some of the lecturers, was unsympathetic in the situation and ignored the lecturers' threat to the point of being prepared to replace them with new appointments if they did not return. The return of white lecturers to work, despite a life-threatening incident that had taken place, reinforced the long-held perception among black students and staff that black universities were staffed with white lecturers who were regarded as not good enough or rejects in white universities. As such, their resignation from black universities would leave them with no place to go to.

The perception of the inferior quality of white staff deployed to black institutions is confirmed by one of the former senior apartheid bureaucrats who served in the new government of national unity between the period 1994 and 1995. In describing the contradictions of transition from apartheid to the new order during the mid-1990s, he argued that the new government had to rely on the cooperation of the apartheid bureaucrats from the Department of Education and Training that was serving black people, and these were regarded as rejects or not good enough during apartheid. As he put it, those who were regarded as no longer good enough to serve in the departments serving whites, would be transferred (dumped) to the Department of Education and Training. These officials behaved in the same way as their colleagues at the University of the North did, by taking advantage of the agreement between the National Party and the ANC during negotiations that guaranteed government employment for all civil servants. They pledged their support to the Government of National Unity and provided a valuable service during the transition period. They also had nowhere to go.

Another factor that contributed to poor quality of teaching in these institutions was the fact that most of the texts that were used were either written by the lecturers, or their former lecturers or friends in white universities. Often, most of the orientation of the courses would be biased against black people. Nkomo points to an example of the Afrikaner orientation in the History subject demonstrated by a student's complaints at the University of Zululand when he said: "We are tired of spending months tracing the origins of apartheid to the English to justify biases of Afrikaner lecturers; we want to learn about achievements of Africans." Official emphasis on South African history and culture was on African ethnic differences and the "backwardness" of the latter while extolling the gallantry of "white Christian civilization."[29]

APARTHEID POLICYMAKING PROCESSES AND STRUCTURES

Inherent in the apartheid government that denied franchise to black people, was also their exclusion in policy-making processes and structures. Where they were involved, they mainly played an advisory role. The purpose of this section is to demonstrate how decision-making processes and structures assumed the almost non-existent role of blacks in this process, the centrality of whites and Afrikaners in decision-making in the country, and the guardianship role they assigned themselves in relation to black people. Education was offered not as a right, but as a privilege that was ensured through the trusteeship bestowed upon the state.

The practice of white supremacy and expertise was also promoted through reliance of the state on Commissions. Commissions always preceded all major policies that were passed by the government. For example, the *Bantu Education Act* of 1953 was preceded by the Eiselen Commission, the *Extension of University Education Act* of 1959 was preceded by the Holloway Commission, the 1983 *White Paper* that introduced the notion of education as an "own affair" was preceded by the De Lange Commission. At the same time, unrest in education was also investigated through the appointment of one-person Commissions. These would always lead to the passing of major policy measures. These Commissions were exclusively white in composition. Along with the increasing central role which Commissions came to play in policy- making, was also the rise of "science"

as a basis for decision-making. Science came to be used dogmatically and assumed an infallible position in decision-making. Setting up Commissions
was one mechanism that enabled governments to use science, or research
knowledge, to contribute to governance. By publicly involving experts and
prominent people outside of government, Commissions were used to provide greater legitimacy because their findings drew on "expertise" and "professionalism" with the added weight of impartiality and consultative
participation.[30] Commissions of inquiry occupied a central place in the formulation of what used to be known as "Native Policy" and during periods
of critical realignments in the structure of empowerment by the South
African state, they were appointed to address the "Native Question" in its
broadest dimensions.[31]

The central role which government played in the appointment of
Commissions, which ensured that it was in line with its policies, was encap-
sulated in the provisions of the Bill on the *Extension of the University
Education Act*. In practice the Act led to the following two types of institutions: state-aided universities for whites and state-university colleges for
blacks. State-aided universities had full councils with decision-making powers, while state-university colleges came under the full control of the state in
terms of policy, procedure and financial matters. These entailed, amongst
others, the appointment of executive and governance bodies, selection and
appointment of staff, provision for academic freedom, provision for courses
and research facilities, construction of the universities. In white universities
these powers were the exclusive right of the councils. This resulted in a direct state control of black universities and some room for intervention in student admission practices in white universities in the event of their violation
of government policy.

The mode of operation in the state in developing policy without the
participation of black people, and the appointment of white people into all
the governance bodies of the black universities, also became a way in which
these institutions came to be run. Put another way, the authoritarian approach to leadership at national level, with its lack of concern to consult the
majority of the people, came to be reproduced in the administrative and
teaching culture in the black institutions. For example, following vehement
protests to the establishment of exclusively racial and ethnic universities that
fell on deaf government ears, students at the University of Durban-Westville
in the 1960s decided to boycott participation in the student governance
structure established by the university, namely the Student Representative
Council (SRC). After a decade of boycott, students decided to engage in the
election of an interim SRC which submitted to the university a constitution

incorporating the wider powers students had sought earlier, such as inviting guest speakers, calling meetings and affiliating with an outside student body of their choice. This was rejected by university authorities on the general principle that they should have a final say in all matters concerning the university. This uncompromising position the authorities adopted should be understood in light of the fact that, as all-White governing structures, entrusted with a guardianship role, they should not take orders from those entrusted to their care.

RESISTING APARTHEID EDUCATION

The black people did not remain passive or docile in the face of oppression. The opposition to apartheid cannot be attributed to one organization or sector. The African National Congress (ANC) has since 1912 been a leading force in challenging the disenfranchisement of black people and has maintained that until its ascendancy to power in 1994, different formations have emerged during the period of white domination that contributed towards challenging the unjust system of oppression. Opposition took the form of student organizations, women's organizations, civic organizations, trade unions, formations with different ideological orientations such as the Black Consciousness Movement (BCM) and the Pan Africanist Congress (PAC) that emerged in the 1960s. Thus analysis of opposition to apartheid would adopt a broad approach that demonstrates the role of these organizations in challenging the system and bringing it to its demise. While analysis will retain a focus on higher education, broader education and social struggles that add value to the anti-apartheid struggles that were waged will also be brought into the discussion.

The analysis will adopt periodization that covers two broad eras: (a) from the inception of apartheid in the 1950s to the introduction of the tri-cameral system in 1983; and (b) from the tri-cameral system in 1983 to the end of apartheid in 1994. The rationale for this periodization lies in the fact that the first was a period characterized by the development of major apartheid laws and cosmetic reforms to adapt to its resistance. The second period was characterized by severe resistance and repression which rendered the country ungovernable. This period saw the imposition of two states of emergency as a result of the heightened level of internal security risks as apartheid tried to survive the inevitable. While the first period draws on general literature written on apartheid education and struggles, the second draws from my personal experience as it coincides with my admission at the University of the North and my subsequent pursuit of post-graduate studies at an historically white university. The latter period draws mainly from my insights in terms of how I experienced apartheid education at the university, being part of the struggles that challenged it and the kind of consciousness acquired through my sojourns in these apartheid institutions.

BANTU EDUCATION IN UNIVERSITIES: FROM THE 1950S TO 1983

The passing of the *Extension of University Education Act* of 1959 was followed by widespread protests against the Act. The historically white universities of Cape Town and the Witwatersrand protested against the passing of the Act which would restrict them from admitting black students. These institutions declared that they were committed to being "open universities" and they decided to hold an "academic freedom lecture" each year. At Fort Hare, staff and students passed resolutions condemning the extension of apartheid to universities. The government responded by dismissing certain staff while others resigned.

The extension of apartheid to universities had unintended consequences as these institutions became centers of resistance to the very policies and laws that established them. From their inception, students in black universities started to organize themselves in ways that helped them to act as a collective in challenging apartheid education. The collective action and resistance they put against apartheid education was fueled by a combination of factors which included their negative attitudes towards black universities which were generally viewed with suspicion owing to the state-imposed restrictions at the white universities and the financial incentives made available through "easy" bursaries and loans. Other factors included the white-dominated staff component, and lack of control of these institutions by black people. As Nkomo observed, absent from these institutions were basic elements that made healthy human organizations: a lack of loyalty to the overall purpose and mission of these institutions, and consequently, a sense of institutional belonging.[32] These institutions were then turned into sites of contestation and struggle for the development of alternative programs, ideology and strategies that would challenge the formal institutional cultures of these institutions. Student organizations became an important vehicle for the mobilization of students and ideas that could give content to alternatives to apartheid practices. The strategies combined and linked campus-based problems with broader socio-political issues in the country.

With the above-described situation prevailing in many black university campuses, it was no surprise that in 1968 there emerged a black student organization based on the Black Consciousness philosophy in the name of the South African Student Organization (SASO). The organization stemmed from a situation at the 1967 National Union of South African Students (NUSAS, a predominantly white liberal student organization) conference where the African delegates were accommodated in the black ghetto and not in the same facilities where white delegates were housed in the white town.[33] For African delegates, this act of segregated facilities demonstrated what was viewed as an example of the failure of NUSAS to implement its rhetoric and the importance of a white liberal organization in bringing meaningful change to South Africa.

This incident, combined with other concerns linked to white liberalism in South Africa, led to the formation of SASO's subscribing to the Black Consciousness philosophy in 1968. The objectives of SASO are described as: First, to promote contact and practical cooperation among students studying at affiliated centers; second, to represent the non-white students nationally; and third, to bring about contact among South African students generally.[34] These objectives cut across the intended goals of apartheid education since they were meant to foster cooperation among students at different black campuses. The role and history of SASO and its Black Consciousness philosophy in the 1970s on black campuses as well as its contribution to challenging apartheid, especially in education, are well documented. Some of these include the speech given by one of the student leaders (Onkgopotse Tiro), representing graduates at the University of the North in 1972, in which he focused attention on the paradoxical nature of the university in which power and authority resided in white hands while the blacks occupied advisory and token positions. This speech led to his expulsion from the university, the reason given for the expulsion being that Tiro chose the wrong occasion to give the types of speech he gave, and so "embarrassed" the authorities.[35] His expulsion led to student boycotts which also spread to other black campuses. This led to the appointment of Commissions of Inquiry in the three black campuses to investigate the causes of the unrest.

SASO also played a leading role in organizing the pro-FRELIMO rallies to celebrate the defeat of the Portuguese colonialists and the attainment of freedom for the people of Mozambique. The students saw in the Frelimo triumph the affirmation, in political terms, of Black Consciousness and the confirmation of black identity on the continent of their birth. This contradicted the very purposes for which these institutions were established, namely, promotion of ethnic pride. Despite government's outlawing of such rallies throughout the country, students at the University of the North went on with their planned rally, which resulted in scuffles with the police. A Commission of Inquiry was appointed to investigate the incident. The Black

Consciousness Movement was also credited for its role in the Soweto uprisings of 1976, which are renowned for having put the struggle against apartheid on an irreversible path towards its demise. SASO and its affiliate organizations were outlawed in 1977. However, this did not deter the continuation of the struggle within these institutions. Apartheid education had given birth to institutions and conditions which were now a thorn in the flesh. When the ideological state apparatus failed, the government resorted to repression and armed forces.

The uprisings of 1976 in Soweto marked a watershed in political relations between the apartheid state and the dominated social groups. Henceforth, a combination of state restructuring of the previous terms of domination of black population, economic recession, the political offensive of the nationally oppressed and the failure of the state to crush the extra-parliamentary mass opposition to apartheid would ensure that the white minority rule, shaken but still secure after 1976, would begin to be negotiated out of existence during and after 1990.[36] The government had also introduced some cosmetic reforms to absorb the pressure exerted against the apartheid system. Among these was the introduction of the quota system for the admission of black students to white universities.

The banning of SASO and other Black Consciousness (BC)-aligned organizations in 1977 left an organizational vacuum among students in universities which came to be filled by the establishment of the Azanian Student Organization (AZASO) which was initially BC aligned but later changed to be Congress (ANC)-aligned. The shift of AZASO from BC to the ANC and its endorsement of the Freedom Charter were significant as it launched the era of non-racial student movements in higher education. From thence, AZASO started hosting joint programs and developing plans of action with NUSAS in challenging the apartheid system. These developments were boosted by the establishment of the United Democratic Front (UDF) in 1983, which was established in opposition to the tri-cameral parliamentary system where Coloreds and Indians were co-opted into apartheid parliament but as junior partners in decision-making. The UDF comprised over 500 decentralized, local and regional civic, youth, women's, political and religious anti-apartheid organizations, together with national student organizations (including AZASO and NUSAS) and trade unions under the Freedom Charter. From 1983 onwards the UDF, as a popular non-racial, multi-class alliance, was to be at the forefront of the resistance to apartheid. [37] With its affiliates AZASO and NUSAS having a presence in almost every higher education institution in South Africa, links between campus-based struggles and community struggles found accord. It was in this political climate that I graduated from high school at the end of 1983 and was admitted to the University of the North, where I came to experience the reality of apartheid in universities and the sophisticated mechanisms devised to undermine it, leading to its ultimate demise in 1990.

RESISTANCE, REPRESSION AND THE DEMISE OF APARTHEID: 1984–1990

I could say that it was having been through different social and state institutions aimed at socializing black people to subservient roles and producing an ethnic consciousness that made me perceive myself as a Motswana, who is different and not part of the broader South African society. Born in the rural village of Marapyane, an exclusively Batswana village belonging to the Bakgatla tribe, the area was declared part of the Bantustan of Bophuthatswana in 1972, the year I started my schooling. In 1977 Bophuthatswana was granted "independent" status and I was therefore stripped of my South African citizenship. We had to carry Bophuthatswana identification documents; at school assembly we sang the Bophuthatswana national anthem twice weekly, we participated in "national" sports and music competitions that featured only Bophuthatswana schools; we had our own Minister of Education; own philosophy of education, namely Popagano, meaning "moulding." Every year there were national youth conventions to which high school pupils were invited and educated about how much they had been "freed" from apartheid in South Africa, that as Batswana youth, we were different and should be proud of our identity, and that we were the best, second to none. The Bantustan had its two "national" radio stations, a television station, its army and police force. All these state apparatuses were habitually put to use to deal with any form of non-compliance or defiance. However, at the end of Grade 12 (matric) we sat for the same examinations with all other black South Africans.

Exposure to that kind of system for 12 years of primary and secondary education had left some traces of allegiance to the homeland system. Political activity, except that which promoted homeland politics, was not allowed. Except for national newspapers and the state-censored South African Broadcasting Cooperation (SABC), which covered broader national events and developments, there was no way of being exposed to broader national and anti-apartheid politics. The state hegemony and legitimacy were further reinforced for me by the fact that my mother was a teacher in the local primary school under the jurisdiction of the Bophuthatswana Education Department, and I therefore became a "beneficiary" of state job provision. With Bophuthatswana having established its own university, there was an expectation that all Batswana students would apply for admission there. Thus in the middle of my final year of high school in 1983, I was faced with a tough decision of which university to apply to: the University of Bophuthatswana (UNIBO) or University of the North (UNIN). My interviews with students from my village who were affiliated to these institutions did not make decision-making easy. Those from (UNIBO) argued that if I were admitted there I would be assured of receiving a proper education without disruptions, whereas at the University of the North there were always boycotts which normally led to the university being closed. The students from UNIN refuted the latter allegation arguing that despite the boycotts, examinations were always written. In the midst of boycotts, students did make time to study. They retaliated by questioning the credentials obtained at a homeland university as at the time there was no certainty about whether the degrees from homeland universities were internationally recognized. I received letters of admission from both institutions, and took the risk of choosing UNIN, despite threats of boycotts, over UNIBO proclaimed as having more stability.

At the University of the North one was welcomed into a culture of resistance, struggle and challenge against the apartheid system. The UDF had been in existence for less than a year and the university facilities were often used as venues for some of its rallies as it spread its activities and influence to different parts of the country. One was surprised at the element of denunciation of the homeland and Bantustan system which was unheard of from where I came. The student culture was that of defiance and of ensuring that every student became part of the army fighting the evil system of apartheid. At the first meeting of the Azanian Student Organization (AZASO) to welcome new students, I was introduced to the real philosophy and approach underpinning the lives of black students at university. In addressing new students, the national president, Tiego Moseneke, explained AZASO's theme for the year, "Organizing for a democratic society," by linking student struggles to broader socio-political struggles. He explained some basic points informing the organizational activities and approaches, namely, that as students (a) we were members of the oppressed black community before we were students, and (b) we were the conscience of the community, and therefore needed to maintain our traditional role as black students in the community. Finally he pointed out the necessity to promote the role of black students as a vanguard in the struggle for liberation. This input led to the internal conflict within me in terms of how one was to relate to it. The perception and ideology one came here with, which was influenced by the kind of education system I had been through, was that I had earned my place/admission at this institution and never before had I heard linkages made between education and liberation in the way they were presented. Secondly, education would lead me to a better life, rather than advancing broader liberation goals. What became apparent was that I was in for a major political education. The role of students in the struggle for liberation and the importance of maintaining our traditional role in our communities were often repeated in mass meetings and rallies organized by the SRC and other political formations on campus. Black universities which were supposed to promote ethnicity were turned into political schools for opposition to apartheid.

I enrolled for a Bachelor of Arts in Education, not out of choice, but because circumstances did not provide me with alternatives. Even though I had been doing well in science and mathematics since elementary school, and would have liked to pursue a career in these fields, the secondary school I went to, which was the only one in my village, did not offer these subjects, since there were no qualified science teachers. This was not an uncommon feature in most black rural schools at the time. Furthermore, none of my teachers was a university graduate and the majority had only passed matric and had two years of teacher training; some were private teachers who had only a matric certificate and had not had any formal training. This situation was caused by the shortage of black and qualified teachers at the time. As a result, their knowledge base was not necessarily superior to that of the students they were teaching. Our school did not have a library or a laboratory, and having a classroom with a door and windowpanes was a luxury. I was thus made to follow the social sciences stream at secondary school, which channeled me into doing an Arts-oriented degree at university.

Even though I looked forward to being taught by white lecturers in the courses I chose, since I had never had that encounter throughout my schooling, I was disappointed by the shallowness of their input, and their poor command of the English language, as explained above. The disappointment was also in the content-heavy and authoritarian approach with which courses were taught. Emphasis was on note-taking, recalling what was in the texts without much emphasis on analysis. Assessment of written work in subjects such as History, put emphasis on punctuation and references, rather than on critique and analysis. A common feature in most courses was the study guide which was often the lecturer's summary of the prescribed texts and was 50–80 pages in size. It sometimes took mastering of those pages each semester for one to make it through the course. In most cases there was never a need to go to the library for references; missing a class was never a big loss. Despite taking this degree in the 1980s, the content of the courses had no relationship to life in the broader community. The History of Education course that I took in my first year and third year covered the period 1652, when the white settlers came to South Africa, to 1953, when the National Party Government introduced Bantu Education. It was history that was written from the white perspective.

While academic life was not that interesting, the social life on campus was more vibrant and I learned a lot more about the history and politics of the country than what the formal education taught me. This was mainly through rallies that were organized, mass meetings called by the SRC where grievances related to the running of the institution, performances of lecturers and the state of the nation would be addressed. More often this would normally lead to class boycotts as the university administrators would refuse to accede to the grievances of students. As students would always openly demonstrate their disapproval of some apartheid practices on campus and in the broader society, this always caught the attention of the apartheid government and the state would unfailingly unleash police on the campus where students would either be beaten by the police or arrested. Cloete et al. noted that from the middle of the 1980s to 1993, higher education protests and disturbances were virtually a weekly occurrence as campuses became "sites of struggle" for various anti-apartheid organizations active on the campuses. The government responded by declaring a state of emergency in July 1985, which led to the arrest of many community leaders and student leaders and activists. As a result of the unrest at the time, the end of first semester exams at UNIN were not written and postponed from July 1985 to January 1986.

The level of violence in the country did not subside and in the early hours of 12 June 1986, we were woken by sirens and floodlights, to find that our campus and halls of residences were surrounded by the apartheid army. They conducted a door-to-door raid of every room which resulted in many students being arrested. The conduct of the police and army during the raid reflects the kinds of prejudices within the South African security services at the time. Many students became victims of beatings during the raids because of posters of white women decorating their walls. They were accused of having a love for white women, which according to apartheid laws, was an anathema. Some were beaten for what was regarded as banned literature. This would be literature of the liberation struggle in the country, anything that purported to be against government. In the review of the raid, it was discovered that any student who was found to have any writing, poster, T-shirt, or banner with a word such as: *freedom, movement, organization, free, rights, liberation,* etc., was subjected to beatings and torture.

Upon reflection, it was apparent that these were the phrases that were also never used during teaching, unless they were used in the context or in support of apartheid policy. The raid lasted from 2 A.M., and was completed at 5 P.M. As the raid occurred, students were confined to room arrest in their halls of residence until the raid was completed. During the raid we learned through radio news that a second state of emergency had been declared. This therefore granted the police and the army the right to conduct these raids. Following the completion of the raid, we further discovered that the army had moved onto campus to establish a base, and did not leave the campus until years later (in 1988) when pressure was exerted on them to leave campus. As a result, the last 18 months of my undergraduate studies were carried out in the presence of the army on campus.

These practices and experiences show the poverty and bankruptcy of scholarship common in black universities during that period. One effect of this practice was that one learned more socially and politically from what was taking place on campus, than in the lecture room. Some of the lessons entailed discipline, in terms of learning to respect and abide by the resolution taken at a student gathering, even though it might appear to threaten some of your aspirations. I learned the art of running away from police and dodging their beatings, as they often visited and raided the campus. Even though I was not a Law student, I came to learn about security laws such as Section 29 of the *Internal Security Act,* which would lead to detention without trial. These were security laws which were often quoted and debated in student mass meetings as they would frequently be used against some student activists. I learned that despite a prolonged period of boycott, studying in the privacy of your room should continue, since examinations would always be written. I graduated at the end of the year feeling more of a South African than a Bophuthatswana citizen. I had been conscientized and my eyes had been opened to the flaws and injustices of the Banstustan system as an extension of apartheid.

In 1988 I was admitted to the University of the Witwatersrand (Wits), an historically white university, which could not admit black students without consent from the Minister of Education. My admission there was not based on clear criteria, since as I later came to discover, white universities were not able to assess the academic potential of black students, as there were no clearly established criteria. In my case, I was admitted on the basis of a distinction pass I had obtained in my first semester Setswana (language) course, even though this had nothing to do with the Bachelor of Education course I was being admitted to. Being at a historically white university was not easy and posed different challenges. Firstly, I was overwhelmed by the city life to which I was being exposed for the first time. The University of the North was based in a small rural township. For the first time in my life I was to be taught by white lecturers who were first-language speakers of English. Their accent was very different from that of my previous lecturers and I had difficulty coping with it. For the first time I was sharing a lecture room with white students; this was an overwhelming experience. As a result, during the first few days of lectures I did not hear anything that was taught. I was trying to adjust to the new environment and settings which were contrary to what I had been exposed to before. I also faced the challenge of having to deal with new subject matter and content which were unrelated to what I had learned in my undergraduate studies.

The different missions, visions and orientations between Afrikaans- and English-speaking universities in South Africa were also reflected in the curriculum. There was critique and analysis which was expected from students at Wits which was not the case at UNIN and other Afrikaans universities. The prescribed texts dealt with contemporary education issues in South Africa such as the People's Education Movement, resistance in education, critique of Bantu Education philosophy and an assault on Fundamental Pedagogics, all of which I had lived through. This brought about a new experience, and a new beginning, that education is not only about the past, but also about the present, and the future. This was never part of what I had learnt throughout my education. Even in my primary and secondary education we were never allowed to give examples that were related to our own life experience at home. We were never allowed to use our African names. But here it was different, and I started finding myself. The overwhelmingly white environment made me appeal to my inner self, to ask myself who I was and what my identity was. Part of that was to recall my African name, Chika, and use it on campus, instead of Trevor, which still continued to be used in the classroom. The challenge I faced was also with the texts which were prescribed, which because of the State of Emergency which was still in force, were regarded as subversive, and if found in my possession by the police would lead to my arrest. This put me in a predicament of having to choose on the one hand between continuing with my studies and carrying those texts with me as I commuted between the Wits campus and Soweto, risking being arrested, and on the other, ignoring the texts and risk failing or stop studying at all. For example, all the writings on socialism and critical pedagogy such as those of Karl Marx and Paolo Freire, and literature of resistance to apartheid which were either banned or regarded as subversive by government, constituted the key and compulsory readings in the courses I took. The challenge was also at another level, the mental shift and adjustment one had to make to come to terms with the reality that that which has been regarded as outlawed by government, can be part of the formal learning content in the classroom. This was not an easy transition to make, especially given that one lived on a militarized campus where such material would result in one being detained if found in one's possession.

Being exposed to a campus environment that had been occupied by the army for a period of over 18 months left within me some fears and phobias which I did not realize until I was at Wits. Cloete *et al.* discuss the level of violence at university campuses during this period and its effects on students as follows: "Although no students were killed on campus, thousands still bear the physical and emotional scars of beatings and tear gassing, and a number paid the ultimate penalty of political struggles that started on campus." [38] Some of the emotional and psychological scars I came to discover at Wits were when I would hear some knock at the door at night, especially if I was not expecting a visitor. I would be filled with distressing fear, thinking that it could be the police. The police used to arrest students randomly for questioning, and given that I was a familiar face at mass meetings and protest meetings, I could not rule out the possibility of being a target. As a result, the learning experience was characterized by the turbulence of having to make social, psychological, pedagogical and environmental adjustments. Coping with the challenges of transition was eased by my contact with a black lecturer at Wits, in whose course I had enrolled; we developed a mentor-mentee relationship and we often had "ventilation" sessions based on shared experience. This relationship blossomed and matured through different phases of our relationship as mentor and advisor through my honors, master's and doctoral studies, and he now is a colleague.

Thus apartheid education took people on different journeys and experiences where some became casualties, and some struggled through the system having to make some adjustments. The separate education practices had long-lasting effects on the broader society. As it was shown, the intended goals of black universities to serve in promoting ethnic identity did not succeed. Students at these institutions faced contending forces of apartheid philosophy, black solidarity and nationalism that cut across ethnic, and urban and rural divides. On the other hand, control of the formal curriculum in school, and the constant use of repressive state apparatuses in the form of police and army to foster compliance with government regulations, left imprints and scars in students which had to be dealt with after graduating or leaving those institutions. It appears that from the experience of the case presented in this chapter, the apartheid environment left contradictory and confusing imprints on school and education graduates. The impact of this depended on where one grew up: rural Bantustan or Homeland setting, black urban township context, which further determined the kind of education and consciousness one would be exposed to. These are the challenges which the new post-apartheid government had to deal with, in building a new non-racial, non-sexist and equal society.

TOWARDS ALTERNATIVES TO APARTHEID EDUCATION

While the apartheid state was continuing with its segregationist policy development, political organizations and civil society formations both inside and outside the country were also involved in policy development initiatives to inform their struggle against apartheid. This was initially done by the liberation movement in exile and came to be appropriated by the mass democratic movement in the 1970s and '80s. The mass democratic movement relied on intellectuals for conducting policy aimed at producing alternative policies to those of apartheid.

Historically, social and political decision-making was concentrated within an apartheid government that believed that its plan for remaking South Africa faced few problems. When, from the mid-1970s, apartheid began to face problems which government decision-makers recognized, they turned to those researchers (aligned to the ruling party) whom they believed could solve their problems.[39] Government opponents knew they had problems, but they did not believe that they could be solved—or at least that they could be solved by policy-making. Since the liberation movement, the liberal opposition and those private interests that opposed government policy were excluded from decision-making in government, they felt no need for policy formulation.[40] In many instances, these organizations were concerned only with formulating their own internal policies with little significance for or impact on general public policies. The policy context began to change when apartheid began to unravel. Firstly, as its difficulties became more intractable, the apartheid government began to realize that it had problems that could not be solved simply by turning to the small groups of researchers who were loyal to apartheid. It began to look beyond its inner circle.

Private interests, such as unions, NGOs and student organizations, also realized that their actions now made a difference, and they needed to know more about the environment in which they acted.[41] The principles governing the organization of these private interests and the research agendas and information they produced were non-racialism, non-sexism, equality, democracy and redress.[42] The approach adopted by extra-parliamentary groups shows a sophisticated approach and multi-pronged strategy for challenging the apartheid system. In education this entailed a demand-led strategy directed at attaining certain educational goals, the use of the class boycott tactic, and the establishment of education policy units which generated alternative education policies. During the 1980s the National Education Coordination Committee (NECC) mobilized and organized the education needs of its sector and constituencies—students, parents, teachers and workers—into a set of principled demands. This demand-led strategy was effective during the repressive years of apartheid in uniting the constituencies behind a common set of goals aimed at challenging the apartheid system. Thus, though the role of research was recognized in the struggle against apartheid education, its contribution was seen as partial. Policy research would be used alongside traditional strategies and tactics which had characterized the struggle against apartheid education. These tactics included school boycotts, opposition to the use of Afrikaans as the medium of instruction, mobilization of students behind the slogan "People's Education for People's Power" and the rejection of the slogan "Liberation Now, Education Later."[43]

The slogan "Liberation Now and Education Later" emerged in the mid-1980s in the context of opposition to apartheid education. As some sections of youth within the liberation movement became frustrated with the repression that was taking place in the broader society and in education, there was a call for youth to stop schooling and take arms to fight for liberation. Once liberation had been attained, they would then continue with their education. This slogan was challenged by the liberation movement aligned to the ANC as education was viewed as an important tool in the struggle for liberation. Schools were also seen as important in keeping the youth occupied in a constructive way and that they could be used as sites of struggle against apartheid. In particular, ways were devised to develop and introduce alternative education in the schools which would empower the youth in their struggle against apartheid. Hence the slogan "People's Education for People's Power" gained currency. As the repression against apartheid education intensified, the slogan "People's Education for People's Power" was transformed into a movement that symbolized opposition and resistance to apartheid education. Attempts were made to give it content and shape with the establishment of curriculum committees (such as in History and English) to write alternative syllabuses and textbooks which were in opposition to the apartheid content that was taught in schools, but also presenting the ideals and values of liberation in a free and democratic society. These initiatives were also short-lived as materials that promoted People's Education were banned from being used in the classrooms. Therefore

People's Education in the late 1980s survived as a movement around which educational and liberation ideals were pursued until the unbanning of the liberation movement.

According to Wolpe, the historic significance of "People's Education for People's Power" lies in the fact that its conceptions not only challenged all previous conceptions of educational transformation in South Africa, but in so doing, placed on the agenda questions which must constitute the necessary point of departure for the future formulation of new policies and new strategies under new conditions.[44] These included a formulation of a vision of a future system of People's Education which, inter alia, enables the oppressed to understand the evils of the apartheid system and prepares them for participation in a non-racial democratic system; eliminates capitalist norms of competition, individualism, and stunted intellectual development, encourages instead collective input and active participation by all, as well as stimulating critical thinking and analysis; eliminates illiteracy, ignorance and exploitation of any person by another; equips and trains all sectors of the people to participate actively and creatively in the struggle to attain People's Power in order to establish a non-racial democratic South Africa; and allows students, parents, teachers and workers to be mobilized into appropriate organizational structures which enable them to enhance the struggle for People's Power and to participate actively in the initiation and management of People's Education in all its forms.[45] In this context, one of the historically black universities, the University of the Western Cape, came to be known as the "People's University" not only because of its history of opposition to apartheid, but also through having become a home for many students that had fled police harassment or had been excluded from other universities. It also became renowned for employing academics who were opposed to apartheid and the level of critique and opposition to the apartheid government led it also to be known as "the intellectual home of the left."

This vision spelled out an alternative to the apartheid education system and informed the future non-racial education system. However, as it will be shown later, while this vision for people's education constituted an alternative to apartheid education, it was emptied of its radical content in the post-1990 period in the name of pragmatism, and sacrificed at the altar of the new post-1994 education policies which were informed by neo-liberal policies that had started to gain currency, and therefore continued to constitute an alternative even under a post-apartheid order. For example, one of the goals of People's Education was to introduce a new curriculum which promoted socialist values and eliminated capitalist values of competition and individualism. These values were abandoned as the post-cold war era affirmed the currency of capitalism based on competitive practices. In the South African context this was affirmed through the adoption of the macro-economic policy based on free-market principles.

The changed post-February 1990 conditions brought about by the un-banning of the liberation movement signaled the beginning of formal demise of the apartheid system. There was a shift in emphasis from what was seen as the politics of protest to what was referred to as the politics of reconstruction. The struggle around policy required new tactics and skills. There was thus an upsurge in the undertaking of policy research which emerged out of a realization that with the prospects of the dawn of democracy in South Africa, there would be a need for alternative policies to apartheid.

Chapter Three
From Resistance to Reconstruction: Preparing to Govern

INTRODUCTION

The aim of this chapter is to analyze the socio-political and policy context of the period 1990–1994 with specific reference to the policy development initiatives that were undertaken during this period. This period was characterized by the emergence of a plethora of policy development initiatives aimed at providing alternative policies to those of apartheid. As a result, the newly elected government inherited a rich legacy of policy development that it drew upon in developing post-apartheid higher education policy. This was not only in terms of the policy content but also some of the principles that underpinned policy development processes that were written into the Interim Constitution. However, the production of these policies was contested and there was a constellation of views and interests that was part of this process. Included here is a critical examination of how some of these views prevailed and became the basis for the development of the new agenda. Furthermore, owing to the lack of capacity, the mass democratic movement privileged the policy process issues at the expense of developing concrete educational policies.

Contrary to past practices where policy development was monopolized by a minority government, new policy development initiatives entailed the broad participation of various stakeholders in the various policy domains. Of importance to this chapter are the new conditions emanating from the unbanning of liberation movements on February 2, 1990, which ushered in the new political dispensation in South Africa. On the educational front this period demanded new sets of strategies and skills in the waging of the struggle against apartheid education. Within the educational organizations aligned to the liberation movement, there was a lack of capacity coupled with the need for democratic discourse to provide alternatives to apartheid educational policies.

This chapter argues that this policy development during this period was characterized by a tension between process approach to policy development within the stakeholders aligned to the liberation movement and technocratization of policy development by government. Despite the limitations caused by the emphasis on the policy process rather than concrete policy proposals, these policy initiatives produced an agenda, principles and values which became the basis for the development of fresh policies by the new government.

SHIFTS IN THE EDUCATIONAL STRUGGLE IN THE EARLY 1990s

February 2 1990 marked an historic date in the history of South Africa as President F.W. de Klerk announced the abolition of apartheid laws and unbanning of the liberation movement. While this was expected, given the crisis of apartheid at the time, the rapidity with which this was done caught many within the liberation movement unprepared. Alongside this was also an announcement of the beginning of negotiations leading to a new South Africa which came to affect every social sphere. A constant feature of educational resistance up to 1990 was what may be termed the politics of resistance and opposition. Key characteristics were mass mobilization and organization and mass action in pursuit of particular immediate objectives of a non-racial and non-sexist democratic social order. This was exemplified by campaigns against state schools, boycotts in higher education institutions against racist lecturers and exclusion of students on financial or academic grounds, linked to national political demands. According to Badat, a notable feature of such oppositional politics was silence on the concrete specification of the means by which the transformation of apartheid education was to be effected. The Freedom Charter and the People's Education Declaration advanced principles and objectives of educational provision. For example, the Freedom Charter declared that "the doors of learning and culture shall be open to all."[1] In elaborating on this, it stated that education should be free, compulsory, universal and equal for all children. Higher education and technical education would be opened to all by means of state allowances and scholarships awarded on the basis of merit. Whereas this principle points to the opening of access of education to everyone, it failed to specify the means and conditions under which this increased access would be realized. This emphasis, coupled with a lack of concentration on policies, while perhaps appropriate during an era of protest and oppositional politics, clearly became inadequate for any project of transformation.[2]

The relative neglect of relations in education and concentration on oppositional politics with inadequate attention to policies was, however, not unrelated to the configuration of economic, political and educational conditions in South Africa. National oppression and class exploitation resulted in the extreme politicization of all spheres of life. Prior to 1990 the prospect of the emergence of an equitable democratic society seemed distant. Consequently, the development of policies for transformation did not feature high on the agenda of the liberation movements or mass educational organizations.[3] The reforms heralded by the unbanning of political organizations in 1990 in turn produced new demands on the democratic movement. For the National Education Coordination Committee (NECC), this meant an oppositional and demands-based strategy would have to be augmented by one which enabled them to engage the state and other powerful groups, such as the business sector, in debates around specific possible alternatives to the apartheid education system.[4] The strategic shift was not something to be accomplished easily. In the immediate post-February 1990 period, the NECC increasingly began to articulate the necessity of moving beyond a politics purely of opposition towards one of transformation and reconstruction. This transformation was conceptualized in terms of the key features of opposition politics—organization-building, popular mobilization and mass action.[5] What this represented was a particular understanding of transformation. Far from being a neutral, purely technical process executed by experts and technocrats, it was viewed as an essentially political process at the core of which active and conscious participation of the masses was needed.

The period also saw the problematization of the notion of transformation. Singh points out that the line between the politics of resistance and that of transformation was not as clear-cut as some might imagine. In the era of resistance politics, transformational concerns were not absent though they may have been differently focused. More crucially, in what was presumed to be an era of transformation, resistance was not off the agenda.[6] She suggests that transformation in the post-1990 period could be understood as the maximum utilization of new political space to push further for popular participation and empowerment. It could also be viewed as an opportunity to insert progressive constituencies (stakeholders) into positions where, through contestations with ruling block forces, they could intervene in the struggle to shape the South Africa of the future.[7] The broader South African community, especially the intellectuals, dealt with the challenges posed by the possibility of the dawn of a post-apartheid social order in different ways. Once the reform process was formalized in February 1990, it became clear that new policies for the post-apartheid era would be required. However, embarking on activities aimed at developing policies for a post-apartheid social order was not easy. Decades of repressive political conditions had left South Africa with a seriously impoverished public discourse about educational possibilities and alternatives. This contributed to the discussions becoming couched in terms of opposition and general demands for redress rather than in terms of positive and attainable alternative policies.

In dealing with the new challenges there was a perspective of policy that emerged that tied issues of its development to those of implementation, drawing from the work of the 1980s. It was realized that the development of micro and macro policies needed to be fully integrated with economic and social policy if they were to be successful. There was also a deep reluctance to propagate specific policies in the absence of full knowledge of available resources or of the executive and administrative authority to carry them out. Chisholm observed at the time that there was a strong commitment, at least among the Congress of South African Trade Unions (COSATU), the ANC, the Education Department and the NEPI researchers, as demonstrated in the substantial consultative forum idea, not only to the policy product, but also to policy process.[8] This was linked to the knowledge that abstractly produced policies had little hope of being carried out without the active support for implementation by all parties involved. This lesson was drawn from other revolutionary situations, where attempts to impose particular policies without the support of those involved in implementation had in many instances led to the collapse of the system they were attempting to reform.

Emphasis on the policy process became important, as there was a realization that the capacity of any movement or party to carry through changes relies on its specific authority and legitimacy to do so. Without proper attention to process, specific policies were highly likely to be worthless. This perception gave rise to the view that effective policy is not produced only by researchers, and/or political parties, but through multiple negotiation and consultation. Unlike imposed blueprints or research conducted outside the process, negotiations were likely to produce effective policy plans. This perspective claims not to promote quick-fix solutions which sound good but signify nothing, culminating in little more than fury. It recognizes that policy is not simply "something that happens, then is over and fixed," but is constantly made and remade at both macro and micro levels by a variety of contending social forces. It adopts a long-term perspective, the most realistic and feasible approach in the then context of devastation, disempowerment and disaffection.[9] This perspective, in linking issues of policy formulation to implementation, favors negotiations and contextual issues. This should be understood in the light of the fact that in the pre-1990 period policy formulation was done in a way that excluded the very people who were to implement it or be affected by it. This new conception of policy would thus lead to a redress of the situation.

POLICY CONTEXT OF THE PERIOD 1990–1994

The post-1990 period saw new developments that changed the educational policy discourse leading to the elections of 1994. New institutional arrangements came into being with the purpose of policy analysis, policy studies and policy generation. One of these was the National Education Policy Investigation (NEPI), conducted under the auspices of the National Education Coordinating Committee (NECC), setting itself the objective of investigating "policy options" as opposed to issues of implementation or "policy choices." The distinction drawn here is between the political act of adopting particular policies (the role of organized constituencies) and the generation of policy options. Policy actors—both constituency and researchers—created a specific discourse that is distinguishable from the ideological positions that had until 1990 dominated ways of representing and addressing fundamental issues in education.

These new developments and realignments in the policy and political landscape were not unique to South Africa. The post February 1990 period brought for the first time in South African history, possibilities of talking about the modalities of building a consensus on education. However, consensus rarely occurs naturally but in some instances has to be "manufactured" to accommodate disparate and conflicting viewpoints and demands. This particular form of policy-making has been under scrutiny in the British education system because of the imminent threat of the historical consensus breakdown.[10]

The other important issue raised by sociologists of policy concerns the transition, which oppositional organizations, as policy actors, have to make in preparation for access to state power, or even the possibility of participating in government. This has been characterized at the level of discourse, from a "discourse of needs" to a "discourse of means." The process of envisioning a post-apartheid education system was certainly something the oppositional movements were involved in, but using different conceptual tools. What the discursive shift revealed was that oppositional movements in most cases were caught unprepared to generate policy. For many it was sufficient to rely on a litany of well-polished slogans, for example, "we demand a democratic non-racial, non-sexist, unified system." The slogans had more than proved their effectiveness by creating and mobilizing politically charged communities that challenged state power and apartheid education. What the slogans failed to do was to automatically translate into policy. They could not be translated until they were mediated through certain processes.[11]

The trajectory of developments between 1990 and 1994 reflects a certain conception of the role of research in policy-making within the liberation movement. While in developed countries such as the United Kingdom (UK) and the United States (US) there had been an established tradition of uses of policy research in policy-making, this was something which had been a monopoly of the apartheid state in South Africa and to which access by educational organizations opposing apartheid had been forbidden. The question that needs to be posed is "why was the NEPI project conceptualized and aimed at producing policy options rather than policy proposals?" Was it because of a lack of capacity or experience in formulating specific policy proposals, or were there other factors that influenced this approach?

Restricted access to information and analysis, and a political climate hostile to free debate and open discussion, had an influence on the approach adopted by the NEPI project. As a result, the discussion within NEPI was couched in terms of opposition and general demands rather than positive and attainable alternative policies. This approach also reflected the kind of expertise that was available within the liberation movement with its limited experience of developing policies for the government and an array of skills for critiquing government policies rather than providing the research necessary for producing specific alternative policies. To change this kind of mindset is not easy to achieve; it entails a process of engagement with and immersion in that which is unfamiliar.

In higher education, the debate within NEPI was how higher education policy could address these twin goals without destroying existing capacities within the sector. There were diverse views that emerged and these polarized the higher education community along racial, sectoral and ideological lines. The outcome of this debacle from the NEPI project was the emergence of policy goals and principles to underpin the future education system, namely equality, development, democracy, efficiency, equity and freedom.[12]

The adoption of these policy principles and goals, especially what they meant in practice, was contested from a diversity of viewpoints. In particular the implementation of these policy principles became a contested issue that characterized policy debates and development leading to the 1994 elections and continued to plague the new DOE in the post-apartheid context.

It led to a constellation of voices, which transcended stakeholder boundaries, with some of the voices becoming un-affirmed, lonely and isolated. The questions to be addressed are "what kinds of voices became legitimized, how and by whom, what is the nature of voices that did not become mainstream and why did they not?" The process of mobilizing resources and expertise and shifting towards development of alternative policies to those of apartheid education was not without difficulties. In particular, it brought about a stark dichotomy between experts or intellectuals on the one hand, and the masses on the other. This dichotomy, which manifested itself in the NEPI project, came to be criticized within sections of the democratic movement. It appears that the unbanning of political organizations and the opening up of space for negotiation had left some mass organizations without any agenda to pursue. As Nzimande observed, the weaknesses of the mass organizations became the strength of policy researchers and intellectuals as organizations started relying more on the latter to deal with the complex situation presented by the post-1990 developments.[13]

There were fierce debates on how intellectuals could use their social skills to make policy accessible to mass-based organizations. In reflecting on this point, Singh identified three possible challenges faced by intellectuals during that period: The first pertained to the role intellectuals could play to facilitate input into policy agendas and formulations by mass- based organizations and constituencies. The second concerned the facilitation of access to policy information, debates and proposals. The dissemination of policy discussion in accessible forms and forums was seen as crucial to a deepening of the democratic process, insofar as it could ensure that such knowledge did not remain the "property" of political decision-makers and experts. The third was that intellectuals who were located at universities and were engaged in policy research were challenged to urge their institutions to play a central role in availing access to policy debates as part of a broader project of using their infrastructure to democratize public access to knowledge.[14]

These views of the roles of intellectuals put forward by Singh are similar to those proposed by Badat in his critique of the roles of researchers and academics in the policy formulation process. He, however, includes two important qualifiers. First, he points out that asserting the importance of researchers and academics to the investigation of policy options does not privilege them in relation to the policy-making process. Rather it recognizes that some kinds of research, such as policy research, are specialist academic activities. Researchers possess particular skills which need to be harnessed in the service of social transformation. Secondly, stressing the importance of academics and researchers does not mean leaving policy-making in their

hands. As he puts it, "there is no direct path from research to policy formulation." He describes the role of academics and researchers in the policy
process as not to formulate or make policies, but to present the democratic
movement with an analysis, firstly of structural and conjunctural conditions, and secondly, with policy options and the implications of such options. He suggests that, armed with the information and analysis about the
range of policy options available, political and social movements will formulate policy.[15]

This conception of the policy process which dichotomizes the two
phases between policy analysis and policy formulation, and ascribes different actors to fulfill the roles, captures some of the politics of the policy
process at the time. There was an understanding amongst academics aligned
to the mass democratic movement that their role was not to formulate policies. Given the tradition of critique which had characterized opposition to
apartheid policies, there was also a certain hostility associated with policy
formulation which was seen as being the prime responsibility of the state.
Since policy-making within the apartheid state was conducted away from the
public domain, and given its ideological underpinning, it was something with
which progressive academics never wished to be associated. This ambiva-
lence with activities associated with the state could have informed some of
the views and models of policy-making which some progressive academics
adopted. However, there were also academics and policy researchers who believed that the new government needed to be supported and presented with
policy recommendations whenever it commissioned work to independent research agencies. Some of the challenges to the relationship between academics and social movements in South Africa were addressed through the NEPI
project. Means were devised to balance the input of intellectuals and mass-
based organizations in the policy research process. This, however, met with
little success. In reflecting on the problem, Nzimande pointed out that NEPI
classically represented the problem of the division of labor where "your experts, academics, university-based people largely, were predominantly white,
while the NECC structures were mass-based community people who were
predominantly black."[16] The former ended up doing most of the research
and writing, while the latter could not effectively participate for lack of skills.

The policy research process undertaken between 1990 and 1994 produced some policy principles and goals which became a source of contestation among intellectuals. Even though these principles and goals were
adopted as a future framework for the transformation of the system, the diversity of views among academics in terms of their implementation continued to characterize the policy process. There were, however, some voices

that prevailed, became legitimized and informed the new government's policies and implementation program. On the other hand, the alternative voices to the mainstream (those that were not legitimized) became isolated, marginal and lonely, even though they were informed by the principles of the democratic movement. This resulted in the policy process becoming characterized by competition and tension between these two voices. It cut across stakeholder boundaries so that sometimes both voices co-existed within the same group. This point is important to remember in the following discussion of stakeholder groups, that they should not be seen as monolithic; rather there are heterogeneous views which always have to be mediated.

POLICY INITIATIVES FROM BELOW

As policy research came to play an important role in the development of alternatives to apartheid education, different stakeholders in higher education, political parties and NGOs started embarking on policy research. The involvement of these agencies outside of the state is characterized as representing policy initiatives from below. This section concentrates on the role which these agencies played in the unfolding of the policy process during the period under review. In particular, it highlights in concrete terms how these agencies contributed to building a legacy of policy research which was to become a resource when the new government came into power in 1994.

The role intellectuals and academic played in the policy process became institutionalized through the work of the Union of Democratic University Staff Associations (UDUSA), formed in a context of academic boycott in the 1980s and which had set itself the objective of organizing its members around that boycott. At the time, there were opposing views on the boycott, some in favor, some against.[17] With the reform initiatives to end formal apartheid in the 1990s, which rendered the boycott principle irrelevant, UDUSA started focusing its attention on policy issues and the restructuring of higher education. While it objected to the segregated nature of higher education and the impact of apartheid on higher education, it went beyond simply asking for all apartheid legislation to be removed and started thinking about what should be put in its place.[18]

The policy work of UDUSA was developed through the following initiatives. First, in 1990 there was a NEPI research initiative that was generated under the auspices of the NECC to look at the possible educational policy options for post-apartheid South Africa. Members of UDUSA played a central role in the work, serving as coordinators of most of the NEPI research groups.[19] The second form in which UDUSA's policy work received a boost was through a national conference on transformation of universities, which it hosted in 1992, and which brought together academics, university management officials, researchers, international academics and students. From there it initiated a transformation agenda on higher education. Following the successful national conference which launched it as an important player in the development of future policies for higher education in post-apartheid South Africa, an UDUSA policy forum was formed in late 1992. The main focus of the policy forum was described as being "to develop policy positions and respond to national restructuring initiatives."[20] Some of the key policy initiatives in which UDUSA members participated were the development of the ANC's Framework for Education and Training (Yellow Book), the Centre for Education and Policy Development's (CEPD's) Implementation Plan for Education and Training (IPET) and the work of the NCHE—both as researchers and as commissioners. These policy documents became a key resource for the new government in the development of new higher education policy. On the other hand, the UDUSA policy forum prided itself on having produced a policy document which was to be used by the Minister on taking office in May 1994.[21]

Shifts in strategies and tactics did not happen only within staff associations, they also took place within the student movement. Prior to 1990, student organizations in South Africa were still organized on the basis of race. One of the first steps undertaken by student organizations that were aligned to the Freedom Charter, namely the South African National Student Congress (SANSCO) and the National Union of South African Students (NUSAS), was to talk about the possible formation of a single non-racial student organization under which higher education students would be organized. Talks of the merger between the two organizations had started as early as 1987 in anticipation of the transformation that was to take place in South Africa. Talks on the merger finally ended in 1991 with the launch of a new student organization, the South African Students' Congress (SASCO). Thereafter, SASCO began participating in the different transformation initiatives organized within the higher education sector as a formal stakeholder.

One of the major activities in which it participated was the NEPI initiative, exposing students to the significance of knowledge and empirical research in influencing policy development. This involved attempts to formalize policy development within the organization by setting up a formal structure in 1992 in the form of the National Transformation Commission (NTC) and charging it with taking care of policy development for this organization.[22] It became a vehicle through which SASCO made some input in the policy initiatives of the period 1992–1994. There were, however, no formal documents produced by the NTC which formed the basis of its input to policy structures. SASCO also participated in such policy initiatives as the drafting of the ANC's Policy Framework for Education and Training and the IPET process of the CEPD.

In 1995, the NCHE was appointed to advise the government on how to restructure and transform higher education. SASCO saw this as another opportunity to make an input into and influence the process of policy development and the transformation of higher education. The Commission created the context and momentum for engagement of students in policy development. In order to combat what was viewed as marginalization of students, SASCO decided to embark on a research capacity-building initiative aimed at assisting the organization to make an input to the NCHE. This heralded a shift in SASCO's approach to policy development from the earlier period of reliance on resolutions and slogans. As the former SASCO policy coordinator put it:

> The NCHE process forced us to put in place a more systematic process than had actually been in the past. We were aware that there is a large danger of students being marginalized. Students have always been involved in spearheading transformation until the 1990s and suddenly there was a huge policy formulating structure called the NCHE, with all these CUPs, CTPs, Business and experts of course who understand more than students could ever.[23]

This new period was characterized by production of policy research which was used to back up students' demands and to influence the process and content of transforming higher education. The significance of the shift is connected to attempts at reconciling the tradition of advocacy with the professional dimension of generating more legitimate knowledge to back up their advocacy and claims. SASCO had come to the realization that some of its forms of knowledge, particularly at that time, would not be recognized as knowledge by the NCHE. Consequently the only way that they could substantiate their claims and make sure that they were recognized was by introducing a professional dimension or scientific approach to their policy-making.

The ANC Education Department also formalized its policy development role in education with the establishment of the Centre for Education Policy Development (CEPD) in late 1992. The CEPD played an important role in the development of the ANC's educational policies, coordinating the research work that led to the production of the ANC's Policy Framework for Education and Training published in January 1994. This was the first formal and comprehensive policy document from within the ANC to be publicized for public comment. It further co-coordinated the preparation of the Implementation Plan for Education and Training (IPET), which was handed over to the ANC when it assumed power. This in turn became the basis on which the ANC addressed policy development when it assumed power in May 1994.

There was also the role played by international development agencies in the policy development process such as the United States Agency for International Development (USAID), the Danish International Development Agency (DANIDA), and the Ford Foundation. Their activities ranged from funding of research, to producing alternative policies to apartheid, to undertaking own research and producing research reports in support of a post-apartheid dispensation. Because of their support of alternative policies to apartheid, and as such did not work with the apartheid government during this period, their position could be regarded as being from below or from the side. According to Jansen, USAID is the best positioned-foreign organization with respect to education policy. He points out that the influence of USAID was established through extensive funding of non-government organizations (NGOs) of which many had well-established anti-apartheid credentials.[24] There were three kinds of interventions through which USAID exercised its influence. The first of these was through the commissioning of the standard "sector assessments" associated with its operations in much of the world. The tertiary education sector provided critical information on the status of higher education in South Africa, including provision of information for policy and planning which had been in short supply in the early 1990s. Second, USAID exercised influence by bringing in cutting-edge technologies for recasting education-policy thinking in the democratic movement. To this end, the Research Triangle Institute (RTI) was contracted to work with the Education Foundation, a local policy think-tank, to generate and apply policy modeling to future educational project needs and financing. According to Jansen, the selling points of these technologies were rationality, discipline and control. He observes that RTI was to continue to be the cover for external expertise in the financing of education late into the 1990s. [25]

Third, USAID influence was extended through direct funding of ANC (and other) leaders, often through the United States Information Service (USIS) on study visits to the USA where they examined educational policy and practice in American schools and universities. Examples included studies of the American community college system, the provision of education for disadvantaged young children, and science and mathematics in high schools.[26] While USAID did not formulate post-apartheid education policy in the same way as other competitors (local policy actors), there can be no question that it played a crucial role in exerting influence on and shaping the landscape within which policy was developed after apartheid.

The policy initiatives taken by different stakeholders discussed above show the extent of policy awareness generated among the South African public in the run-up to the 1994 elections, and they constituted a rich legacy inherited by the new government when it came to power. Not only was there an awareness of policy that was generated within society, but also one of the significances of these initiatives was that there was a particular agenda for the transformation of higher education that emerged.

POLICY INITIATIVES FROM ABOVE

While organizations not formally related to the state embarked on policy initiatives aimed at producing alternative policies to those of apartheid, the apartheid education department and the statutory structures aligned to it also embarked on reform initiatives. However, these initiatives took place unevenly across these structures. While the Department of National Education and the Committee of University Principals (CUP) embarked on minor reforms aimed at keeping their structures and practices intact during transition, the Committee of Technikon Principals (CTP) embarked on a radical reform agenda aimed at creating space for the technikon sector to play a role in higher education which would be equally important to that played by the university sector in a new South Africa.

The apartheid Department of National Education (DNE) had been the *de facto* policy instrument for education during apartheid. While the ferocity of political oppression continued through official and "third force" instruments of state power in the townships, the DNE provided a much more open and accessible forum for deliberating on reformist policies.[27] For example, access was provided for ANC-aligned academics to the DNE's policy deliberations, including the attempts to formulate a new teacher education policy for South Africa. Progressive academics at first steered clear of these invitations but gradually became part of these policy forums in the form of the Committee on Teacher Education Policy (COTEP). The outcome of these policy deliberations was the release of the Education Renewal Strategy (ERS) in 1991, which appeared in two versions, the second following public criticisms of the first publication. The second policy document was the Curriculum Model for Education in South Africa (CUMSA) in 1992, which later led to a review of school syllabuses with a view to reducing the content-heavy emphasis that characterized curriculum restructuring. Driven by the need to change, the ERS document proposed a reform program based on three principles: race was not to feature in the provision of education; justice in education opportunities had to be ensured; and the new model had to promote and express national unity.[28] Given the history of apartheid education as characterized by racial divisions and injustice in the provision of education, the new values proposed by the ERS represented an intention on the part of the National Party government to shift from apartheid-based education. However, this move was not easy as it was accompanied by intentions to retain as much privilege as possible for the white minority groups.

In March 1994, on the eve of the first all-race general election in South Africa, the Department of National Education, under the National Party government, hosted a conference on higher education titled "Tertiary Education Conference" that provided a forum for debating higher education in the post-apartheid dispensation. It brought together academics, non-government organizations, government officials, officials of higher education institutions, business and political organizations. That an apartheid education department was able to bring together such a broad spectrum of higher education role players, from both the left and right, shows the extent of political maturity and "openness" in debating issues pertaining to the future of higher education in South Africa.

Statutory bodies in higher education, such as the Committee of Technikon Principals (CTP) and the Committee of University Principals (CUP), embarked on policy development initiatives aimed at preparing for the post-apartheid social order. The following were some of the milestones achieved by the CTP between 1991 and 1994. In 1991 the CTP working group on qualification structure (which included degrees) completed its investigation into the possibility of technikons offering some degrees. This was discussed with the Minister of Education in 1992. Permission to offer degrees was granted to technikons in 1993 with the proclamation of the Technikon Act which brought former black technikons and former white technikons l under one Act. The right to offer degrees also included the right to offer master's and doctoral degrees. Not only was CTP given the right to offer degrees but they also claimed the right to use the title "Professor" and to offer honorary degrees.[29] In explaining the timing of the writing of the proposal to offer degrees and to have all technikons under one Act, Figaji, a former chairperson of the CTP, commented that:

> In 1991–1992, the writing was on the wall about the new elections. There was going to be a change in government and we took the opportunity to write one Act, to put all the technikons under one Act and make a political statement saying we unify our sector of higher education in one Act. And it is that Act in which we wrote the qualifications.[30]

There is no evidence of a major preoccupation with development of alternative policies within the CUP. However, the changes did have an impact on its operations as exemplified by the challenge of language policy. The official languages of the CUP had historically been Afrikaans and English. With the admission of more black vice-chancellors, it was for the first time faced with a situation where it had members who did not understand Afrikaans. Some of the members insisted on using it even though others could not understand. The drama this brought about is captured in the following statement:

> Afrikaans [language] was a huge issue, and the chair of CUP used to conduct one meeting in Afrikaans and next time would conduct it in English. We started getting members who couldn't speak Afrikaans and people who simply insisted on speaking in Afrikaans. It created dissonance just in itself. I just couldn't believe that people who could speak perfectly good English spoke Afrikaans just to make a point, even though some people at the table couldn't understand it. It set the tone for the meeting. You try and conduct a conversation in Afrikaans with half the people enraged with you with speaking Afrikaans in the first place. How do you create an environment with that kind of thing going on?[31]

The language factor as illustrated in the above quote shows the extent of heterogeneity within the CUP. At the same time there was an emergence of the seeds of what later became known as the forum of historically disadvantaged institutions (HDI forum) within the CUP, with a new group of black vice-chancellors. These academics were concerned with trying to find ways of re-engineering their institutions and making them even stronger.[32] According to Reddy, a former vice-chancellor of the University of Durban-Westville, the decision at the time was not to form a separate association, but as he put it:

> We felt that we had common things in the form of disadvantages to discuss; we wanted to be a pressure group. It had a lot of significance and merit because HDIs were the growth point at that time. They were growing rapidly and were the centers of change and opposition to the government at that time.[33]

The emergence of these different voices within the CUP informed the ways in which this body responded to issues pertaining to higher education restructuring. For example, the appointment of the NCHE and the need for input from various sectors led to the establishment of an HDI forum which made a submission separate to that of official statutory bodies. In its background statement in its submission to the NCHE, the forum of the fifteen universities and technikons stated that it realized that:

> They have in common in that they were all founded in the apartheid era
> to cater for exclusively black [variously African, Colored and Indian]
> students; that they continue to admit mainly educationally disadvan-
> taged students; and that for all their diversity, they exhibit a set of shared
> characteristics which are fundamentally specific to historically disad-
> vantaged institutions. Because of their similar concerns and experiences,
> these institutions believed that it would be valuable to submit a joint
> statement to the NCHE.[34]

The identity which the HDI forum carved for itself in terms of how it defined itself in relation to its affiliate institutions, its clientele and service it
provided, highlights the fact that policy debates were racially based even
well into the post-1994 period.

SETTING THE AGENDA FOR HIGHER EDUCATION TRANS-
FORMATION: PROCESS VERSUS CONTENT

Analysis of policy development leading to the 1994 elections and the first
five years of the newly elected government shows emphasis on the policy
process with a high level of consultation with and participation from the
various stakeholders. As pointed out earlier, this ultimately became the basis
on which the legitimacy of the process and product came to be judged. For
example, one of the bases on which the NEPI project gained legitimacy was
the extent to which it was conducted in a consultative, participatory and accountable manner. Though there was still emphasis on process issues, policies developed during the period closer to the 1994 elections entailed a less
consultative process. In his analysis of the process of production of major
policy documents during this period, starting with the People's Education
discourse of the late 1980s and ending with the first *White Paper on
Education and Training* produced as a draft in September 1994, Greenstein
identifies a consistent move away from a populist emphasis on process, consultation and equality, to a more technocratic emphasis on performance,
outcome and economic competitiveness.[35] This could be related to the urgency to deliver more concrete policies in preparation for ascendancy to
power by the new government.

    Despite this observed shift, emphasis on process continued to hold
sway in policy formulation in education. There are a number of reasons that
can be advanced to explain why process issues were important during this
period. First, it could be a demonstration of lack of capacity within the democratic movement to deal with the challenge of formulation of specific policies. One such was the conceptual difficulty of formulating policies for a
unitary education and training system. Chisholm explains this by citing the

conditions that existed in the immediate post-1990 period, where there were different and separate budgets dealing with education and training and nonformal education. An integrated approach to the entire educational question, including literacy, was one that required conceptual leaps that at the time few people were making.[36] Thus holding onto that which was familiar, namely struggle politics as informed by participation, consultation and representivity, would assist the movement to retain a grip on the policy development endeavor. This assertion is supported by Morris, who points out that emphasis on the policy process was a response to a lack of capacity from within civil society organizations and the intellectual community to deliver on policy. As he put it, "they placed stress on instituting correct process rather than concentrating on the substantive detailed content in alternative policy options."[37] He argues that what followed was a concentration on setting up a number of representative forums covering a wide variety of socioeconomic issues. This delayed the process of formulating acceptable policies and implementing them.

Second, the concentration on the policy process could be a way of buying time by the democratic movement since there was hesitancy within the movement to take the initiative and put forward specific policy proposals. It was only in 1994 with the release of the ANC Framework Document that the first policy proposals came from within the democratic movement. Before then the policy domain was characterized by critiques and policy options. A preoccupation with resistance and later with critiques and provision of policy options did little to prepare the disadvantaged constituencies for the challenges of formulating concrete policy proposals. Talk of educational transformation after 1990 had to be about budgets, fiscal transfers, efficiency or cost effectiveness—not simply grievances. According to Chetty, good politics (particularly those on the left) had to an extent been presumed to be a substitute for policy analysis based on hard evidence and strategies to deal with the inheritance of apartheid-style mismanagement, inefficiency and mediocrity.[38]

The emphasis put on process issues rather than on concrete policy proposals had the positive effect of producing policy principles and frameworks that later informed the development of post-apartheid policies by the new government. The emergence of the core principles of non-racialism, non-sexism, democracy, equity, quality, and redress from the NEPI research reports later informed the writing of the ANC's Policy Framework for Education and Training. These principles also made their way into the writing of the White Paper 1 on Education and Training which was produced by the DOE in 1995.[39]

The developments leading to the 1994 elections did not see only the shifts in the ways educational struggles were waged and the greater involvement of stakeholders and other role players in the development of alternative educational policies. The focus on policy work happened within a context of the realization, after February 1990, that imminent negotiations were going to demand more detailed policy than previously advanced. If there was going to be a democratic government in place soon, it was also going to need a set of policies to be put in place.[40] Singh explained the situation as follows:

> There was a realization that we were entering a decade where the reconstructive task might be a much more critical and needed intervention given the direction the negotiations were going. It was in that context that we started to turn our minds to some alternative policy frameworks and positions for higher education.[41]

There are three key documents through which this agenda has been shaped, namely: (a) the NEPI reports, especially the post-secondary report released in 1993, which produced values and principles to underpin the future education system, as well as the policy options for the macro aspects of the higher education system; (b) the ANC's *A Policy Framework for Education and Training,* which became popularly known as the Yellow Book, which outlined a vision and policy framework for the future education system; and (c) the *Higher Education Implementation Plan Report* that was produced by the CEPD's Higher Education Task Team (HETT), which outlined implementation plans which the ANC government had to follow when it came into office. The significance of the three documents for analysis of the educational policy process is that they represent maturity within the mass democratic movement, from talking about policy abstractly in terms of options, to concretizing it in terms of clearly articulated principles, policy goals, values, vision and practical policy proposals and recommendations.

THE NEW POLICY AGENDA

This section discusses the policy agenda that emerged through this process in terms of the values and principles, policy goals and implementation plans adopted. The NEPI reports distilled five principles against which the policy options presented were analyzed and which were intended to underpin the future education system, namely: non-racism, non-sexism, democracy, unitary system and redress.[42] The higher education research group of NEPI identified the following five elements of the higher education sector in formulating the new higher education policy:[43] (a) governance of higher education; (b) the nature of and function of higher education; (c) access to higher education; (d) financing higher education institutions and students; and (e) the shape and size of the higher education system.[44] The logic that informed the choice of these policy areas, the rationale for focusing on them are explained by Singh in the following statement:

> If you look at the kind of emphasis that we had at the time, governance was an important concern, and this had to do with the fact that arrangements of governance within higher education were offensive. Clearly we had to think about what would be the more democratized governance arrangements in higher education. Instead of saying that "you did not want that vice-chancellor making decisions in this unilateral fashion," then what did you want as an alternative governance arrangement?[45]

The funding and allocation of resources were regarded as constituting an important element in the reconstruction and transformation of higher education. In addressing this issue Singh elaborates:

> The financial issue, for instance, if you take the case of the University of the North, which ended at certain point enrolling 18 thousand students for a campus designed for a smaller number of students [six thousand]; this was Bantu Education at the university level. The way the subsidy formula was organized was that you got money on a calculation of entry of inputs and outputs. With the large failure rate we had at the Historically Black Universities [HBUs], the output component did generate income that was expected from large enrolment. Academic development was not funded. So it was quite clear that students at HBUs were getting a raw deal in terms of financing education. So parity in financing on financial principles was going to be an issue to be addressed in the same way as spending on health, welfare and housing was absolutely determined by apartheid policy.[46]

With respect to access, various indicators such as enrolment patterns between various sectors, across institutions and within disciplines showed that access to higher education was unequal, and this was thus a logical policy area on which to concentrate. The central issue facing a future higher education system was determining what its shape and size should be. "Shape" refers to the proportion of higher education enrolments in the different sectors or programs (in a unitary system) and in different subject areas. It also refers to the relative emphasis given to undergraduate, postgraduate, and research programs in the higher education system.[47] On the other hand, the "size" of the higher education system refers to the number of institutions and number of enrolled students across the higher education institutions. The final size of the system would depend chiefly on an access option by a future government.

The work done by NEPI was carried forward in the ANC's policy document on education unveiled in January 1994. It presented the following issues as dominant and affecting all policy questions in the sector: First, higher education institutions ought to be representative of the South African population. That meant that black students should enter and succeed in higher education in proportion to their strength in higher education. Students and academic and administrative staff should reflect the country's racial, gender, class, and rural-urban balance. Second, the effect of the apartheid social order on HBIs had left them disadvantaged financially, in the range of disciplines offered, and by the underdevelopment of graduate studies and research capacities. Third, the higher education system should be transformed to enable it to contribute to the reconstruction of society through close linkage with a development policy aimed at economic growth, the enhancement of a democratic political system and promotion of cultural and intellectual life. [48]

These points raised above show a bias towards addressing those issues that had historically disadvantaged some members of the higher education community on the basis of their race. This point seems to be reflected in its vision for higher education which is presented as follows: "There will be a well planned and integrated, high quality national system of higher education whose students and staff are increasingly representative of South African society."[49]

With respect to principles that were identified, the national government was tasked with the central responsibility for the provision of higher education. The redressing of historical imbalances will be a priority; the higher education system, and individual institutions, will be required to be effective and have clearly defined objectives linked to the national development; and democratic values of representivity, accountability, transparency, freedom of association, and academic freedom will underpin the higher education system.[50]

The Higher Education Task Team of the CEPD recommended the following immediate action to be undertaken by the national Minister of Education. With respect to legislative actions it recommended that the Minister proclaim the National Commission on Higher Education and revise the appropriate action to transform the Advisory Council on Universities and Technikons (AUT) into a Higher Education Council (HEC), in the interim, reconstituting AUT to have broader stakeholder participation. With respect to executive actions the new Minister was to reorganize the Ministry to create a Division of Higher Education and appoint key personnel; issue an instruction to universities and technikons to provide information on 1994

enrolments and 1995 admission policies; issue guidelines to stabilize enrolments at Historically Black Universities (HBUs); issue guidelines to increase
black enrolments at all technikons and Historically White Universities
(HWUs); allocate a substantial sum (approximately R100 million) in supple-
mentary funds for the academic year 1995 for loans and bursaries to universities and technikons.

CONTESTATION OVER THE POLICY AGENDA

The development of this policy agenda was not without problems, but was
contested throughout the process. The policy agenda highlighted the inequities of the higher education system and a commitment was made to address them. While there was agreement on some of the features and
principles of higher education, there was no unanimity on how to address
some of the challenges. For example, with respect to ensuring that higher education addresses equity, quality and development goals, there were fierce
debates about how these could be attained. One argument was that strategies designed to improve equity in higher education could lead in certain circumstances to a decline in the quality of the system, particularly if the
demands of equity were taken to imply that all resource allocations in the
system should be equalized.

The problem with this argument may be that it could have an unacceptable effect on the socio-economic development of the country—high equity plus low quality could lead to low economic growth. Flowing from this
perspective were therefore two central issues facing the higher education system: How could the demands for equity be made consistent with South
Africa's need for a higher education system of higher quality? How could the
development needs of the country be met if priority was given to elimination
of inequalities in the higher education system? [51] The contestations tended
to polarize higher education along racial lines with the Historically White
Universities (HWIs) favoring development and quality goals and the
Historically Black Institutions (HBIs) favoring the equity goals. This point
in succinctly captured by Wolpe and Sehoole, in pointing out that:

> The argument has been advanced from the side of the HWIs that they
> should continue to be funded at certain levels because they embody
> teaching and research capacities required to develop the new South
> Africa, and from the side of the HBIs, that funds should be shifted to
> them because they have been historically disadvantaged.[52]

Neither of these positions was acceptable in this form since, in one way or
another, funding had to be attached to new redirected functions. Simply to

fund the institutions in a manner which enabled them to perform better according to an agenda under a previous dispensation was inadequate.

CONCLUDING REMARKS

This chapter has explored the policy arena in the post-1990 period leading to the 1994 elections, with specific reference to the shifts which the democratic movement had to make from resistance to transformation and engagement, the policy development initiatives from below and above, and the higher education transformation agenda that emerged from these initiatives. The shifts led many stakeholders to be involved in different policy initiatives that were aimed at influencing post-apartheid education policy.

The ways in which stakeholders were involved have helped to reveal the extent to which policy initiatives were pursued both inside and outside government and how this led to competing discourses of the vision and content for the post-apartheid education system. The policy initiatives of the organizations that were aligned to the mass democratic movement structures were fed into the major policy documents produced by the liberation movement, led by the ANC. Capacity was therefore built in terms of human resources, as well as policy options and positions which the new government could use as a basis for policy development. As a result, when the new Government of National Unity came into office in 1994, it inherited a rich legacy of policy development, and some clear policy guidelines that formed a basis for development of new policies in the post-apartheid era. This is different from the experiences of many developing countries where post-colonial governments had to start virtually from scratch with respect to the development of new policies.

Despite the contribution made by agencies associated with the liberation movement in principles and values, frameworks and policy recommendations in informing post-apartheid education, the work produced suffered from the following deficiencies: First, the NEPI work was conducted under the assumption that there would be a unitary system of education and they could not anticipate the political terms of the South African transition from apartheid. For example, possibilities of having general education controlled by provincial governments never featured in the discussion. In fact it was only in early 1994 that this reality presented itself. Second, The NEPI researchers had limited access to the inner workings of the education bureaucracy and the kinds of legislation and practice governing policy formulation on a day-to-day basis. Third, the IPET policy recommendations also suffered from attempts to develop close-to-realistic plans outside the conditions of education, such as would exist after the political negotiations. Neither

NEPI nor IPET could anticipate the formation of the provinces with political and legislative autonomy enshrined in the Interim Constitution of South Africa as the single most important factor that would undermine the delivery of education in the first five years of the new government. Nor could all these policies have anticipated the lack of bureaucratic capacity to engage and to implement national policy within each of the nine provinces.[53] This lack of capacity impacted on and compromised the ability of the public service to act on policy. Fourth, neither NEPI nor IPET could anticipate the personnel costs in education and the expenditure patterns and deficits in the nine provinces which emerged after the dismantling of the 19 apartheid-era education departments and the establishment of a single education department.[54] Fifth, the policy proposals and agenda did not address curriculum issues in higher education.

Of importance during this period was the emergence of a policy agenda that contained principles, values, goals, vision, proposals and an implementation plan for the future education system. Some of these principles and values made their way into the writing of the first White Paper for Education and Training, and were adopted by the NCHE as operational principles for its work and further adopted in the writing of the White Paper for higher education transformation and the *Higher Education Act*. Despite the challenges entailed and the some of the weaknesses of the process, the transformation agenda that emerged during this period further informed the subsequent policy development initiatives of the new government.

Chapter Four
Assuming the Power of the State

INTRODUCTION

The ANC came into power with strong ideals of democracy and delivery promises made to the electorate. However, there were issues that militated against the realization of these democratic ideals. These include the pact as finding expression through the government of national unity, the constitutionality of the state, and the neo-liberal global pressures. This resulted in the emergence of a relatively weak state that was constrained to deliver the realization of democratic goals, especially in the first five years of the new government in power. This chapter explores how the romanticized view of the state was constrained both from within and without, and why it was difficult for the government to realize its goals. It argues therefore that critiques of the South African government's failure to deliver on the promises during the first five years should be understood within the context of the complexities of a new government that was constrained by the effects of the pact, the interim Constitution and the shifts in macroeconomic policies towards a neo-liberal agenda.

THEORIES OF SOUTH AFRICA'S TRANSITION TO DEMOCRACY

Different theories have been advanced to explain South Africa's transition to democracy. This section will explore three of them, namely: the liberal democracy theory, the popular democracy theory and the elite pact theory. Saul suggests there are two approaches that explain this transition, namely liberal democracy and popular democracy. Liberal democracy happens in the context of the left or when the liberation movement accepts the necessity for a carefully negotiated transition to obviate the risk of civil war.[1] In the South African context, this posed challenges for the ANC as the leading organization in negotiating a way to democracy. As Saul posits, first, it had to retain the "confidence" of local and external capital and foreign governments. Second, it had to demobilize its (non-electoral) popular support. Third, it had to abandon a social redistributive strategy in favor of one dominated by neo-liberal "market solutions." This led to a form of democracy which Saul refers to as liberal, and which he claims does not empower the people.[2] Shivji argues that "liberal democracy" draws its inspiration from western liberalism centered on notions of limited government, individual rights, parliamentary and party institutions, and the centrality of the economic and political entrepreneur of the market place.[3] This form of liberal democracy is, as Saul puts it, hegemonic in South Africa, arguing that a progressive agenda is kept alive in these conditions by pressures from trade unions, civic organizations such as women, students and other community-based organizations, where there are growing signs at grassroots level of resistance to the ANC's government and its development strategy. Within education the student movement and teacher unions were active in keeping this progressive voice alive in the immediate post-1994 period. They were, however, weakened as the liberal democratic discourse came to be accepted as the norm.

The second explanation of transition is a popular democracy theory, which Saul refers to as "the missing alternative." This is a form of democracy that is said to be genuine and that leads to empowerment of the people. It is a bottom-up form of democracy rooted in civil society. Barber refers to this alternative to liberal democracy as "strong democracy" defined by politics in the participatory mode, a politics through which active citizens govern themselves directly. He adds that a strong democracy is one in which consensus, and a sense of the "public realm," is won through political interaction and not imposed from above. This form of politics can best be pursued in a context where "we make government our own through recasting our civic attitudes."[4] This in turn is possible only in a vibrant civil society where responsibilities and rights are joined together in a seamless web of community self-government. Attaining this goal entails forging civil society in an international environment and is a challenge indeed.

In South Africa, there is a realization of the need for such strong democracy, especially among those who have struggled against apartheid. With all the challenges inherent in the struggle for popular democracy and empowerment there is no short cut to popular democracy, nor any elite pact or refined constitutional dispensation that can guarantee it, however important these latter accomplishments can sometimes be in opening up space for the pursuit of a more deep-cutting radical process of democratization. The weakness of Barber's theory of democratization, as Saul sees it, is that his writings run the risk of valuing democratic activity for its own sake, or for that of producing a more meaningful community, without spelling out the concrete policy ends that a more effectively empowered citizenry might be expected to produce.[5] Whereas some of the ideas expressed by Barber formed part of the struggle for democracy in South Africa, they are viewed as unfeasible and remain rhetorical since they fail to spell out how subordinately the capitalist classes respond and behave in the interests of society.

A third explanation for South Africa's transition to democracy arises from an elite pact theory. According to Adler and Webster, this is premised on a theory that for democratic transition to succeed, democracy itself must be limited. Radical expectations for democracy as a means to remake society, perhaps to institute socialism, are not only unfeasible but also threaten the transition process as a whole. As a consequence of the risk they provoke of an anti-democratic reaction, pro-democratic forces have to offer concessions on their economic and social programs. Thus, successful transitions from authoritarianism can be brought about only as a result of negotiations and of pacts between adversarial elites.[6] In the view of Przeworski, this entails negotiation and alliance between the reformers inside the authoritarian block and the moderates in the pro-democracy opposition. He argues that conflicts inherent in transitions to democracy occur on two fronts: between the opponents and defenders of the authoritarian regime about democracy and between differing groups of pro-democratic actors against one another for the best chance under democracy. But societies are divided in many ways, and the very essence of democracy is competition among political forces with conflicting interests. This situation causes a dilemma: to bring about democracy, anti-authoritarian forces must unite against authoritarianism, but victory under democracy always takes place on two fronts: against the authoritarian regime for democracy and against one's allies for the best place under democracy.[7]

For Przeworski, the process of democratization entails two aspects, namely: extrication from the authoritarian regime and the constitution of a democratic one. The relative importance of extrication and constitution depends on the place within the authoritarian regime of those political forces that control the apparatus of repression, most often the armed forces. Wherever the military remains cohesive in defense of the regime, elements of extrication dominate the process of transition.

Przeworski identifies four political actors in this debacle: hardliners and reformers inside the authoritarian block and moderates and radicals in the opposition. Each distances itself from the extremists in its own camp—reformers from hardliners and moderates from radicals—and seeks a suboptimal solution that will nonetheless allow themselves and their society to survive. Przeworski points out that extrication can result only from an understanding between reformers and moderates. He argues that extrication is possible only if: an agreement can be reached between reformers and moderates to establish institutions under which the social forces they represent would have a significant political presence in the democratic system; reformers can deliver the consent of hardliners or neutralize them; and moderates can control radicals.[8] This solution is encouraged by the threat of chaos implicit in a continued stalemate or in the costs to be incurred by attempting maximalist socialist solutions. Political actors, argues Przeworski, calculate that whatever difference in their welfare could result from a more favorable institutional framework is not worth the risk inherent in continued conflict.[9]

Adler and Webster's model captures the social relationships between the four groups, namely reformers and hardliners on the one hand and moderates and radicals on the other. They posit that there are two kinds of social relationships between the four actors. The first is where one group can marginalize or dominate its challengers. The second is the relationship between two groups that can be characterized by a more or less reciprocal interaction. In the case of the latter, reformers marginalize hardliners and moderates marginalize radicals, thus creating space for reformers and moderates to negotiate a constrained transition. The two then find their common cause in a limited notion of democracy in which government "must be strong enough to govern effectively, but weak enough not to be able to govern against important interests."[10] Adler and Webster further argue that a theory of democratic elitism finds new currency as the alliance between reformers and moderates commits itself to a form of democracy that preserves the central pillars of capitalist society, ensuring the entrenched power-holders—especially the bourgeoisie—maintain a veto over the pace, content, and institutional form of democracy.[11] In Przeworski's words, successful transitions require a pact that is inevitably conservative, economically and socially. The *ancien régime* gives up unilateral control in exchange for a system in which it continues to wield considerable influence while, in agreeing to such an elite-pacted transition, the pro-democracy forces accept a limited form of democracy and postpone, if not abandon, aspirations for equality.[12]

Przeworski suggests that this balance can be engineered through the familiar institutions of elite-pacted democracy, which insulate the government from the people by making politics the permanent business of a small number of specialized personnel. In such situations, governments are confronted with two options in relation to social movements, and, in the South African context, civil society. They can either work to undermine and weaken civil society or work with civil society to garner support for their programmes. Where there is strong civil society, the first option can be pursued only at great risk as it threatens to compromise the democratic character of transition. Thus governments attempt to draw on these social movements through corporatist-type arrangements on the assumption that these will demobilize and moderate popular movements. In this respect, transition theory reproduces classic assumptions about the relationship between structure and agency common to social movements and corporatist theory.

There is a notion of elite-pacting that is integral to transition theory and is premised on two theoretical assumptions. Firstly, that negotiations cannot be conducted by the masses themselves at venues other than the bargaining table but must be entered into on their behalf by a leadership (elite) that ostensibly speaks for them. Secondly, it is assumed that not all members of the contending factions are enamored with the idea of negotiations, or pacting. Hardliners within the authoritarian block, and radicals among the pro-democracy forces, might well wish to pursue maximalist solutions in the sense of provoking, or intensifying, a civil war that each believes can be won in a final decisive battle. However, for reformers within the authoritarian ranks who recognize that the retention of power requires the apparent sharing of it, and for moderates within the pro-democracy movement who recognize the futility of inheriting ashes of a once viable society, or who prize governance above all else, the prospects of chaos so defined are unacceptable. The resolution of this stalemate lies in an alliance between reformers within an authoritarian bloc and moderates in the pro-democracy opposition. Both distance themselves from extremists in their own camps. Both seek a sub-optimal solution that will nonetheless allow themselves and their society to survive.[13]

At the heart of transition theory is the argument that reformers and moderates eventually find a common cause in a limited, or attenuated notion of democracy. That is to say, reformers and moderates reach a conservative compromise, a pact, expressed in and through "liberal" democratic institutions that insulate the government from the broad mass of the people. In this way they allow existing power-holders to retain much of their control over such levers of power in society as property, the military and—not least—the state bureaucracy. In effect, the reformers and the moderates make a political trade-off that ultimately allows a small number of specialized political personnel to govern on behalf of the few rather than the majority. Thus political transition, as explained through elite pact theory, leads to the form of democracy or outcome that is similar to Saul's definition of liberal democracy. Building on this premise, transition theorists explicitly recognize that reformers in the state and moderates in the opposition are willing to settle for a form of politics that preserves the central pillars of a specifically capitalist society.[14]

The elite pact theory is a useful contribution to understanding transition to democracy in South Africa. Indeed, an ANC-led negotiating team spent days and nights courting a negotiating team from the National Party (NP) in an attempt to find a solution and way forward towards democratization. In the process deals were made that entailed making compromises on both sides. The National Party had to abandon its demand for regionalism in favor of a unitary state. On the other hand, the ANC let go of a "winner takes all" system of majority rule, and instead had to settle for a Government of National Unity (GNU) where all parties would be proportionally represented in government according to how they had fared in elections.[15] In addition it dropped demands for nationalization in support of protection of individual and property rights. As a result of this compromise, or pact, between the reformers led by the NP and the moderates led by the ANC, the power of government to seize some of the national resources and put them under government control was limited. Furthermore, it resulted in the notion of a government of national unity which allowed the social forces they represented to have a significant political presence in the new dispensation.[16]

However, this theory has its own limitations. As Adler and Webster indicate, the elite pact theory overlooks the role of other players, in particular the labor movement, as an important actor in precipitating and securing transition to a democratic order.[17] Thus the game was not only between the elite in the two camps, reformers had also to negotiate with the radicals in the opposition, and in this case the labor movement was an important player. The role played by the labor movement in South Africa, in the campaign for the rewriting of the Labor Relations Act, is a case in point. The theory further fails to account for the role played by some other important players outside the two main negotiating parties, namely civil society organizations such as the National Education Coordinating Committee (NECC), which had been mobilizing students in schools and higher education institutions to resist and reject apartheid education. The impact of this movement culminated in the formation of the National Education and Training Forum (NETF) in 1993 that brought different stakeholders from government, business, labor, education and the MDM to find solutions to the crisis in education. It further fails to account for the role of political parties such as the Inkatha Freedom Party (IFP), which operated outside the main negotiating frameowrk. With its threats of secession and mobilization on the basis of Zulu ethnicity and nationalism, and of convergence with the National Party, and also through the pressure exerted by the international community, the IFP managed to secure important concessions at the negotiating table that helped shape the subsequent political landscape of South Africa. It played an important role in securing the devolution of powers to provinces that ensured the central state did not have absolute power in all the affairs of the provinces. This entailed a provision that provinces could have their own constitutions, thus leading to a strong federal element in the interim constitution.[18]

Freund and Padayachee point out that federalism was held out as a significant concession. The ANC was prepared to accept the institution of provincial legislatures (vested in nine provinces) as well as another five-year deal allowing minority parties parity in elections.[19] A former Director-General of Education captured the impact of this compromise on the operations of government when he reflected on some of the challenges encountered within the Department of Education. He commented that:

> The problem in this country is that we have a system of government that is not centralized. People talk about the government as if it is centralized. We have provincial governments that have executive responsibilities, but there is a continuing pretence that we have a centrally-run administration. We don't have that, and we have failed in our critique of even the transition to appreciate the fact that we have inter-government relations that are constitutionally defined. So you either started in the beginning to ignore your own Constitution or you respected the Constitution and tried to find a way of helping the provinces on the basis of the constitution.[20]

Habib draws a distinction between South Africa's transition and the decolonization process in that it did not involve the physical retreat of a colonizing nation and settler class.[21] He argues that while analyses suggesting the distinctiveness of South Africa's political evolution manage to capture the "exceptionalism" of the country's conflict and the innovativeness of its social movements, they have not demonstratively proved what is unique in this transition trajectory. Too often these analyses glibly take for granted the rhetoric of the leadership and the activist base of social and political movements. In the process, what is said is interpreted as what is true. The net result is that the forces underlying the transition, its character, and its possibilities and limitations, all become hidden in the mountain of propaganda that attempts to legitimize the current political trajectory of the transition. He points out that despite the distinctive strengths these analyses have, the problem with them is that, by emphasizing either the "normalcy" or the "exceptionalism" of the transition, they oversimplify a complex process, and therefore are incapable of developing a holistic picture of transition.

Any attempt to understand the transition in South Africa, he argues, must simultaneously recognize the distinctiveness of the country's conflict and the nature of its resolution, while being flexible enough to capture the similarities of aspects of this transition with those that have occurred at different times, in different parts of the world. Having highlighted the inadequacies of attempts to explain transition in South Africa, he then proposes a dynamic model of explaining transition in South Africa, which he argues should address three central questions: What is the principal character of the conflict in South Africa? How do we theoretically account for the form, pace and content of the transition? What are the conditions that should be met to facilitate the consolidation of democracy? That means a model of the transition must address issues of the nature of the conflict, extrapolate the forces and factors that influence and direct transition, and outline conditions that facilitate its consolidation. He asserts that the model becomes an analytical tool that enables scholars to dabble in the past, explain the present, and speculate on the future.[22]

The analysis of transition provided by Habib is useful for the approach and argument pursued in this chapter in that it appeals against oversimplification of the nature of transition in South Africa while at the same time highlighting its distinctiveness. Although a critique of the similarities and differences between South Africa's transition to democracy and that of other countries falls outside the scope of this chapter, the internal accounts of challenges faced in the creation of the new state will be the focus of the chapter. The emergence of the South African state in the context of transition will be analyzed with specific reference to the Interim Constitution and the macro-economic policy framework with their neo-liberal orientations, all products of the negotiations that characterized the transition to democracy.

THE NEW SOUTH AFRICAN STATE AND THE CONSTITUTIONAL PACT

One of the challenges of the birth of a new democracy in South Africa in the aftermath of the 1994 elections was the formation of a new state. After the 1994 elections it was difficult to categorize the state because it was an old one whose entire philosophy and way of doing things—such as its culture and approach—were still intact. It was completely different from the kind of state that was finding expression in a new democracy. It was not only in transition at that point but also in limbo and entrenched in the apartheid social order, in terms of legislation and policies. The only thing that had changed was the Constitution. The policies that guided the daily activities of government during that period were still the policies of the old apartheid state. That impacted on the operations of the new government because, since the old authority was not fitting into the new agenda, it did not have the enabling authority through legislation to do certain things or to effect certain strategic changes without changing the legislation. Therefore the new government had to prioritize the formulation of enabling legislation to effect change. As Mseleku explained:

> This tension [between the old and the new culture within the state] created delays, frustrations and problems for the new order. But on the other hand the fact that the new order [and] the state that was in the making was still very young and had just been born, it lacked the sophistication of a state, the knowledge and had no history. The only history it had was its commitment to a new order.[23]

The new state had a history outside the state based on anti-apartheid policy development, campaigns, and mobilization, and in some cases education programs for members. There are four key elements that characterize the nature of the new state which are defined in the interim constitution. These are important for understanding the possibilities and constraints for transformation which the state could effect and include the continuation of old departments, old laws, the employment of old bureaucrats, and of the apartheid Public Service Commission. The first deals with the continuation of the old laws, in which section 229 of the Interim Constitution stipulates that:

> Subject to this Constitution, all laws which immediately before the commencement of this Constitution were in force in any area which forms part of the national territory, shall continue in force in such area, subject to any repeal or amendment of such laws by a competent authority.[24]

The effect of this clause was that when the new government came into office in 1994, it inherited and operated on the basis of apartheid laws and its challenge was to repeal them in line with the provisions of the new Interim Constitution. In reflecting on the implications of these for education, and responding to the criticism of lack of delivery by government in the first five years of democracy, the former Director-General of Education said:

> The Mandela administration [which was in office during the five years of the new government] is rightly seen as having a lot of policies and

laws. But it was inevitable because we had apartheid laws and policies and we had to change them. You could not run this system without changing the laws. There was no way you could run this process without going through the process of changing South Africa's Acts, otherwise we would just have continued to run with the old apartheid system and the government structure that was in place.[25]

However, the passing of the new laws did not mean an overnight transformation of the system, and embracing the new ways of seeing and doing things. In reflecting on what this meant for higher education, Manganyi added:

> Now that there is a new government we are not succeeding in saying now all the institutions are South African institutions. We are failing to make the link and therefore we are still operating on the basis of old categories which are difficult to dislodge because in some ways things are still very much what they used to be. That is the challenge of change, unless you have had a real revolution where everything was destroyed and you start from scratch, you are bound to have this past as part of the future as well. That is one of the enduring dilemmas of the new dispensation.[26]

The comment by Manganyi raises an important theoretical challenge in terms of approach to organizational change. That is, the approach to change that was adopted was not premised on disregard of the past: it acknowledged the existence of the past and the challenge it faced was how to negotiate the new within the old. Part of this was achieved through the passing of legislation where relevant.

The second deals with the continuation of old apartheid departments, in which the Interim Constitution stipulates in section 236 (1) that:

> A public service, department of state administration or other institution . . . which immediately before the commence of this [Interim] Constitution performed governmental functions under the control of an authority referred to in section 236 [apartheid structures] shall, subject to subsections governing rationalization of public administration, continue to function as such in accordance with the laws applicable to it until it is abolished or incorporated or integrated into any appropriate institution or is rationalized. . . .[27].

What this meant for education was that the Minister of Education inherited 19 racially and ethnically defined education departments which continued to operate until they were amalgamated into new provincial departments or

to page 78.

the national department. The implications and operationalization of this are explored in the next chapter. One of the compromises agreed to at the negotiating table was for the continued employment of civil servants, even after the election of the new government, which represents the third element. This was provided for in the Interim Constitution in clause 236 (2), which stipulated that:

> A person who immediately before the commencement of this Constitution was employed by an institution referred to in subject section (1) [a public service, state department] shall continue in such employment subject to and in accordance with this Constitution and other applicable laws.[28]

This became popularly known as the "sunset clause" and accounted for the continued employment of the apartheid civil service in the new bureaucracy in the first five years of the new government. The effect of this was that it became difficult for the new government to employ its new people in strategic positions in the early months of its coming into office. This situation is similar to that faced by the Zimbabwean government when it came to office and was unable to appoint new people from outside the existing civil servants. The result of this was that Zimbabwe had to rely on appointing teachers to become ministers in order to bring new faces into government.[29] Even though this appears to be an obvious constraint on the part of government to effect transformation in key appointments and strategic positions, there are those in the new government who saw the merits of the "sunset clause," especially in education. These merits are related to the logistical and administrative sense of running the education system. In illustrating its value within the education context, Metcalfe commented:

> Education is unlike any other sector in that it has such a defined calendar. It starts at the beginning of the year and ends at the end of the year. So you have this very rigid time-scale that you're working with all of the time. I cannot see how we would have managed at the practical level to get the bare bones that kept education going in place without some continuity. 1994 happened, the end of the year examinations had to happen, children were expecting to write exams and complete. Children were going to start school the next year and expected to have stationery and books. There is no way that you could have managed the very rudimentary forms of educational life, which is all that we were left with, which is still all that we are left with, without some kind of basic continuity. If anyone imagines that you could have just said "new government, there is no continuation" who would have paid the teachers? So the sunset clause was not such a restraint on us. [30]

This observation highlights an important feature of transition which found expression in the maintenance of continuity in effecting change within government; that is the fact that despite aspirations for change there were certain features of government administration which had to be maintained or practiced, irrespective of whether that government was democratic or undemocratic. Despite the sentiments expressed above on the value of the "sunset clause," especially its continuity, there is some sense in which it was a constraint for the new government and this is explored later in the chapter.

The fourth and last constitutional provision relevant to an understanding of the nature of the state in 1994 was that which provided for the continuation of the Public Service Commission. Clause 268 stipulated that: "A public service commission established for a public service referred to in section 236 (1), shall subject to subsections (3) and (4), after the commencement of this Constitution continue to function as such in accordance with the laws applicable to it."[31] The implications of this provision were that in the new government's early days, employment, which entailed the creation, advertising and filling of new posts, was governed by the apartheid Public Service Commission. The relevance of the clauses in the Constitution which protected the jobs of the existing civil service for higher education was that, despite the higher levels of inequalities in the racial composition of staff (in 1991, 76 percent of the permanent academic or research staff in higher education were white),[32] they could not be dismissed arbitrarily in order to effect redress. On top of the fact that the majority of them could have had good qualifications, which made them indispensable to the system, the Constitution also guaranteed their jobs.

With respect to higher education, section 247 stipulated:

> The national government shall not alter the rights, powers and functions of the controlling bodies of universities and technikons under laws existing immediately before the commencement of this Constitution, unless agreement resulting from bona fide negotiation has been reached with such bodies, and reasonable notice of said proposed alteration has been given.[33]

The effect of this law was that the DOE was constrained in intervening in the affairs of higher education institutions as they continued to operate on the basis of old laws. These left the introduction of changes to the discretion of individual institutions until new laws had been passed which would be the basis on which government would act in providing leadership for these institutions. As this study demonstrates, these laws in the form of the *White Paper on Higher Education* and the *Higher Education Act* were passed after three years of government being in office and left with less than two years before its term expired. As a result, the government missed out on an important opportunity premium to provide leadership when institutions were still prone to change and willing to follow the leadership provided by the DOE. However, this was later achieved in the operationalization of policy, as was the case with announcement of mergers of higher education institutions that started in 2002.

NEO-LIBERAL GLOBAL PRESSURES AND THE BATTLE FOR THE SOUL OF THE SOUTH AFRICAN MACROECONOMIC POLICY FRAMEWORK

South Africa's transition to democracy took place in the context of a changing global economic environment that put pressures on nation states. As such, analysis of the South African state should include not only internal factors but also external influences. This section will provide a brief analysis of globalization, South Africa' macroeconomic framework and the impact both had on higher education. The role of the state as a mediator in shaping the emerging macroeconomic policy and higher education will come under scrutiny. The context in which South Africa emerged from apartheid to democracy was of a world which was becoming increasingly globalized. As such the South African state had to deal with the internal challenges of transformation while at the same time responding to the challenges of globalization. Castells characterizes this world as a new economy which could be defined as the combination of three inter-related characteristics unable to function without one another:

- It is an economy in which productivity and competitiveness are based on knowledge and information.
- Jobs are influenced by what happens at the core of its economy.
- Capacity of this economy is technological, organizational and institutional.[34]

Technological capacity refers to the economy's ability to structure the entire planet through telecommunications and information systems. The new economy has organizational capacity because the firms and networks working in this economy organize themselves to be active globally, both in terms of the supplies they receive and the markets they look for. It is also based on institutional capacity which means deregulation and liberalization, which opens up the possibility for it to operate globally. In that sense governments are the main globalizers because they create the institutions of the new economy throughout the world. After that they lose control.[35] One of the challenges of South Africa's transition to democracy has been the development of the macroeconomic policy, which took place in the economic context described by Castells as globalized. For that reason, these global factors could not be ignored and the analysis of the development of the ANC's economic policy and the government's macroeconomic policy should reflect on how they exhibit the features of the global economy.

The macroeconomic policies of a government are important for understanding the social and public policies which that government introduces. In Friedman's words, they are the "operating system" for your "hardware," which in the South African context is supposedly a free-market hardware.[36] Macroeconomic policies are what allow governments to pursue certain social or economic goals by applying particular strategies and instruments (software). They also help in understanding the nature of the state that oversees those policies, i.e., whether it is a welfare, capitalist or neo-liberal state. The question of the nature of the state in South Africa and the outcome thereof from the negotiating table should be seen against the background of some developments from the unbanning of the liberation movement in 1990. In particular, debates around the economic policy of South Africa had a profound influence on the outcome and nature of the state being discussed at the negotiating table.

The discussion in this section will shift to analysis of the evolution of the African National Congress's (ANC's) economic policies and the kinds of shifts in macroeconomic policies of the new government from the Reconstruction and Development Programme (RDP) to a neo-liberal Growth, Employment and Redistribution (GEAR) policy. The use of neoliberalism in this study draws from the insights provided by Adelzadeh in his critique of the GEAR policy document in which he uses it to refer to a shift the ANC made in its economic policy from a Keynesian economic paradigm as finding expression in the Reconstruction and Development Progamme (RDP) to a neo-liberal framework that had long been the alternative that had been offered by big business in South Africa, the International Monetary Fund (IMF) and the World Bank in its structural adjustment programs. He argues that in the departure from the Keynesian towards the neo-liberal framework, the RDP White Paper transformed the role of fiscal prudence from a means to achieve the RDP objectives to an objective of the RDP; the goal of redistribution was dropped as a main objective, and the government's role in the economy was reduced to the task of managing transformation.[37] Politically and educationally, the term neo-liberalism is used in this book to refer to a departure from the policy goals and intentions that informed the liberation and educational struggles which aimed at empowering the former oppressed, with the state playing a central role. Instead the new policy frameworks that were adopted represent the essential tenets and policy recommendations that are oriented towards subjecting all government policies to market forces with the state playing a regulatory role. This definition of neo-liberalism inextricably links educational policies with socio-economic and political policies and the links between these are crucial in the framework and analysis adopted in this book.

According to Marais, when the ANC was unbanned in 1990, it had no economic policy, a peculiar situation for an eight-decade-old liberation organization which had gone to the trouble of internationally training a cadre of ANC exile economists.[38] Instead the development of the ANC's macroeconomic framework has to be traced largely through three documents published after the period of transition had begun, namely: the Macroeconomic Research Group (MERG), the Reconstruction and Development Programme (RDP) and the Growth, Employment and Redistribution (GEAR) policy documents. The major initiative to develop economic policy within the ANC was the Macroeconomic Research Group (MERG), a project established by the ANC to develop its alternative macroeconomic vision. The project was controlled by a steering committee that included representatives of the ANC, COSATU representing labor, the civics movement represented by the South Africa National Civics Organisation (SANCO) as well as participating universities, i.e., the Universities of the Witwatersrand, Western Cape and Fort Hare.[39]

MERG produced its report in 1993 and at the core stood an argument that the economy could best be restructured through the labor market (improved training and higher wages), and through interventions aimed at improving the structure and operation of business. A new economic model would depend on a "strong private sector interacting with a strong public sector."[40] If its key proposals were implemented, the MERG model predicted annual growth of 5 percent by 2004 and the creation of 300 000 new jobs a year. According to Marais, it presented a two-phase growth plan (comprising a "public-investment-led phase" and a "sustained growth phase") that tied growth to expanded and efficiently deployed savings and investment (rather than a demand-led path of large increases in state spending advocated under a "growth through redistribution" formula).[41] The report advocated state investment in social and physical infrastructure (housing, school education, health services, electrification and road development) in the first phase. This would account for more than half of the growth and trigger sustained, growth-inducing effects throughout the economy. In addition, it proposed that the state strategically apply a mix of incentives and regulations to re-structure and improve industrial performance. It recommended a minimum wage pegged at two-thirds the subsistence level for a household of five. MERG argued that the minimum wage would improve productivity "by re-ducing absenteeism, illness and labour turn-over," and provide the incentive for firms "to undertake the necessary adjustments to make human resources more productive."[42] It proclaimed a need for the state to "provide leader-ship and co-ordination for widely-based economic development" and to in-tervene directly in key areas. This included the argument that no coherent macro-policy could be operated without more control or oversight by the Reserve Bank.[43]

Marais suggests that the MERG plan represented the most sophisti-cated popular economic strategy ever devised in South Africa, yet it was al-lowed to die an ignominious death soon after the report's release. He points out that mainstream economists savaged it in the media, with some ANC leaders reportedly joining in. Two years later, the ANC government's Growth Employment and Redistribution (GEAR) strategy would adminis-ter the document's *coup de grâce*.[44] The demise of MERG could be attrib-uted to the fact that it advocated an economic framework comparable to those of welfare states at a time when they were becoming unfashionable in the context of the new global economy. The interventionist strategy of the state in terms of initial investment, followed by growth, runs contrary to the ideology of the market which advocates that investment in the economy should be left to and led by the private sector.

In the run-up to the 1994 elections the ANC, through its alliance struc-tures, produced a development program in the form of the Reconstruction and Development Programme (RDP). This was also to form a basis for the ANC's macroeconomic plan when it became the government. More than a development framework, it aimed at completely reordering the politics, the economy and society.[45] In the shape of the RDP Base Document, its policy focus was around five sub-programs: Meeting Basic Needs, Developing Human Resources, Building the Economy, Democratizing the State, and im-plementing the RDP.[46] After the ANC came into power, the RDP was adopted as a government programme. The seriousness with which the ANC government regarded the RDP was evidenced by the establishment of an RPD Office in the President's Office. After it was adopted as the govern-ment's development plan, the RDP had to undergo a governmentalization process whereby it was adapted from being a party policy to becoming offi-cial government policy. In the governmentalization of the RDP there was a shift, not only from the RDP base document to the RDP White Paper, but also from the RPD document as a whole to the Growth Employment and Redistribution (GEAR) framework. These shifts were, however, not clear to lay people or outsiders as they continued to operate on the assumption that the RDP base document remained the development strategy.

The struggles that characterized the shifts have been presented as riddled by conflicts and tensions between "pragmatists" and "socialists," allegedly battling for the soul of the ANC. They included policy differences between "conservatives" and "interventionists" in the GNU, deep methodological and ideological differences between the two sets of economic modelers used by the government (the "supply-side" team) on the one hand and (the "demand led" team) on the other. [47] The shifts have been explained in different ways by commentators. The reason for these shifts should be understood in the light of a sophisticated process of influence to which the ANC was exposed as early as 1990. First, the ANC was forced into a dialogue with a variety of other interest groups and constituencies, including western governments, international financial institutions and local conglomerate capital. According to Freund and Padayachee, through these dialogues a message was passed to the ANC regarding the need to understand that the world had become globalized and that policy options unacceptable to the international capital markets and its key players could no longer be countenanced.[48]

Second, some of these institutions arranged for key ANC economic advisers and politicians to receive training at business schools and international banks and investment houses in the West, which introduced them to neo-liberal values and principles. The effect of these pressures had already been felt long before the ANC came into power. It had been manifested in concessions made by the ANC in respect of economic policy at the negotiation table where, for example, it agreed to the independence of the Reserve Bank. This decision would affect issues such as monetary and exchange rate policy, as well as macroeconomic and industrial policy. It is also argued that these pressures led the ANC leadership to ditch the interventionist recommendations of MERG by late 1993.[49] The result of these influences was that when it came to power the ANC went further to compromise the essence of the RDP and MERG, and opened a way for a neo-liberal macroeconomic framework. This was manifested in the ANC's acceptance of the importance of privatization in principle, its implementation of a program of trade liberalization, phasing out export incentive measures, and the gradual elimination of protective measures to support the currency.[50] At the same time, the GNU supported a program of black economic empowerment, which was to see a dramatic growth in the income, wealth and asset base of a tiny group of black businessmen.

Third, the shifts may be attributed to a weak or poor development of economic policy within the ANC while still in exile. It was only after its unbanning that the ANC started giving serious thought to economic policy. Even then their economic policy was only debated within the ANC and its alliance structures. The MERG report and the RDP document were the first public documents to make public in a coherent fashion the ANC's economic policy, and they had to come under scrutiny beyond its alliance structures. This happened in the context of some influential ANC leaders having already bought into a liberal discourse of capital concerning what would work for South Africa. Thus at the time of the release of the MERG report in 1993, amid controversy over the strong foreign economists on the team and, more tellingly, resistance from members of the ANC's Department of Economic Policy (DEP) felt that MERG was usurping their roles,[51] it was easy for those influential leaders to marginalize the report and pursue their newly earned neo-liberal discourse alongside plans for the ANC.

The pursuit of the neo-liberal discourse was done in a context of concerns to make South Africa investor-friendly. For this to happen shifts were made in the nature of the growth path South Africa was to pursue, from growth through redistribution as advocated in the RDP document, to redistribution with growth. With this shift, there was a minimal role ascribed to the state in terms of redistribution and driving the growth path. Instead, this role was shifted to the private sector and favorable conditions for the operation of capital had to be created. Redistribution would be effected from the "trickle down" effects that accrued from growth driven approach and dependent upon the private sector. The shifts from MERG to GEAR ultimately reached a point where, according to Saul, influential ANC leaders came to adopt a "there is no alternative" (TINA) position. In other words, a neo-liberal route was the only way, with capital leading along the growth path. The production of rival policy frameworks by Business and Labor in the first few months of 1996, and the sudden and dramatic fall in the value of the currency (the Rand), forced the GNU to accelerate the production of its own macroeconomic policy document. In June 1996 the government publicly unveiled the Growth Employment and Redistribution (GEAR) strategy, announcing that it was not negotiable as policy. GEAR's approach was based on the view that if the GNU demonstrated its commitment to fiscal and monetary discipline, the much-needed private investment (both local and foreign) would materialize.[52]

While earlier explanations for the shifts from RDP to GEAR have emphasized factors external to government, there has so far been little focus on those factors internal to government that led to the demise of the RDP and hence a shift to GEAR. In explaining the shift, Coombe links it to the central question of where planning in the new government should be located. Should it be in a separate ministry or in the Ministry of Finance? When the ministries of the new government were announced, an RDP office given the responsibility for planning and development was established and based in the Office of the President. Coombe argues that planning and budgeting are necessarily part of the same process. The budgeting process is a planning process and to separate the locations of the two offices, in the President's Office (planning) and the Ministry of Finance (budgeting) caused unnecessary difficulties in government.[53] He further asserted that, bureaucratically speaking, there needed to be an identity in these functions, or at least a very close alignment. Because of its importance, to put the planning function within the Presidency was an error because the Presidency was not an executive ministry. In his view, this invited contestation and tension between the Office of the President, which should be above such things and able to resolve them, and the major ministry of government, the Ministry of Finance.[54]

Coombe's view has been challenged by Pillay who saw the RDP as a sound development framework which was never given a chance. Disagreeing with Coombe, who saw planning and budgeting belonging together in the Ministry of Finance, Pillay saw them as belonging apart. Development planning, according to Pillay, belongs to the Chief Executive Officer of government, i.e., the President.[55] In his view, the RDP office was supposed to be a planning office that would identify the needs and developmental plans of government and be financed by the budget managed by the Ministry of Finance. Instead of playing this role, the role of the RDP office became confused by the establishment of an RDP fund. This led to the situation where the RDP office failed to perform its planning function and concentrated instead on a funding role. The question that needs to be posed is: what is the significance of the location of such a government priority as the RDP in terms of ensuring delivery? The two perspectives highlighted above represent the kinds of tensions that have characterized government's approaches to addressing development needs. They further highlight the contestations that were taking place within a state that was still young and striving to find shape and form. Pillay's perspective can be regarded as representing those who believed in the RDP's potential to meet the basic needs, a perspective out of tune with the emerging global economic trends. On the other hand Coombe's perspective, even though it draws from experiences of developing countries, such as Zambia, seems to be compatible with the new global trends that subject development needs to the dictates of the finance ministries.

The problem of the location of the RDP was addressed with the appointment of the task team that was to review this problem. The outcome was the establishment of a coordination and implementation unit in the Office of the President. A decision was also taken to close down the RDP office and absorb its functions within the Finance Ministry. The *de facto* situation was that expenditure planning, a function of the budget office through the Medium Term Expenditure Framework (MTEF), became the planning mechanism for government. The MTEF, located in the Ministry of Finance, is a rolling three-year phase of planning used in managing state expenditure. By default it became the planning mechanism of government whereby the formulation of the strategic purposes of government in relation to resource allocation and management was undertaken. The MTEF became a planning implementation strategy of GEAR, and its introduction coincided with the demise of the RDP office. At a macro-political level, the period of the shift from the RDP to GEAR also caused a number of developments within the GNU which warrant closer investigation.

In May 1996, the National Party announced its withdrawal from the GNU and the next month President Mandela announced GEAR as the government' s macroeconomic policy. It was non-negotiable. In the same year, the RDP office was closed and its functions transferred to the offices of the Deputy President and the Finance Minister.[56] The MTEF was then introduced as a medium through which the formulation of the strategic purposes of government in relation to resource allocation was carried out. Given the contestations that have characterized the negotiations in the early years of the GNU, could the chronology of events outlined above, wherein the National Party withdrew from the GNU, be a coincidence? One would argue that they were not. It appears that the National Party had secured its purpose of being in the GNU by securing the economic interests of its allies such that it would no longer be necessary to fight for this as a partner in the GNU, but as part of the opposition.

This chapter suggests that there is a relationship between the adoption of the RDP as a macro-plan for the new government and its institutionalization in the Office of the President. This envisaged an arrangement wherein a development plan would be driven from the Office of the President and the Ministry of Finance would perform a financing function. The demise of the RDP on the other hand coincided with the demise of the Office of the President's role in development planning. These functions were transferred to the Ministry of Finance, which was more concerned with global economic trends and ensuring the economy was aligned to global trends. Neo-liberal economic policies became the order of the day at the expense of the meeting of basic needs as advocated by the RDP.

IMPLICATIONS OF THE NEO-LIBERAL ECONOMIC REGIME FOR EDUCATION REFORM

Carnoy provides an analysis of the impact globalization has had on the role of the nation-state in knowledge production and distribution, and in education systems. He points out that in developing societies, knowledge has been a monopoly of the national state, with education systems defined by the state and almost all research and development done by state-owned enterprises. In contrast, in a globalized information technology (IT) environment, knowledge formation and power over knowledge move out of the control of the nation state.[57] He further points out that the modern capitalist state has developed into a successful market "softener." That is, it is managing to create favorable conditions for the development and expansion of globalization. State policies are fundamentally constituted by political choices made by state managers in response to domestic and international political and ideological /cultural pressures.[58] After all, it was the decision of state authorities to restructure state organs and institutionalize the power of the financial, transnational corporate elite and the managers of the multilateral institutions of the global debt crisis management.[59] According to Atasoy and Carroll, local cultural values, political practices and historical legacies are very much part of the developing policies and the making of political choices.[60]

Further, globalization has eroded the nation state's monopoly of scientific knowledge and its ability to use that knowledge to reproduce class power, even as the nature of the class power relations itself moves away from nation-state control. Despite all of these factors—and at the time of writing Carnoy was probably not fully aware of the reversals in the information technology (IT) market—the state still has an important, albeit changing, role in defining knowledge, distributing it, and using it to shape power relations. The state-financed and run educational system continues to dominate the educational process, hence the transmission of knowledge to the young as well as the production of new knowledge in universities. Those who want to acquire new knowledge therefore still have to pass through the apparatuses of the state.[61]

Some major policy documents in education after 1994 in South Africa contain a preamble statement about the country's role in the global economy, the importance of economic and educational competitiveness within a globalized community, the growth of new technologies and innovation, demands for new kinds of workers that should be prepared for the globalized realities of the 21ˢᵗ century, and the proliferation of new modes of knowledge production based on international partnerships norms, to which South African knowledge industries should aspire.[62]

Indeed, some of the factors pointed out by Carnoy were those the South African state had to contend with as it negotiated itself into power. The global forces then expressing themselves in the form of neo-liberal policies that favors minimal state intervention in the economy, reduction of the budget deficit, outsourcing of services and the use of casual labor, were all very much part of the debate around the embryonic macroeconomic policies as well as education reforms in South Africa.

The dropping of the RDP and adoption of GEAR is viewed by some critics as part of a bigger and alien agenda, aimed at protecting the interests of a white constituency whose capital would facilitate greater participation in the global economy. According to the proponents of this view, in education it found expression through foreign agencies such as USAID and the Ford Foundation. These philanthropic organizations were seen as implementing the foreign policy of the United States by funding projects and ideas they wished to see happening. The funding of activities was an effective strategy for launching an attack on alternative ideas that might have emerged as a counter to the policy agenda they themselves had. In elaborating on how this strategy was implemented, Nevhutalo commented that:

> Not only do they fund policy development, they fund major policy conferences. So it is a disseminating strategy, they try and influence thinking by having it written, by having it distributed, by having it communicated, by having media in that communication, by inviting other people to try and legitimize it, because when you invite people to come and attend that conference, they are legitimizing the outcome of that work. Whether they have anything to say about the outcome of the conference, they are legitimizing it.[63]

The view expressed above comes across as conspiracy theory in being suspicious of the genuineness of foreign agencies in supporting local development initiatives. This could be drawing lessons from past experiences of the operation of multinational corporations in developing countries where rather than serving the best interests of these countries, they created markets for their products which benefited their home countries (metropole) rather than the recipient countries (periphery). Indeed, the Ford Foundation and USAID have been the major funders of policy work from the early days of UDUSA's involvement in policy work. They funded the NCHE, and the Ford Foundation was responsible for the creation and funding of the Centre for Higher Education Transformation, one of the influential policy organizations in higher education outside of government in the period 1996–2001.

The use of the Medium Term Expenditure Framework (MTEF) as a planning tool became prevalent across all government departments, and also saw the increasing role of the Ministry of Finance in the operations of line departments. For example, in April 1997 a draft White Paper on higher education was released, proposing, *inter alia,* the introduction of three-year rolling institutional plans in the Department of Education as a planning tool. These would be used in developing the National Plan for Higher Education to establish indicative targets for the size and shape of the system, overall growth and participation rates, and institutional and program mixes to advance the vision, principles and policy goals of the system. On the other hand, the approval of institutional plans would lead to the allocation of funded student places to institutions for approved programs in particular levels and fields of learning.[64] The White Paper 3 introduces the new planning strategy in higher education as follows:

> The key instrument in the planning process will be the development of national and institutional three-year "rolling plans," indicative plans which facilitate the setting of objectives and implementation targets that can be adjusted, updated, and revised annually. A participatory, multi-year planning process will avoid the inherent defects of the old top-down central budgeting system. This is in line with the government's budget development process as reflected in the Medium-Term Expenditure Framework.[65]

Though the White Paper justifies the use of three-year rolling plans and the use of the MTEF, and sees these as a departure from the old top-down budgeting system, this chapter argues that this development was in line with the new government's policy of GEAR. It gave the Ministry of Finance powers to intervene and have a final say in the policies of all government departments. The flexibility that would be adopted to adjust, update and revise objectives and targets was mainly aimed at fitting higher education planning into what government resources could support and afford, rather than being driven by the need to address higher education needs. For example, it is unlikely that the budget allocation for higher education could be substantially increased to address the emerging needs (e.g., the Financial Aid Scheme for higher education). Instead, education needs would be adjusted to meet the realities of available resources. This was demonstrated by a decrease in the subsidies of higher education institutions that were announced in December 1996 for the academic year 1997 which reduced the subsidy levels of institutions from 68 percent down to 60 percent. This was accompanied by a decrease in the state contribution to the National Student Financial Aid Scheme (NSFAS) from R300m for 1996/97 to R250m for 1997/98. Thus, rather than more resources made available to support deserving needy students, these were reduced, thus constraining government's capacity to deliver on providing access to disadvantaged students. This prompted the heads of higher education institutions to request a meeting with the Minister of Education to plead for an increase, or at least retention of the funding levels for 1996.[66]

The Committee of University Principals (CUP) warned of the dire consequences to students and institutions alike if the need for financial aid by students was not met. The CUP further raised a point with the Minister that the cuts in NSFAS and their implications for students and institutions were exacerbated by the subsidy cuts for 1997 which, as they put it, "leave all institutions strapped for cash, and incapable of attempting to meet the shortfalls in student aid out of own resources."[67] Following their meeting with the Minister on 28 January 1997, in which they managed to solicit his support and a promise to make a plea to cabinet for the increase of funds, the joint leadership of the CTP and the CUP took their appeal to the Cabinet meeting of February 5, 1997. In its letter to Cabinet the joint leadership warned of the possible closure of some institutions as a result of a cut in funding levels to 60 percent.[68]

The introduction of GEAR did not just immediately reframe a policy process; it immediately set constraints on what was feasible regarding availability of resources to address the transformation agenda. It derailed the popular views held within the Mass Democratic Movement (MDM) structures of the reconstructive role the state was supposed to play in promoting access, and pursuing redress and equity goals. The goals needed new resources to be made available to higher education, and these resources would not be forthcoming within the GEAR framework. The above developments suggest a relationship between the GEAR policy that was adopted in June 1996, and its emphasis on cuts in spending and the announcement of cuts in funding to higher education. These measures reflect the influence of the MTEF's fiscal austerity policy on the higher education policy.

The introduction of GEAR has come under criticism from some quarters where it is regarded as an enemy of higher education. Mosala commented on its impact on the writing of the White Paper on higher education, following its shift from the RDP which had informed the work of the

Commission and the writing of the Green Paper. He attributes the involvement of the Ministry of Finance as follows:

> When we started to write the White Paper, the Finance Department started to sit [on] some of our meetings and we started to talk to them about some of the things in the funding framework chapter that we were proposing. Whenever we talked about the need to avail more funding in order to achieve the objectives, every part of the draft White Paper where we talked about new funding, the Finance Department would scratch out that part. They told us to not make any mention whatsoever about the new funding. And that's why in the White Paper there is nowhere the new funding is talked about. Everywhere where we talked about what implements and new structures we were going to create which implied new funding we could not actually say so in the White Paper. And that was because the Finance Department at that point had already launched GEAR in 1996. They were already operating in the framework of cutting the public spending budget, and that was frustrating. And here was the enemy of higher education.[69]

The position adopted by the Department of Finance had an impact on higher education transformation in that, since there was no new funding available, the Department of Education could also not produce implementation mechanisms that would require new funding. Its immediate impact was experienced in the cut in the subsidies formula and the government's contribution to the NSFAS. The redress fund for institutional and individual transformation that the Commission had proposed was not made available.[70]

The introduction of GEAR and of the MTEF strategy gave the Ministry of Finance a strong influence on policy development and operations of government departments. It may be regarded as an unduly powerful organ of State, according to the perceptions of some government ministries and other commentators.[71] To ensure that the Ministry of Finance was able to fulfill its role of management of resources, after GEAR was introduced, the Minister of Finance became a member of government structures, executive structures and clusters of cabinet that dealt with government policies. As a member of these clusters, he received information about what was going to be discussed beforehand and if he was not able to attend he could advise one of his officials to represent him and push for the stoppage of policies that were not in line with government's policy plan and resources.[72]

The power wielded by the Finance Ministry was critical because it was supposed to be used to manage the resources of the country. Its power was demonstrated by its ability to veto or stop certain policies of some government departments from being approved if, for example, there might not be resources to support them. The Director-General of Education, in his reflection on its impact on government ministries in general and education in particular, stated:

> The Ministry of Finance is powerful in the sense that it has to be able to say to everybody "are these policies that you are putting in front of cabinet affordable, or are you promising something that we can't deliver because the resources are not there?" Now, to have that kind of power is to be sometimes super-powerful, because you may find that some of the policies are desirable and you are told by Finance that the country doesn't have the money. I think the Department of Finance carries a critical [and] important role just to check on the resources.[73]

The ascendancy of the role the Ministry of Finance in policy making across government departments was not something uniquely South African, but is a phenomenon that is associated with global neo-liberal policies aimed at enforcing fiscal austerity. In their analysis of the activities of the World Bank in higher education in Africa, Samoff and Carrol point out that like most external support, World Bank loans are to governments, not directly to education institutions or the education sector. As such, they are commonly administered by the Finance Ministry, which thereby also secures a seat at the policy table. Along this pathway, the World Bank's messages are presented in education policy debates by the national Finance Ministry. Thus, as the reliance on foreign funds increases, so does the influence of both the Finance Ministry and the external agencies. Representing the government in negotiations with those agencies, the Finance Ministry tends to become much more directly involved in policy and programmatic details across all government departments. As they point out, that increased role may suit well the external agencies.[74]

Especially concerned with reducing government spending, those agencies are likely to see the Finance Ministry as their ally, in contrast with ministries of, say, health or education, whose general mandate requires them to be more concerned with spending than with saving. The alliance between external agency and Finance (and perhaps Planning) ministry may be structured as a powerful lever for influencing national policy. As this occurs, the concerns, orientations, and priorities of the funding agencies are internalized in the policy process, both in the analyses and diagnoses that become the platform for policy and in the recommendations that shape the policy itself. As the distinction between insider and outsider becomes blurred, the homogenization of perspective and the adoption of universal verities, ostensibly with sound research support, proceed apace.[75]

The introduction of GEAR also confronted the new government, and all those from within the MDM who had assumed that there would be sufficient resources to address transformation goals, with a new reality. The policy planning had to be related to availability of resources. Though those who operated within the redistribution framework that was advocated by the RDP could see this perspective as reactionary, it brought about a sobering of mind within government and the bureaucracy, since a framework for policy-making was now being presented from above.

The fulfillment of a role of a super-ministry that managed the resources of the country was not without challenges. There could be conflict of interests of the ideological orientation of the Department of Finance and the rest of the party in relation to how it saw the policy issues. As Mseleku put it:

> Finance Departments are not just about how much money you have, they are about macroeconomic policy; they are about development policy. In other words, they are about the very issues that government is about, issues of growth and development, sometimes seen by many as obstructionist.[75]

Because of the tensions that characterized the overseer role that the Ministry of Finance was supposed to play, there was a continuous contestation, depending on whether there was convergence around the macroeconomic policy. The macroeconomic framework continued to be debated within some clusters of government in order to influence its content. This was to avoid some progressive policies from becoming blocked by the macroeconomic policy framework. In the dawn of the new millennium, it has become an area of contestation between government and labor and this threatens cooperative government arrangement and the basis of the tripartite alliance involving the ANC, SACP and COSATU.

CONCLUDING REMARKS

This chapter has analyzed the emergence of the new South African state using transition theories, theories of the state, the global context in which this state operated, the interim constitution of the GNU, and the changing macroeconomic policies and their impact on the development of higher education policy, and has come to a number of conclusions: (a) analysis of post-apartheid educational policies should take into account the context within which they were developed; (b) part of the context entails understanding the nature of the state, which in the light of the reviews of theories of the state has been described as a weak state and operating under severe constraints as a result of the local and global conditions under which it was being established; and (c) while transition that took place in South Africa is similar to that which occurred elsewhere in the world, there is some distinctiveness that characterizes this transition and helps to explain its nature. In particular, the nature of the settlement that was written into the interim constitution contributed to shaping the nature of the new state, and determined the pace and content of transformation.

The chapter also has explored the evolving macroeconomic policies of the new government. The changes that took place from the RDP to GEAR demonstrate the kinds of external and internal influences which the ANC as the ruling party and new government was exposed to. These help to shed some light on the compromises that the ANC was forced into and that reinforced those written into the Interim Constitution. In particular, the adoption of GEAR and the MTEF as planning tools brought with it the increased influence of the Ministry of Finance in the work and plans of other government departments. This took the form of all other departments' plans being subjected to the approval of the Ministry of Finance, based on whether or not there were resources to support them. With respect to higher education, GEAR reframed the policy process in terms of relating policies to available resources. In that context it implied that no new resources would be made available for higher education, thus derailing the process initiated by the NCHE to draw a framework for addressing equity and redress imperatives, as demonstrated by the cuts in the subsidies and in the NSFAS.

The significance of this chapter is threefold. First, it has contextualized South Africa's transition in the context of both nation state and of globalization, showing both similarities and distinctiveness. This lays the basis for dismissing the myth that South Africa's transition to democracy was unique. Second, it has outlined some of the constitutional provisions that have determined the character of the state in terms of what it could and could not do in the immediate post-1994 period. This has determined the nature, pace and content of transition that had an impact on the development of policy across government departments. Third, it has examined the evolution of the government's economic policy and the ultimate triumph of the neo-liberal economic agenda. This further reinforced the constraint of the transition framework under which the GNU was operating. The triumph of a neo-liberal economic agenda in the form of GEAR meant that the GNU had to operate under strict fiscal discipline, leaving few resources available to address the transformation needs of the country.

This chapter concludes that the state that emerged out of this transition was constraied and lacked the power and capacity to address the transformation needs which had informed the struggle for democracy. This conclusion is based on the following observations: (a) constraints were put on the new government in terms of appointing new people in line with the "sunset clause"; (b) the continued existence of new departments, old laws and appointments from the old bureaucracy, made room for resistance to and sabotage of the new government's transformation agenda; (c) the abandonment of the MERG and RDP policy frameworks, which accorded the new state a central role in the reconstruction and development of the country, and the adoption of the neo-liberal policy of GEAR, left economic development and reconstruction to the dictates of the market; and (d) the directive that government had to negotiate with higher education institutions before introducing any changes in them.

These conditions provided the framework for the establishment of institutional structures and development of policy which had to be in line with this framework. The impact of this on the establishment of the Department of Education, as a government department supposed to lead the transformation of education in general, and higher education in particular, as well as on the development of higher education policy, is explored in the next chapter.

Chapter Five
Bureaucratic Past and Democratic Future

INTRODUCTION

Discussion about the nature of the state and the understanding of how it operates should not only be at a theoretical level, but should also be grounded on the daily operations of the state as it finds expression through its organs. In this respect, this chapter focuses on the Department of Education as an important organ of the state that sheds light on understanding the nature of the South African state and the constraints under which it was operating. Analysis of the DOE is relevant to this study for three reasons. First, the Interim Constitution of South Africa made higher education a national competence under the Department of Education. As a result policy development in higher education became the responsibility of the national Department of Education.[1] Second, the consensus that prevailed during transition concerning the need to abolish apartheid necessitated the dismantling and rebuilding of many institutional structures and practices that had promoted apartheid. The apartheid education departments had to be dismantled and reconstituted to form the new national Department of Education and nine provincial education Departments. Third, the Higher Education Task Team had recommended the establishment of the Higher Education Division as one of the immediate actions to be implemented by the new Minister of Education. This did not occur immediately and it left a vacuum of sectoral leadership in higher education which was filled only in 1996, after the NCHE had reiterated the need for the establishment of a Higher Education Branch.

This chapter contends that education policy development took place in the context of the restructuring of the apartheid education departments and the pressures for change, and therefore the complexities of restructuring and the constraints under which policy development took place, should form part of the critique of policies developed during the transition period. There was further contestation over power and who is in control as the old bureaucracy held on to power and the new struggled to seize power. This partly explains the sustained reproduction of the existing institutional culture and modus operandi of the DOE during this period. Two factors could help to explain this: (a) the focus on concentration power and control was an important feature of the building of the new state and its instruments; and (b) the inexperience and lack of understanding of the nature of the bureaucracies and how they operate. In explaining the challenges and pressures under which it took place, and the need to formulate new policies, Du Preez, who acted as the Director-General of Education during the first four months of the new government, equates the challenges involved with "changing the wheel of the car while the car is moving."[2] Once the new Department was established, it drove education policies and the restructuring process.

The aim of this chapter is to analyze and assess the processes and challenges encountered in the establishment of the new Department of Education, particularly the new bureaucracy as an organ of state, in order to explain the complexity of the state formation and policy development during transition. It argues that these processes were characterized on the one hand by resistance to change by clinging to the bureaucratic past and attempts to democratize the functioning of the bureaucracy in line with the democratic vision and goals pursued by the new government. Using Max Weber's theory of bureaucracy, this chapter shows how the old apartheid bureaucrats struggled and even resisted change, as a result of their allegiance to the values of logic, efficiency and reason that had informed the apartheid system. On the other hand, the new incumbents, with a lack of experience in how the bureaucracy operated, came with idealistic notions of democracy and transparency, failing to recognize that democratization of the system is better driven by the bureaucracy which has its own culture, tradition, values, principles, and most importantly, memory. How the old memory had to be dislodged and replaced by the new one, lies at the heart of the establishment of the new Department of Education.

The establishment of the Department of Education thus saw a shift from impenetrable polity, as represented by the old institutional structures and cultures, to accessible polity, as represented by the culture being forged in establishing the new Department of Education. Impenetrable polity refers to the extent of the closure of polity controlling the centralized decision-making system whereas accessible polity refers to the openness of the decision-making system. According to Archer, these have an influence on the nature and patterns of change.[3] She argues that the patterns of change vary depending on the nature of polity controlling the centralized decision system which could either be closed (impenetrable) or open (accessible). Given the sunset clause that guaranteed the existence of the old bureaucracy, the new DOE was characterized by the coexistence of the old and the new bureaucracy, and the old and the new institutional culture. The contestation that characterized the appointment of officials by the new government and the creation of institutional practices in line with the vision, principles and values it espoused, saw a shift within the DOE from an impenetrable polity to an accessible polity. This transformation was important in ensuring that policy development took place in an environment conducive to serving the objectives of the new government.

THEORIZING BUREAUCRACY

Max Weber's theory of bureaucracy describes a new organizational form (bureaucracy) that Weber had noticed emerging in Western society during the second half of the nineteenth century. According to Weber, in this new type of organization, leadership and authority were derived from a more "rational" framework than was the case before that period. Previously, authority was derived from either charisma or tradition. In charismatic authority, followers obeyed gifted leaders out of devotion, loyalty and respect. Traditional authority, on the other hand existed due to historical reasons and people obeyed a person in power for the simple reason that a person was in a position of traditional power, for example, in a position of monarchical or other hereditary leadership positions.[4]

Weber believed that authority in the new organizational form was rational because leaders were recognized and obeyed for subscribing to values of reason, logic and efficiency. Such organizations functioned on a basis of "legitimately" derived laws, rules and regulations. He pointed out that bureaucratic action was typically oriented towards solving problems and that bureaucratic decision-making was guided by the objectives of efficiency, calculability and predictability. Consequently, decisions were more rational because they were made "without regard to persons," and were immune to personal, irrational and emotional aspects. Three key features of bureaucracy identified by Weber are worth exploring. First that bureaucracies had a formal and an unambiguous hierarchical structure of power and authority. Second, bureaucracies had an elaborate, rationally derived and systematic division of labor. Third, bureaucracies were governed by a set of general, formal, explicit and exhaustive and largely stable rules that were impersonally applied in decision-making. The goal of bureaucracy is, according to

Weber, efficiency. He posited that bureaucracies were technically efficient instruments of administration because their institutionalized rules and regulations enabled all employees to learn to perform their duties optimally.

The apartheid bureaucracy displayed a level of complexity which falls beyond Weber's theory in that it reflected features of the old (charismatic tradition) and the new (rationality). These were interchangeably applied in support and sustenance of the apartheid system. As pointed out earlier in the first chapter, one of the features of apartheid ideology was its link to religion in which the Afrikaners saw themselves as the chosen of God, called to civilize the black people. As the chosen generation, they had to be separate from other "races" in their execution of "God's calling." Concomitantly, leaders were seen as chosen and called of God, and therefore had to be revered, respected and followed. This laid the basis of charismatic leadership and authority. With the bureaucratization of the apartheid system through separate development policies, rational elements of the bureaucracy were built into the system to bolster the efficiency of the system. The combination of these elements account for the bourgeoning of and survival of apartheid over four decades.

On the other hand, the liberation movement, having suffered suppression and exclusion from decision-making, had evolved principles and a culture that fostered participation, consultation and representation, which came to be understood as democratization. The transitional pact which formed the basis of the new Government of National Unity (GNU), led to former adversaries having to work together in government. Using Weber's theory of bureaucracy, this chapter will show the tension that ensued in the establishment of the new Department of Education through the interplay of hierarchy, division of labor and established rules, on the one hand, and the consultative, consensus-building and participatory culture of the new bureaucracy and the challenges it poses to the logic of rationality, performance and efficiency, on the other hand.

ISSUES OF BUREAUCRATIC INHERITANCE

One development that came out of the appointment of the new Minister of Education was that on his taking office, there was no Department of Education. He had to create one. The implication of the transitional pact and the sunset clause was not on the "inevitability" of building on the existing Departments, but on how the Minister should go about doing this. Building by engaging with the legacy was a historical necessity. The new Minister had to create the new department from the existing ones since he had inherited all their personnel, infrastructure and laws. The process of this creation needs to be unpacked in order to appreciate the complexity it entailed. The apartheid education system had 14 education departments consisting of the Department of National Education (DNE), the three Departments of Education and Culture (House of Assembly for Whites, House of Delegates for Indians and House of Representatives for Coloreds), the Department of Education and Training (DET) for Africans, the four education departments in the "independent" African homelands of Transkei, Bophuthatswana, Venda and Ciskei (TBVC), and six education departments in what was known as the self-governing territories of Lebowa, Gazankulu, Qwaqwa, Kan-Gwane, Kwa-Ndebele and Kwazulu, which also served Africans. The significance of these different Departments of Education for Africans under apartheid is that they were used to serve the different ethnic groups in line with the separate development policy of the National Party government.[5] These "national" departments all fell under the new Minister of Education after the appointment of the cabinet in May 1994. The creation of the new Department of Education was a complex and elaborate process, and while the new systems were being put in place for its establishment, the old departments still continued to operate until they were formally integrated.

The creation of the new department not only entailed creating the national Department of Education, but also establishing nine provincial education departments. Given the elements of federalism in the Interim Constitution, the provision and control of education in the provinces was a provincial competence and was to be headed by a provincial cabinet official referred to as a Member of Executive Council (MEC).[6] Given a lack of capacity within the provinces to deal with the creation of new structures, in the case of education this responsibility was retained by the DOE at national level. The bringing of the old homeland departments under the national Minister also produced challenges, especially for the creation of provincial departments. In the interim the national Minister of Education became the political office-bearer over all the provinces.[7] The continued operations of the old apartheid education departments also meant that the locus of power at the center of contestation vested in the old bureaucracy and remained intact.

Secondly, all the ex-homeland and ex-provincial departments and the DET were devolved to the newly established provinces. This was a very controlled process where a survey was made of all the functions that were done under each department and how they would be continued or discontinued under the new dispensation. A provincialization unit was created in late 1994 to de-establish the 14 apartheid-era education departments and establish a single system of education. According to Manganyi, this provided the national Department of Education with a new and interesting perspective on the personnel costs in the education system and the expenditure patterns and deficits in the provinces.[8]

Apart from some of the systemic problems the new Department of Education had to address, there were other constitutional measures, administrative procedures and interim plans which it had to consider in managing transition. These account for elements of continuity and discontinuity between the old and new structures. The aforementioned "sunset clause" was one of the compromises to come out of a negotiated settlement with its provision for the old bureaucrats to retain their jobs after the election of the new government. The retention of certain positions by former bureaucrats accounts for their continued presence within the new Department of Education. The implication of the "sunset clause" here, and the interim measures put in place to deal with policy, meant the new system faced many challenges as people resisted change. Du Preez explains this resistance as follows:

> There were people from the old dispensation who did not want to cooperate. Bengu [first post-apartheid Minister of Education] said in an article in the *Beeld* last year that his stroke was caused by the shock that he got when he saw what was in that 1994 budget. An amount had to be shifted to the more disadvantaged areas of education, and it was not shifted in the draft. And when he got his draft budget and saw that it was not, that gave him a stroke. There were outbursts, because people couldn't accept change, there were few who could not accept that they have not got the power now.[9]

The non-compliance of officials who failed to carry out the Minister's directives highlights the problem of old officials in the new department who impeded the new policy agenda. Their behavior could be construed as bordering on sabotage. This could further be related to dissonance, which was related to the racial nature of the apartheid bureaucracy which had always been led by a white person, and now white senior officials had to take orders from a black Minister. Thus change in this instance became too much to bear as not only were orders coming from "someone not of our own" but were also giving directives to remove resources "from our own [whites]" to "others [blacks]." In reflecting on this phenomenon, Burns and Stalker point to how highly bureaucratized organizations are resistant to change. A prevailing atmosphere of hierarchy, control, efficiency and predictability meant that organizational members favored self-continuity and felt threatened by change. Thus, such organizations are poor in innovating or at embracing new ideas.[10]

The resistance of the former apartheid bureaucrats to change was also manifested in dealing with the appointment of new officials under the government, where old rules became an impediment to effecting change. The establishment of the new bureaucracy was done through the amalgamation of old departments (bureaucrats) and appointment of new officials. The process of appointing new officials had to follow certain processes and procedures to be approved by cabinet. This meant that while some of those positions were still occupied, no new positions could be created. The appointment of new officials was governed by the Public Service Commission with regulations across the board in every government department. The Public Service Commission was still based on apartheid rules and procedures. This hamstrung the new government in terms of appointing new people into strategic positions. For example, as a result of this arrangement, it was not possible for the ANC government to appoint a new Director-General of Education before the post was created, and that appointment had to be made in terms of the Public Service Commission procedures. The interim measure devised was that one of the senior National Party officials in the Department of Education had to act in that position for up to four months until the new Director-General was appointed. This led to a situation in the first four months of the new ANC-led government where there was an ANC Minister of Education, working with a National Party Deputy Minister and a National Party Director-General of Education.

Once an organogram was drawn and new positions created, the appointment of officials became a contested issue in government. As well as the "sunset clause" there was contestation around the appointment of Directors-General to the point that all Director-General appointments had to be approved by cabinet. In the case of education, the National Party was trying to retain Bernard Louw, the Director-General in the old apartheid Education Department as the new Director-General.[11] However, the appointment finally went to the ANC preferred candidate, Dr N.C. Manganyi. The new organogram also made provision for the creation of three deputy Director-General posts. These positions were also fiercely contested between the ANC and the National Party. The compromise position was that two would go to ANC appointees and the remaining one would go the National Party appointee. The National Party candidate was given the position of Deputy Director-General, Support Services, a strategic move on the part of the National Party since the post had to do with control of money and resources.

Regarding the "sunset clause," Mosala, who was one of the first new people to be appointed to head higher education, explained that the biggest challenge he faced was to appoint new people since the department had inherited a bureaucracy with existing personnel, and people who were already in those positions. He elaborated that the directors he worked with were not his choice as they were from the previous dispensation. As he puts it:

> The most difficult thing was to try and get them to hire relevant people in my directorate and they did not. There was an ideological discord. So I had to rely not on them in trying to drive new things. I had to rely on other people in the Department in general who were new to government and were in other sectors other than higher education. They [old bureaucrats] had to be reduced to just carrying out instructions. But in the end they defended and protected existing rules and processes.[12]

The coexistence of the old and the new bureaucracies in the DOE posed challenges for all the people involved in the restructuring of education since there was a period where there was a vacuum in terms of what the new agenda of the new government was. Once the new agenda was created, there was an insufficient leadership capacity among the new incumbents to lead the old bureaucrats. But as Mosala points out in the statement above, some old bureaucrats not only continued to operate by the old rules, but they also defended and protected them. Though the old bureaucracy might seem to be protecting the old rules, there was no indication of what the new rules were by which they were supposed to operate. Change is not easy; it takes time, patience and commitment to be effected. In the absence of direction and effective leadership from above, the old bureaucrats were bound to stick to what was familiar to them and to protect it as their livelihood.

Once appointed, the new incumbents were also under pressure from the higher education sector as they were seen as new and had to spearhead progressive policies towards visible transformation. The dilemma they faced was that most were appointed at senior level and had the old bureaucrats working under them, interacting directly with institutions. Mosala illustrates the differences, stressing that he "would find out about things long after they had said no to a person, and I would have said yes to."[13] The challenges that were experienced by the new government highlight the impact of the pacts that were underwritten into the negotiated settlement, making it difficult for the new government to operate effectively. The fact that the apartheid Public Service Commission continued to be the basis for the appointment of new government officials, coupled with the imperatives of the "sunset clause," reveals the extent of the continued closure of the system, despite there being a new government. It can help to understand the challenges of restructuring which entailed both the utilization of existing personnel and the establishment of new structures and procedures by examining them through a theory of organizational change. Having good ideas about change does not mean an understanding of what is to be changed. In the context of the DOE, there was no way of understanding how a bureaucracy operates without being a part of it. So the presence of the old bureaucracy not only had a negative impact in the sense of blocking change, but also had a positive effect, especially from those who were willing to listen and to be open, in that they were able to provide some continuity. This entailed the training of the new appointees, providing information to consultants who were assisting the DOE in restructuring, on just how the organization operated.

STATE AND CIVIL SOCIETY RELATIONS IN THE NEW STATE

The ANC government did not succumb to the constraints imposed on it by the Interim Constitution and it devised some means to overcome these. When the limits of the framework within which government was operating became clear, the internal Department of Education of the ANC both nationally and provincially began to develop a strategic direction and perspective relating to the restructuring of the bureaucracy. Intense discussions were held with legal and constitutional advisors to clarify different options available to the Minister of Education.

The strategy whereby the ANC could have access to the workings of the bureaucracy in order to ensure the implementation of the RDP was through the establishment of Strategic Management Teams (SMTs) at both national and provincial levels. Their introduction would draw membership from MDM structures, and would ensure continuity in the agents of MDM policies and the policies that were to be pursued within government. In other words, it would draw from the policy think-tanks of the liberation movement and deploy them as a source of support and policy advice for the new ministers. In that way, continuity would flow from the old bureaucracy into a new set of policies over which the new appointees would be custodians. This strategy had its own limitations in that each provincial and national minister was allowed to take not more than six members into the new bureaucracy. The limit placed on the new numbers within each SMT was determined by the national budget.

At national level SMT members were appointed by the Minister of Education on political grounds and were drawn from the political formations of the MDM. The creation of SMTs was a political compromise and a way of getting around the bureaucratic procedures and constraints imposed by the Interim Constitution for new appointees. They were expected to drive the MDM policy agenda and were politically accountable to the Minister and to the democratic movement structures.[14] One of the first things that the SMT in the national Department of Education had to work on was construction of the organogram for the new Department of Education. The Minister of Education, through members of the SMT, put in place a process of engagement that brought people together from both the previous government and also members of the strategic management team, into what came to be known as interim strategic management teams made of the old bureaucrats and new appointees.[15] The interim SMT helped to bring about a meeting of minds between the old bureaucrats and the new appointees who were providing support to the minister. It also served the important function of fulfilling the role of a political clearing structure where different positions between the old and the new dispensations could be mediated. It was a mechanism for opening up the system to make it more accessible. However, the impact of the SMT in terms of wielding power was insignificant given that the Minister of Education was allowed to have only six members of the SMT on his side, which appeared limited in a context of bloated inherited bureaucracy and the challenge of providing effective leadership.

With respect to higher education policy, the impetus of the pre-1994 period and the developments in the new government was maintained when the convener of the Higher Education Task Team (HETT), Dr Moja, was appointed to the Interim Strategic Planning Team. This ensured that the implementation of the recommendations by the HETT started immediately. This entailed, among other things, ensuring that the proposals for the appointment of the Commission were acted on with establishment of a Task Team that drafted the terms of reference. With the appointment of new people into the bureaucracy, continuity was established between the pre-election policy recommendations proposed and their implementation. A critical look at the implementation issues that were acted upon shows that these were not touching at the core of the system, but were only scratching the surface, hence there was little resistance (except for the NCHE terms of reference)[16] from the old bureaucracy.

Alongside contestations in the appointment and creation of the new bureaucracy, was the imperative to create the Institutional Culture that would inform the operation of the bureaucracy. Given the relative weakness of the new state, and the constraints of the Interim Constitution and sunset clause which gave the old bureaucracy a numerical advantage within the new government, the institutional culture of the apartheid system continued to be the basis on which the daily business of the Department was carried out. This institutional culture could be referred to as the invisible expression of the closure of the system. The use of the concept of closure of the political system is not only related to centralization of power in the hands of a few people, it has to do with the institutional cultures that characterized the operations of the Department of Education. It addresses the extent to which these institutional cultures were open to changes and had to be transformed. Thus the transformation of this institutional culture to make it more open and in line with the values and principles of the new government, was one of the challenges facing the new Ministry of Education. Given the nature of these challenges, it had problems in translating the old structures and cultures into what might become levers or organs of state power.

The creation of the new institutional culture was informed by the new vision but also drew from the backgrounds of the individuals, from their individual memories. This process of creating this new culture was not linear but drew on various sources, including the individual memories of the new appointees. In some cases those memories were new to the system and not even integrated; they had to go through the "melting pot" process where individual memories would be merged into the new memory of the state.

By institutional memory is meant the background that individuals bring to the context. It has to do with the past and what they can remember. It is an established form of practice and draws from the principles, values and norms that inform it. It influences the way things are done. The challenge was how to draw on this (institutional memory) in a way that shapes the present and future institutional culture. How these memories are negotiated into the new institutional culture depends on the vision, leadership and strategies. Attaining this transformation took a number of steps. First there was a need to create an institutional culture and to identify the levers of state that needed to be brought under control in order to accelerate the pace of change.[17] Mseleku explains institutional culture as:

> How people go about doing things, the systems, the operations, and the procedures for doing basic things, what leads to the development of those systems and what is it that they were actually trying to create, what were their objectives for creating all those things? Without understanding them or without having somebody who understood what this system was meant to do, you weren't able to break into it because you need to understand the dynamics of the system in order to know where to change it.[18]

In organizational change, a primary step is to understand the nature of the organization and the key dimensions in it. Rensburg elaborates on the notion of institutional culture by relating it to:

Policies and laws which are a formal representation of the memory, ideas, vision, mission, values, and frameworks for change, the strategies for change, objectives, and of the implementation strategies attached to those objectives. And so someone has to write it, or groups of people have to write it.[19]

The challenge was to create a conducive environment for these backgrounds and memories to be expressed in order to lay the basis for the establishment of an institutional culture that would inform the new institutional practices and new policy development. There are different levels through which institutional memory mediates new practices and the development of new institutional culture. The first level is of senior public servants (bureaucrats) who express it through ideas, mediate it through interpretation, give meaning to it and implement it on the basis of their own weaknesses and strengths. It needs to be pointed out that the new senior bureaucrats were also not necessarily constituting a homogenous entity. They came from different backgrounds, had different levels of experiences and expertise and also subscribed to different ideological orientations. For example, the new Director-General (DG), Dr C. Manganyi, came from a background of scholarship and academic leadership, but also grounded in activism as expressed through his literary work; Dr T. Coombe, Deputy Director General, brought knowledge and expertise of how bureaucracies functioned, how the planning and systems operations should be coordinated, whereas Dr Ihron Rensburg and Mr T. Mseleku came from mass democratic structures that were at the centre of opposition to apartheid, especially through the National Education Coordinating Committee (NECC). All these subscribed to the Freedom Charter and were aligned to the ANC. On the other hand, Dr Mosala came from the Black Consciousness Movement and an academic background, and had a particular way of how transformation had to be effected that was informed by his personal biography and politics. These personal biographies, combined with the biographies of the old apartheid bureaucrats, made the building of the new institutional culture based on backgrounds and memories a difficult task.

The next level of mediation is institutions themselves, according to their capacity to respond to policy which had been selected from a range of options. The policy process and implementation itself involve interpreting this memory. The new policies and laws were developed, written, understood and implemented by bureaucrats and the public. They were not only written, they were also mediated.

The creation of the new institutional culture in government departments became a contested domain, given the fact that liberation was not attained through a revolution but through negotiations. The GNU arrangement forced members of opposing camps to work together, even though it was difficult for this to happen given the history of adversarial relations among members of the GNU. In reflecting on the impact of the coexistence of institutional cultures within the DOE on writing the White Paper 1 on Education and Training, Coombe comments that:

> Stakeholder organizations from the past regime were still using the structures and personnel of the old departments as their conduit into the new political dispensation. They were putting their own views across through the officials from the previous departments and likewise those officials who were feeding drafts of the new White Paper through those lobby groups, teacher organizations in order to protect their own familiar base from the previous dispensation. Those structures were by no means dissolved through the process of the election and the formation of the new department. The process within the bureaucracy was not simply a bureaucratic process at all, given the political context. Just as the SMT members were aware that they had been appointed by Minister Bengu on political grounds, they were drawn from the political formation of the mass democratic movement, and they were expected to drive the mass democratic movement policy agenda and they had a political accountability to the Minister and to the democratic movement structures.[20]

Another feature of creating a new institutional culture was the recruitment of a new crop of bureaucrats who quickly had to drop unrealistic expectations such as shifting of resources from the advantaged to the disadvantaged without formal policy, or not following procedures for decision-making within the bureaucracy and facing the challenges of state and state power. This required a realistic understanding of the old bureaucracy and how it worked in order either to work against it or imbue it with a new style. Failure to have this sobering kind of experience in order to understand the nature of bureaucracy, and relying only on the fresher values and approaches that might have been inappropriate, would not have been relevant for state power. On the other hand, they would have been appropriate for what Mseleku calls "an anti-state movement, in other words, they are good for a revolutionary state because their mobilization strategy is not necessarily appropriate in the context of a democratic state."[21]

DILEMMAS OF BUREAUCRATIC EXPERTISE AND DEMOCRATIC POLITICS

Different views have been expressed concerning the usefulness of relying either on the old or the new bureaucracy in the development of policy in South

Africa during the transition period. Arguments in favor of both views have been advanced which add to the complexity of creating a new institutional culture. They range from putting primacy on skills (bureaucratic expertise), to putting primacy on politics (democratic politics) in effecting change and managing transition. The former sees the problems of the policies developed in the first five years of the new government as caused by a reliance on the new, visionary but inexperienced bureaucrats, at the expense of the old and experienced. Morris, one of the proponents of the use of the old bureaucrats, argues that they were not utilized and in the process were sidelined and became alienated. He highlights their unused skills in the new context in the following statement:

> They actually have all the institutional knowledge of how to work something through a system. There are rules that say how to do this, and everybody knows that if you want to do it through the state you do it this way and that way in order to get it through. Those people know all of that; they have all the implicit knowledge to do it. If they do not participate in the process, then you do not know how to guide things through a particular system. So on the one hand, it's a lack of capacity by new people coming in with the correct ideas of policy formulation. On the other hand, people in the institution who don't understand what the new policy is about, but understand the institutional arrangements about how to get it through. So if you don't create those linkages you have a big problem.[22]

The use of rules by bureaucrats and the skills they possessed in maintaining the system, typifies what Weber refers to as the basis of the operation of bureaucracies which are "legitimately" derived laws, rules and regulations. The non-utilization of these personnel and expertise in the new South African context resulted in their alienation and demoralization and some of them eventually left the system, thus contributing to the loss of important expertise for the new government.

From the opposite standpoint, those who put primacy on politics believed the skills possessed by the old bureaucrats were not appropriate to the new policy context. Elaborating on this view, Mosala points out that:

> When you drew them [old bureaucrats] in, they had no understanding of the political objectives of the new government. Even where they did understand, they had an ideological difference with it. They did not have the technical expertise and capacity that was required to drive the new system. So they were unqualified to be there. They were not suited, not as persons, but they were not qualified to run with the new policy intentions of the new government. Their world was just another world.

It is not true that they were not brought in, but they were not useful at all. In fact, we did use them but predominantly to do manual things like taking minutes and sending them. They were robots. They were trained in another type of world. They were used to taking instructions. They refused to think. That is the bureaucracy the new government could never have used.[23]

This view of their "uselessness" in the new policy context highlights some points about the nature of the bureaucracy in such centralized and impenetrable polities as was the case in the apartheid political system. It could be argued that the top-down approach used in these polities required a type of bureaucracy that efficiently carried out instructions for the system to run effectively. It could further be inferred that this type of personnel might have been trained with the sole purpose of carrying out instructions unquestioningly. Whether or not such an inference is valid, the appointment of replacements to build new capacities did not provide instant solutions to the problems described by Mosala. The new bureaucrats were also found to be wanting in terms of management skills that were required to run the system. In outlining some of the problems, Badsha explains that:

> We had the challenges of bringing in capacity. At a very basic practical level it was a case of people coming into the Department who had some experience and some sense of the policy process but now had to deal with being managers in the public service where you had to now manage projects and manage processes in particular. You had to work in different ways with agencies like non-governmental organizations (NGOs) or whomever you had to now draw on to take your work further. So where you were before a researcher yourself, you now had to manage that research process and guide it and lead it. So that posed new challenges for a lot of people. Another challenge people faced was to be able to find their feet in the bureaucracy. Some people found it more difficult to leave behind some of their activist background. There was a sense of helping people respond now to issues in a much more realistic way rather than as activists. It has also been important to recognize skills gaps of colleagues and help them to develop those areas.[24]

A third perspective incorporated both views, putting primacy on both politics and skills. It related the use of the old bureaucrats to a certain caliber of leadership. Metcalfe argues that:

> In terms of utilizing the expertise of experienced officials it required a particular caliber of leadership in order to effectively use such people. That particular caliber would have been a person with vision, who was able to hold that vision, communicate that vision, and get them to use

their skills in a very well-managed way to achieve that vision. That happened infrequently. If you look at the case histories of the particular sections within the new bureaucracy what you would more often find is an alienation between the two with no real leadership in terms of taking people along, marginalization of the old guard and constant irritation at their display of old attitudes without a meaningful engagement or taking them along. There were relationships which were rooted much more in suspicion and people who were unable to accept the new leadership and vision.[25]

This highlights the different perceptions, assumptions and positions that prevailed and which posed challenges for the establishment of the bureaucracy. These inevitably impacted on the creation of a new institutional culture necessary for stability within the DOE. The different perspectives on the role and use of the old bureaucracy in the new political context highlight two important points concerning the bureaucracy in relation to the relative openness and closure of the system. The first concerns the power the old bureaucracy wielded in terms of knowledge of the system which could be used to block the transformation agenda, and hence ensure the continued closure of the system. The other is related to the relevance of the operational skills within the system which the old bureaucracy had but which could be used only on the basis of direction and leadership offered from elsewhere.

Some of the ways in which skills have been spoken of show the heterogeneity required in this context. The views expressed about them entailed, *inter alia,* knowledge of the system, the new policy, the political objectives of government, managerial skills, technical skills to drive the new system, thinking skills, leadership, vision and communication of that vision to the bureaucrats. It appears that for the purpose of continuity within the new bureaucracy, a combination of the old and the new bureaucracy was required in the department. However, this needed to be drawn from people who were committed to the new vision of government and prepared to use their skills or acquire new skills for the benefit of the new government.

Creating a new institutional culture also entailed the management of crisis entailed in transition from the old bureaucratic culture to the new one. According to Mseleku, the new government was faced with an old order that did not want to change, and actually wanted to entrench itself by saying "we are the institutional memory," and the new order that was saying "we cannot trust the old at all and therefore it has no reason for claim [*sic*] to an institutional memory."[26] The interface between those two had to be managed. The new state was faced with contending institutional memories and cultures, one rooted in the old apartheid bureaucratic order, the other in the historical struggle against apartheid, and had no history of dealing with formal government bureaucracy. The interface between the two was actually what the managers were faced with. Some of these difficulties of dealing with the two institutional cultures in relation to the notion of democracy and participation are highlighted by the Director-General of Education in the following statement:

> You have a situation where participation in democracy is what you want to come with, but the institutional memory that exists tells you that you cannot go and discuss with the structures and the people out there your intentions as government before they have been approved by democratic structures of government. So you are frustrated because you believe that in the policy development stage that the principle of democracy which is participatory, is quite critical and crucial. Yet the institutional memory which exists tells you that "to do that is to undermine your power as government because you would actually have sold your position. You cannot do this without losing your authority as government."[27]

This statement reflects the tension embedded in the nature of the bureaucracy in terms of hierarchy and rules on the hand, and pursuit of democratic goals and ideals on the other as finding expression in the coexistence of the old and the new bureaucracies with different ideological orientations. The challenge facing the new managers within the DOE was how to deal with these two cultures without abandoning the principles of democracy, participation and consultation, and how ultimately to forge the new institutional culture. Mseleku's response here reveals the tension and the struggle that characterized the transition from the closed and impenetrable polity of the apartheid order to the open and accessible polity the new government was committed to. The new bureaucracy comprised people from different backgrounds, political persuasions and ideological orientations. According to Mosala, the coexistence of such diversity did not impact on policy formulation, but on implementation. This could be attributed to the period in the early days of the establishment of the DOE when it mainly outsourced the development of higher education policy and only senior government officials were involved in the final stages of policy development. The outsourcing could be related to the lack of capacity of human resources to deal with the demands being made on the bureaucracy within the DOE. On the other hand, it opened a window of opportunity for the public or stakeholders, other than the bureaucracy, to participate in the policy development process, thereby democratizing it and making it more accessible.

The situation of having the old and the new bureaucracy working together in pursuit of the government's new vision for education raises the question of what measures were put in place to prepare or reorient the bureaucracy so as to be able to operate under these new conditions. There does not seem to be any evidence of such preparation being put in place. While the new bureaucracy was lacking in a full understanding of how organisations operated and how to change them, the challenge lay in getting the old bureaucrats to understand where government and the new policies were trying to go. Mosala expresses this challenge in conspiratorial terms:

> The language of the new policies was another world to most people [old bureaucrats] and they didn't identify with that world. In fact, at other times I had the distinct impression that those people worked against what we were trying to do, consciously or unconsciously. For example, when we were deciding whether or not we were going to continue to have the CTP and the CUP as statutory bodies, those people were working together with technikons and universities to try and force us to maintain the statutory status of those bodies. Many a time they were in cahoots with the sector [higher education] against the Department in trying to push the line of the sector which was predominantly status quo, traditional, white, old guard sector at the time. [28]

Here expression of the frustrations and contestations entailed in the creation of a new institutional culture reveal part of the struggle involved. It could be mediated only through sophisticated staff recruitment, writing of policies and provision of leadership. Against this were the limitations of appointing too few people within the directorate with the desire or ability to attempt transformation. For the process to succeed, more people were needed who shared the same vision and would be prepared to work in new ways to achieve it. More broadly than the details of recruitment, creating a new institutional culture would have to entail putting in place a new conception of democracy. Not only would the right human resources have to be found, their effective mobilization would require matching them with the appropriate responsibilities. This called for the establishment of systems and processes of finance, procurement, workflow and decision-making across a range of specialized areas. There was no escaping the fact that some of these skills were found within the old bureaucracy and again this reinforced the notion of their indispensability within many departments, including the DOE. Even though there was a need for change to be effected, it did not mean that everything had to change. The key to creating continuity lay in balancing the bureaucratic skills of the old with a willingness to pass them down to the new.

One illustration of the complexity involved in this balancing act involved a chief education specialist who had served the apartheid education department for thirteen years and had reached retirement age even before 1994. Mr. H. Davies was retained by the DOE because he was the only person who understood the Technikon funding formula. He continued to serve as consultant for the Department in this field, thus maintaining an element of continuity. By 1999, a number of other senior officials of the DOE who had served in the first five years and had left, had been retained as consultants. Even though this practice could be viewed with skepticism, given the cost of using consultants, it points to a perceived difficulty in substituting experience.

A particularly sinister aspect of the institutional culture of the apartheid bureaucracy was the need to guard against enemies. Whether collectively from outside the country, or individually from within, the apartheid government was always under attack. Even, perhaps especially, the ministers were not safe, and ranged among their most obstructive opponents were the bureaucrats. What the Director-General colloquially refers to below, as "covering the Minister or Director-General's back" could be translated formally as loyalty. Or, it could reveal something more profound about the culture of apartheid. As Mseleku explains:

> Mainly all the practices here were based on this main principle of covering the Minister or Director-General's back. How does it translate itself? No one, for example, could speak to the press, could write a letter or anything on behalf of this Department, could do anything without the consent of people who were on top because it was important to cover the Minister's back or the DG's back. And the culture that existed in decision-making among the people from the Director level was to push paper upwards. The locus of decision-making was centered at the top, [and was] very closed.[29]

To change such a culture of paranoia and subservience and put in a system that was both vertical and horizontal in decision-making was something the DOE had to do urgently. It meant no less than putting in place what the Director-General refers to as a new culture of democracy. This entailed establishing the new rules and procedures for decision-making. In line with the principles of transparency, democracy, and accountability, which the new government had committed itself to, the new culture that was forged in the Department was, according to Mseleku, not about protecting the Director-General or the Minister, but about facilitating delivery, which technically could mean efficiency. What is not clear is whether giving up protection for the Minister also meant giving up loyalty. Would allowing departmental officials to go out and do their work lead in the process to their making mistakes?

Obviously making mistakes was not encouraged but the significance lay in what was intended when the mistakes were made. As Mseleku put it: "The culture was that the DG would cover your back rather than you covering his. It allowed people to experiment and be creative as long as they operated within the established parameters."[30]

Though past practices discouraged officials of the Department from talking to the public without authorization, Davies rightly argues that this was still the practice within the new Department.[31] Even though it was cultivating a culture of democracy for itself, it did not necessarily mean that any official could go out and say anything on behalf of the Department without authorization. An incident described by Mosala in which he was castigated for speaking to the press without formal authorization, illustrates this point succinctly:

> The new appointees, particularly blacks that came in, suffered from an inferiority complex of not having worked in government before and fitted into what they found in an uncritical way and as the way government works. We were told all the time by the people who were there that "this is what you do and this is how you do it." The first problem I had in the Department was I gave an interview to a newspaper, the *Business Day*, on the indicative funding figures for higher education. My colleagues who were all white at that time felt that the rule and the tradition was that we don't divulge that information until April the following year after the Minister has made the budget speech.[32]

Mosala argued that in his view, universities, technikons and the public were awaiting these figures to help in their planning. Since he knew them and explained that these figures were only indicative and not yet approved by cabinet, he found no problem in divulging them. But, as he explains:

> I got into such trouble about that because these people then told the Minister and the Director-General who then wanted to know who divulged this information. And people were surprised that I did it, and I said "Why can't I?" And they said "no, it is not done." "But who was saying it is not done?" The old guard. "But why shouldn't it be done?" I asked.[33]

The incident landed Mosala in trouble within the DOE, with even the Minister not endorsing his action. The practice was for these figures to be divulged only after planning had been endorsed by parliament. However, in Mosala's view, they were still the figures that were to be worked with. By the time parliament endorsed them in March, major political decisions would already have been made by the councils of higher education institutions. Mosala viewed this veil of secrecy as unhelpful.

The experience of Mosala highlights three important features of the DOE at the time. Firstly, it indicates the inadequacies and challenges of the new bureaucracy in the new context. Though the issue might be dismissed as procedural and having nothing to do with transformation, it however highlights discord among the old and new bureaucrats in terms of procedures to be followed in doing things. Secondly, the lack of transformation was similar to the process which existed in the old days. In Mosala's view, the functioning and workings of the Department should have been completely reconceptualized and redesigned so that the new people could come in with new ideas and that the departments could be made to respond more timeously. Thirdly, it shows the continuation of the old institutional culture in the new context. As a final point to be made from the incident, contrary to the view that the Minister or Director-General would cover the staff's back, Mosala was expected to cover the department by not divulging funding figures. This demonstrates the relative closure of the system in terms of decision-making and access to information.

So there was a fresh ethos and, as far as South Africa was concerned, unprecedented democratic practices which the DOE had to forge. They were not to be served up on a plate but contested, negotiated and, in the rhetoric of the time, "struggled over." As Mseleku put it, "democracy is actually people, culture, thinking, approaches, and processes, everything that you find in a government Department. That's a democracy."[34] This definition may appear simplistic and may fail to draw on the insights provided earlier in terms of the different discourses and people coexisting within the Department. To say "democracy is people" is not enough. The question then for government was what kind of people do you have and what kind of practices do you have in place? Democracy could be defined in terms of the kinds of people, cultures, processes and approaches that were supposedly being established in the Department. However, as pointed out earlier, what might be regarded as democracy by some people, others might regard as weakness?

CONCLUSION

This chapter has analyzed the creation of the Department of Education in terms of the challenges entailed. Using Weber's theory of bureaucracy, especially in relation to hierarchy, rules and division of labor, it showed the tensions that characterized the establishment of the post-apartheid Department of Education and its bureaucracy, and in particular, that bureaucracies could be stumbling blocks to change as they try to cling to power or what is familiar. In the South African context, resistance was also compounded with the challenge of dealing with the new conditions brought about by the post-apartheid era, which particularly old bureaucrats who used to be loyal to the apartheid regime were never prepared for. The experience further supports Blau's view that in bureaucratic organizations, certain people who know how "to play by the rules" become gradually more powerful, resulting in power shifting from leaders of organizations, who did not know how to play by the rules, to people who did.[35] In this case, it made it more difficult to seize power from them. However, the ruling party did not succumb to this resistance but tackled it until it managed to have a handle on the levers of power.

For a number of reasons enumerated above, including a global move away from the associated ideologies, radical revolution was not an option. Rather the choice lay in various forms of restructuring old apartheid structures, dismantling some, amalgamating others. To create the new educational system envisaged by the ANC activists would have required a very different culture within the department. While the appointment of new people accompanied by retention of the old gave an element of continuity to government, and therefore arguably some stability to the process of transition, the so-called "sunset clause" also impeded progress in implementing the ideals enshrined in the Constitution.

Transition and transformation were not only at the level of people and structures; they also involved institutional practices, which in a broad sense have been termed cultures. The challenges entailed in creating these new institutional cultures have been explored. The DOE did manage to challenge the operations of the old, closed and impenetrable polity at the level of structures and personnel appointment. However, at the level of daily institutional practices, there was initially little evidence of transparency within the bureaucracy in terms of change or embracing a new way of doing things in line with government policy. Coupled with a lack of capacity within the DOE, these conditions resulted in this responsibility being mainly outsourced to external agencies, and departmental involvement began only in the final stages of the development of these policies. Ironically, it was this outsourcing in the early stages of policy development that was to create space for the creation of an accessible polity framework in the development of policy. Analysis of the policy process should therefore take into consideration some of these contextual factors which constrained the operation of the new government. A critique of policies that fails to take into account these factors, will run into the problem of oversimplifying the challenges entailed in the development of these policies.

Chapter Six
Change Commisioned

INTRODUCTION

The examination of state formation in the previous chapter focused on the establishment of the Department of Education, with the purpose of outlining a key component in the nature of the state in South Africa with respect to education in general and higher education policy in particular during the transition period. The principle underpinning the establishment of the GNU, which fostered participation of minority parties and made consultation mandatory with all its partners in major decision-making, also enhanced the opening up of these processes in government. However, the institutional practices of the apartheid state and some Constitutional provisions that underpinned the transition to democracy also constrained the DOE in effecting any rapid transition to democracy.

What the government failed to achieve in opening up space for greater participation of the people in decision-making within formal government structures, it achieved by outsourcing policy development initiatives to external agencies. In this way, it managed to keep decision-making away from possible obstructionists and simultaneously created a context for public participation in policy formulation. Thus there was continuity between the processes of public participation and consultation in the policy process that was developed in the pre-1994 era and the policy development processes that were outsourced by the DOE. In this case, the DOE relied on Task Teams, Commissions, Technical Committees and Reference Groups to do the initial work of researching and making policy proposals to it. Almost all draft policy documents it released contained a call for the public to participate by making written responses and attending public consultative meetings. Significantly, the development of the higher education policy leading to the passing of important legislation was also developed within this framework.

This chapter focuses on NCHE as a change agent commissioned to undertake research and advise government on how the higher education system could be transformed. It posits the following two arguments: First, the concept of "commission" was not new, but had been part of the apartheid system, and has also been used by democratic societies elsewhere. It was appropriated and re-created in the light of the principles and values generated in the struggle against the old regime and during the negotiation process. Its significance and the way it was constituted should be understood with reference to the politics of compromise and consensus building embraced by the new government. Second, given the political and social context in which the NCHE was established and operated, its policy project, including the process and procedures entailed, were conceptualized, planned and implemented as participatory, consultative and dialogical to enable policy input by the public. However, in practice the process translated itself into an expert-dominated one in which the voices of stakeholders were mediated by commissioners. This is not to downplay the significance of this process. In this regard, it will be argued that policy development as dialogue also had unintended consequences with far-reaching impact on the field in which stakeholders operated. This has been demonstrated in the experience and learning acquired by stakeholders who interacted with the Commission and which created conditions for participation in the subsequent stages of the policy process and implementation.

BACKGROUND TO THE ESTABLISHMENT OF THE NATIONAL COMMISSION ON HIGHER EDUCATION

When the new government came to power in 1994 it inherited an inequitable, racially skewed, undemocratic and inefficient education system. The need for redress of these inequities was expressed in 1992 by the National Education Policy Investigation (NEPI), conducted under the auspices of the National Education Coordinating Committee (NECC) which was aligned to the liberation movement, especially the ANC. This need was further articulated in the ANC's Discussion Document, *A Policy Framework for Education and Training* (1994), which identified three features of the education and training system under apartheid:

- The system was fragmented along racial and ethnic lines, and had been saturated by the racial ideology and educational doctrines of apartheid.

- There was a lack of, or unequal access to, education and training at all levels of education with large disparities along race and gender lines.
- There was a lack of democratic control within the education and training system.[1]

The idea of the Commission was first mooted within the education sector of the mass democratic movement as policy proposals for post-apartheid South Africa were discussed. In commenting on the emergence of the idea within the MDM structures, the former chairperson of the parliamentary Portfolio Committee on Education pointed out that:

> The Commission was mooted in what was initially referred to as the Yellow Book (ANC's Policy Document on Education) as a means of saying "there is so much in the restructuring of higher education that is needed that we will need a very thorough investigation into the state of higher education. [This was important] . . . because whilst we knew in broad terms what the state of higher education was under apartheid, we needed to find out some finer details. The idea of the Commission was also informed by the fact that once you start the process of restructuring, you have to consult as widely as possible.[2]

The legitimacy that comes with the involvement of experts and public participation in the policy process can be given as reasons for the importance attached to the Commission by the MDM. It also needed to maintain the continuity of public participation in policy-making within the liberation movement in the run-up to the 1994 elections. The former Director-General expressed this at length:

> If we had the kind of government that came in posturing itself and believed that it knew the answers to every social issue, public concern, then we could have had other options other than the Commission. It could have simply proclaimed that this or that is going to happen with regard to higher education. But we didn't have that kind of outcome from our negotiations. Instead we have had both a history of democratic practice in terms of the liberation movements. We were asserting a moral position and it almost seems like a logical consequence in that approach to statehood and nationhood that we would have had a process that would have created not only conditions for proper investigation of the issues but participation of the public in both understanding the issues and trying to help create a new framework for the system. So it was necessary both in terms of the political logic of liberation and democratic imperatives, and also because it is a fairly large system and it is complex and had not been treated in the past as a national system, and someone needed to look at it as a national system to see what it has to offer.[3]

The ANC's intention of dealing with the restructuring and transformation of higher education was carried into government. The new Minister of Education (S. Bengu, an ANC Minister), appointed a working group within the Interim Strategic Management Team in the new DOE to draft the terms of reference for the Commission.[4] The government's intention to appoint the Commission was also expressed in the first *Draft White Paper on Education and Training* released in September 1994.[5] In discussing the importance of the Commission, the Draft White Paper stated that:

> The Ministry has the responsibility to advise the government on whether this vast infrastructure of intellectual and professional endeavour, substantially supported by public funds, is yielding a good return to the nation and how it might be assisted to do better. No official inquiry into the whole of the post-secondary sector has ever been undertaken in this country.[6] The new democracy needs to have confidence in its senior institutions of learning, especially given the massive influence which higher education exerts on the cultural, social, scientific, technological and professional formation of the country's leadership. Accordingly, after a prolonged period of consultation, a proposal by the Minister of Education to appoint a National Commission on Higher Education has been approved.[7]

The process was put in place for the appointment of Commissioners. Even though the CEPD's Higher Education Task Team (HETT) had fleshed out the framework and details of the appointment of the Commission, these still had to undergo a formal governmental process and be adopted as a government program. The process entailed circulating draft terms of reference for public comment, appointment of a nominations committee, inviting nominations for the Commission, shortlisting of nominees, and the appointment of the Commission.[8] The NCHE was finally appointed in February 1995 following a presidential proclamation.[9] Its terms of reference were to advise the Minister of Education on:

- What constitutes higher education?
- The immediate and long-term national goals of the system of higher education.
- The institutional types required for the system, their particular functions and missions, their respective inter-relationships and their relationship with the state, professional bodies, the private sector, NGOs, etc., whether national and/or provincial.
- The structure required by the Minister of Education or any other governing authority to provide ongoing policy on higher education.

- The steps required to establish advisory and administrative structures.
- Funding mechanisms for institutions and students in higher education.[10]

Different issues impacted on the appointment and composition of the Commission. Apart from those of professionalism and expertise, which were obvious considerations, the political context of the appointment of the Commission, namely the government of national unity, became crucial in terms of its composition. This qualitative difference in the composition and nature of the Commission is important to note since it had an impact on the way the Commission was to operate and how it would relate to stakeholders and their submissions. As one of the commissioners later commented, it was established under a Presidential proclamation and was accountable to the President and the Minister, not to the stakeholders.[11] This represented a paradigmatic shift in the way in which policies were now going to be developed. Contrary to the past practices within the MDM structures, where policy-makers were accountable to the masses and their constituencies or stakeholders on the ground, the new context of policy-making made them accountable to the leadership (the President and Parliament.) This approach to policy development laid the basis for protracted tensions and conflicts that were to characterize its work.

In the composition of the committee that drew up the shortlist of nominees, diversity, inclusivity and nation building issues prevailed as the new Minister of Education tapped into the expertise of the old bureaucracy. Moja, who later became the executive director of the NCHE, noted some of the surprises that came out of this process, which are in some way the outcome of the democratic process of the appointment of the commissioners: "What was interesting was that the top three candidates on that list, in the order of priority that they had listed, were three white Afrikaner males . . . which shocked all of us. That is why I emphasize the democratic process of selecting commissioners."[12]

The question that needs to be posed is, given the history of opposition to apartheid and the extent to which apartheid ideologues were discredited within the liberation movement, how did they come to be accorded such prominence in this Commission? Several answers could help explain this. Firstly, it could be a reflection of the inclusive policies and consensus-building approach that underpinned the operation of the GNU. Secondly, it could also be related to the influence of the old bureaucracy in the decision-making process of the new government since the Commission was appointed within the first year of the GNU. Thirdly, perhaps recognition of the expertise and experience which the three experts would bring to the Commission would serve both the purpose of continuity and the indispensability of their qualities.

Given that this new Commission was established within the framework of the GNU, where politics of compromise and consensus seeking were the order of the day, representing the diversity of political orientation, race and gender was a necessary consideration. Thus, after an initial shortlist of 101 nominees,[13] 13 commissioners were appointed drawing from a number of sectors including technikons, colleges, universities, NGOs, business and the old apartheid administration.[14] Accommodation of the latter symbolized the prevailing politics of compromise and consensus seeking at the time. A comment by Coombe best characterizes the prevailing approach within government:

> Although he was an ANC Minister and advancing an ANC policy and would never depart from that, he was trying to build a broad consensus around that policy. That was a necessity in that specific time because the Government of National Unity was new, it functioned as a tri-partite political set-up within the cabinet and the doctrine of sufficient consensus from the negotiations was still the doctrine that applied at the cabinet level. The Minister knew that he would need to get [that] sufficient consensus at cabinet level in order to avoid significant disruptive political tensions when he would ask the cabinet to approve, and then the members of the public to implement, that policy. He was convinced that the open warfare, open contestation around education changes that had occurred prior to 1994, could not be the basis for transformation post-1994 with any success.[15]

It was in this context that people from the opposition camps came to be appointed to the Commission. Though the recommendation of the Task Team was for the appointment of an expert commission,[16] and the Commission saw itself as such, the nature of its composition in terms of membership shows that both expertise *and* representivity were considered. It needs to be pointed out that the composition was not only a departure from the apartheid approach which was exclusive to the state ideologues, but also a departure from some of the prevailing conceptions within the MDM structures as it now had to reflect the new conditions of the GNU.

DIALOGUE AND EMERGING IDEAS
WITHIN THE COMMISSION

There are three dimensions of dialogue in relation to the NCHE process and how it carried out its work. The first is the Commission in a dialogue with itself, mediated by the competing discourses within (internal dynamics). The second is the Commission in dialogue with stakeholders, (external dynamics) and the third is the changing ideas emerging from the interaction with stakeholders and dynamics in the Commission.

With respect to the internal dynamics of the Commission, one of the first things commissioners had to do upon assuming office was to clarify their understanding of the terms of reference and develop a shared vision to inform their work.[17] This is in line with the views of Callan, who headed the California Commission, when he pointed out that the general charge should be established prior to its formal establishment and appointment of commissioners. He regarded this as important since members should know, when they agreed to serve, how much time they would have to accomplish their charge. He observed that the most effective commissions begin by focusing on the task at the beginning.[18] It the case of the NCHE, appointment took place alongside the drafting of the terms of reference, so establishing a common understanding was a logical starting point. There was convergence between the Commission's definition of higher education and the ANC's proposed parameters defining higher education, namely that higher education represents all forms of education beyond secondary school level.[19] This served as a framework within which dialogue among commissioners would be conducted.

Secondly, structural arrangements in the form of research groups and technical committees were put in place to supply research information to the Commission. These also became the means through which dialogue within the Commission was facilitated. The research groups were chaired or co-chaired by commissioners who would update the Commission about issues arising from them. This was deliberately done so that the research agenda would not have a life of its own. There were also conveners of different research groups who came together with the chair of the Commission as coordinating committee. Their arrangements facilitated dialogue within the commission from the technical committee level.

Despite attempts to make the process representative on the basis of race and gender, the policy process of the Commission continued to be dominated by white and male researchers. This was reflected in the composition of the task teams and technical committees of the Commission which shows that of the 192 members of different task groups and technical committee members, Blacks constituted 31.7 percent whereas Whites constituted 68.3 percent. The output of Task Teams and Technical Committees was also dominated by whites. Of the 140 papers produced, blacks produced only 35 or 25 percent[20] while whites produced 75 percent of the papers.[21] The domination of

whites should be understood in the light of policies of apartheid which privileged whites in general and males in particular in terms of access to privilege and power.

The internal dynamics were also connected to authorship of policy.
Writing was done by whoever had the time and this should not be taken at
face value. Underlying factors such as who wrote what should be taken into
consideration. As a former commissioner explained:

> If I were to do an analysis of the Commission's report, I would be able
> to show you which bits were influenced centrally by which individual.
> People who were drafting would use this power to shape the terms of
> the debates. So what that actually comes to is not only the different per-
> spectives among the commissioners, sort of national unity perspectives,
> but also the question of who had more time to spend on this work and
> who had less time. Technically we were all part-time commissioners but
> in practice some people were retired and were contracted by the
> Commission to write certain sections or to work on certain issues and
> to prepare drafts for the Commission. Other people were located in the
> institutions, which made it possible for them to spend almost all the
> time or 80 percent of the time on the work of the Commission.[22]

Institutions such the Human Sciences Research Council (HSRC) and the
University of Cape Town (UCT) are examples of those bodies that released
their staff to spend more time on the Commission. On the other hand, some
of the commissioners continued with their full-time jobs and did the work
of the Commission on a part-time basis. This brought about imbalances in
terms of the quantity and sometimes the quality of input commissioners
could make.

The divergence of views within the Commission was demonstrated by
the way in which it dealt with the type of system for higher education to rec-
ommend. The choice was between a trinary system (made of college, technikon and university sectors), the binary system (made of two sectors,
namely, universities and technikons) and a unitary system (where all institutions offer the same programs). After some protracted debates within the
Commission, which was divided between favoring retention of the binary
system and the unitary system, the Commission proposed a single coordinated system as a compromise. The proposal for a single coordinated system, which departs from the binary system which has been part of the South
African higher education system, was a contested issue both within and outside the Commission, and between different sectors. This debate first started
within the technikon movement in the Committee of Technikon Principals
(CTP), and was later carried over into the Commission. Figaji, as a member

of the technikon movement, was opposed to the idea of a unitary system because it implied sameness and the possibility of technikons being called universities. His concerns were based on the fact that in a unitary system the technikons would have lost their competitive edge over universities, which was based on the career-focused and vocational education they offered. He elaborated that:

> If we as technikons now call ourselves universities there is going to be an expectation that we do what universities do, and to become even better. In the CTP there was a strong feeling that the binary divide is unnecessary and that we should eradicate it and have a unitary system. I just kept on asking for the logic. I said "show me anywhere in the world where you have the unitary system. Let us look at what happened in Britain where we had the binary system closed and we had the polytechnics becoming universities. What happened is many of them have become bad copies of the previous universities, and lost their career purpose. Can we at this stage of our country afford to have this? The answer is no."[23]

The compromise solution to this impasse was that the Commission proposed something different and unique in the form of a single coordinated and differentiated system. Despite this compromise, there was still concern on the part of Figaji about the proposal of a single coordinated system and how diverse sets of programs and research functions would be distributed across institutions. His objection to this development was so serious that he wrote a minority report for the NCHE in which he warned about the consequence of having instructional programs as a fundamental building block of the new higher education system. In his submission he argued that:

> While this provides a very useful mechanism for planning, funding and steering the higher education system as a single coordinated system, it sacrifices the notion of institutional mission, such as career education. A university can apply to offer what is currently a technikon programme and vice versa. From experience we know that this type of system only benefits those institutions with more resources, greater capacity and better facilities, that is, universities. The chance that a technikon will be granted approval for a medical school, for example, is quite remote.[24]

The debates within the Commission illustrate its internal dynamics, revealing that it was not homogeneous and that the consensus-seeking mode had become a way of resolving difficult issues. The mode of operation of the Commission is linked to an understanding of its brief and the political climate of the time, which was characterized by transition and consensus seeking. In commenting on the impact of transition and a consensus-seeking mode on the work of the Commission, Omar elaborated that:

> We had to operate on the basis of sufficient consensus, and that persisted for the first three or four years after the elections of 1994. We did not have a majority rule principle, if we had a majority rule in the country, then we would have operated differently in the Commission . . . we would have been able to get much harder positions on issues like redress, payment of fees for higher education and access issues. And that would have got into the Commission itself. But it didn't, it was transition, government of national unity, consensus and so on. So that shaped the way in which the Commission discussed some of the issues.[25]

This highlights that apart from the principles and values that came out of the MDM policy process, and the constitutional provisions in the Interim Constitution, there were some values and operational principles that underpinned the operation of the GNU, such as sufficient consensus which a policy institution like the Commission had to consider. The exchanges that characterized the debate regarding the unitary and binary systems and the compromises that came out of it, highlight some of the elements of policymaking. Threats, for instance, could be used to influence some policy outcomes. In the event of these not succeeding, a minority report could be written in which one's own position was stated in objection to the widely held view.

The external dynamics of the Commission are discussed with specific reference to the relationship commissioners had with the sectors they were drawn from, the different opportunities for participation the Commission created for stakeholders, the different perspectives of stakeholders and how the Commission dealt with them. Despite the view that the Commission was made up of experts, it has been demonstrated that in the appointment of commissioners, the issue of diversity across the higher education sector seems to have influenced its composition. As experts, they would have the space to make decisions based on their expertise, irrespective of the sectors they were drawn from, while as representatives of stakeholders or sectors they would have to reflect the views of those parties rather than the expert views. There are three related questions that need to be raised in this respect. Firstly, what kind of relationship did the individual commissioners have with the sectors they were drawn from? Secondly, what was the nature of the relationship which commissioners had with the individual institutions from which they were drawn? Thirdly, what kind of support did they receive from these institutions in relation to the Commission's work?

For dialogue to be facilitated between the Commission and stakeholders or the sectors commissioners were drawn from, it was important for commissioners to clarify their identities. For example, in what capacity were they operating in the Commission—as experts or were they operating as representatives of their sectors? Interviews with some commissioners reveal that there was no common identity that they assumed as commissioners. Some saw themselves as experts who operated independently of the sectors they were drawn from. For example, Figaji explained his position in the Commission in the following words: "I was not in the Commission sent by the CTP so I did not owe them anything. I was there in my own right."[26] Despite being there in his own right, Figaji however ensured that the interests of the technikon sector were taken care of: "I was a CTP member and I would tell them what was happening in the Commission and try as far as possible to ensure that the CTP people were represented in research groups, and that in their appointments there would be a technikon person. That was my duty."[27]

On the other hand, Ngcobo, who was drawn from the college sector, saw himself not only as an expert but also as representing the interests of teacher education. In his view, expertise and representivity went together and it was impossible to have one at the expense of the other. He described his position in the Commission as follows:

> I couldn't be independent. The drive was to ensure that teacher education was represented, was put in the higher education sector. My view in terms of the NCHE is that it was driven by both considerations— representivity and also expertise. You couldn't have one at the expense of the other.[28]

Despite the claims that the Commission was an expert one, the available evidence suggests that it was a combination of both experts and representatives of different sectors, as suggested by Ngcobo. Even though Figaji saw himself as an expert in his own right, the fact that he ensured that the interests of the technikon sector were taken care of suggests that he also acted as a representative of the sector. To complicate matters, there is also evidence that Figaji demonstrated his independence from the technikon sector by adopting policy positions different from those of his sector. The difference between him and his sector centered around the proposal of having a unitary system which would make it possible for technikons to become universities, as explained above. The experiences of the two commissioners and their interaction with the sectors they were drawn from represent a form in which dialogue between the Commission and the stakeholders took place. It further reveals the multi-leveled nature of debate that took place around the work of the Commission.

That is, debates took place within the Commission but also among members of different sectors in an attempt to influence its work.

Another form of dialogue and interaction between the Commission and stakeholders was interaction between the individual commissioners and the institutions they were drawn from. On an ongoing basis they kept their institutions informed about what was going on, helping to promote awareness of policy. By the time the Commission released its report, these institutions were able to align their policies with those proposed by the Commission. As Cloete put it:

> Institutions that had people working for the Commission had them sharing the views with their institutions. They in a way prepared the institutions for what was coming. They also defended the position of the Commission as well as the White Paper. Thus institutions saw the policy coming and were ready.[29]

Apart from these informal interactions there was a formal process put in place by the Commission which facilitated dialogue with the public. The Commission adopted an interactive mode of operation aimed at involving higher education policy stakeholders in policy formulation. The NCHE report indicates that stakeholders contributed to three broadly based national consultative conferences, responded to calls for submissions, made presentations at scheduled meetings and provided research.[30] This is how the mode of operation is explained in its report:

> In its first ten months of operation, the Commission received 123 written submissions, conducted hearings and heard verbal presentations. Visits were made to all the nine provinces, and not necessarily all institutions. A broader stakeholder reception was hosted by the Member of the Executive Council (MEC) for education in each province to enable stakeholders outside institutions to make inputs. The Commission also provided an opportunity for stakeholders to discuss their submissions with commissioners at hearings scheduled over three days during which submissions were debated. Since students had not yet made written submissions at that stage, special arrangements were made for their organizations to address the Commission.[31]

Extensive use was made of international higher education policy organizations such as the Center for Higher Education Policy Studies in the Netherlands, the Commonwealth Higher Education Management Services, the American Council on Education, and the World Bank, as well as numerous individuals, supported by international funders. The Commission mentions in its report that it recognized the need for policy feedback on its policy proposals. To create opportunities for this, the Discussion Document was prepared, published and submitted for scrutiny by the widest possible range of stakeholders. The purpose of the Discussion Document was said to be "to consult on the policy positions being considered."[32] What is significant about this Discussion Document was that it was referred to as "A Framework for Transformation." This title reflects the prevailing views within the Commission in terms of what they were expected to produce, that is a framework within which specific proposals would be formulated.

CONSULTATIONS OVER THE NCHE'S DISCUSSION DOCUMENT

There was a consultative conference organized to discuss the Discussion Document with the aim of receiving feedback but not to collect ideas from the public and record them in the report. The challenge this posed to the NCHE and subsequent policy development processes was that this conception of consultation and how it was applied was understood in this way only by commissioners and policy-makers. Stakeholders had different expectations of how the consultative process could be used in the policy process. The consultative meetings and conferences became important means through which dialogue between the Commission and stakeholders took place, and it is thus worth reflecting on three of these. Following its work of 15 months, the Commission released a preliminary working document on 15 April 1996, called "the Discussion Document." Two meetings the Commission held around the Discussion Document, namely the national stakeholders' feedback conference and the Salzburg meeting with international experts, and another conference organized by black professors at the University of Venda in response to the NCHE's report, are analyzed. The latter did not involve the participation of commissioners.

The national stakeholders feedback conference was held on 28 and 29 April 1996 and attended by 350 delegates representing a wide range of stakeholders. The Discussion Document was criticized for its failure to reflect the views of some stakeholders who had made submissions and whom the Commission met for discussion during the site visits. Students, led by SASCO, argued that the Document reflected mainly the views of commissioners and the experts who had conducted research for the Commission. This development was attributed to what students referred to as the non-accountability of experts. To this effect SASCO argued that:

> The problem with public policy that is driven by unaccountable experts
> with no strong popular participation is that most of the time experts

smuggle their own ideological positions in the final policies. The NCHE is worse than most—it does not even attempt to put forward the views of other stakeholders, except in few instances, where the commissioners disagree with one of the powerful stakeholders.[33]

The view expressed by students provides a perspective of what stakeholders expected from participating in the work of the NCHE. The thrust of the argument is that some stakeholders would have loved to see different perspectives emerge from the submissions. As SASCO put it:

> True consensus, as the Constitution-making and parliamentary processes show, evolves out of public disclosure of differences and head-on confrontation of areas of disagreements, not sweeping them aside. This often leads to an unsustainable false consensus which can only serve to postpone rather than resolve conflict.[34]

The concerns raised by SASCO lead to the posing of a question about the nature of the policy process and how to present policy recommendations in the context of a consultative process. Should policy documents reflect the views of all participants or just those who have been consulted, or should they present a distillation of the main views and perspectives by commissioners emanating from the consultative process? It appears that SASCO and other stakeholders subscribed to the former perspective and they rejected the Discussion Document, arguing that it was a submission by the commissioners. As SASCO put it, "it should be seen as a starting point for further deliberations, rather than as a compilation of stakeholder opinions and general consensus."[35] They questioned the process of consultation followed by the Commission, stating that it was not people-driven or people-centered, because it was seen as comprising "unaccountable experts with no popular participation and overt individual vested interests."[36]

The views advanced by SASCO illustrate the discord that existed between the Commission and some stakeholders in terms of the brief of the Commission, the process of carrying out its brief and expectations of the process, especially of the meaning and implications of being consulted and participating in the policy process of the Commission. Students rejected this notion of consultation. The major critique of the consultative process was the fact it was seen as a legitimizing process, rather than a serious consideration of inputs from the stakeholders.

In response to the accusation that the NCHE had failed to incorporate the views of stakeholders, and therefore had a flawed process of consultation, Stumpf argued that the Commission had used an after-consultation approach to substitute policy development, which gave commissioners the right to formulate policy recommendations as they saw fit. He argued that it would have been impossible to incorporate every stakeholder's view, which would imply using an in-consultation approach. The latter approach implies that, "if you consult me, then you are bound to reflect my views in the report." According to Stumpf, an in-consultation approach would have caused total mayhem and there would have been no need for a Commission.[37] Stumpf explains it as follows:

> There is a legal difference between what one calls "in consultation" and "after-consultation." "In consultation" with someone means you have to accept and reflect the views of the party you are consulting with. "After-consultation" means you consult with a party and after your consultation you formulate the views as informed by your consultation. The model of the Commission was most definitely an "after-consultation." An "in consultation" model would have been total mayhem. There was absolutely no possibility to reflect every stakeholder's proposals and that was never an undertaking of the Commission.[38]

This explanation puts final decision-making powers on the policy-makers to decide what goes into policy and how it is presented. It also seems to have been the prevalent view within the DOE as the former Director-General echoed the same sentiments in relation to the role of stakeholders in writing the White Papers:

> Well the stakeholders did not write White Papers, but like all democratic processes they use whatever expertise they can find to deal with certain issues. So they would make their contribution on the best possible sources of information they can find. But it is certainly not their job to write White Papers. The White Paper is a government document and ultimately the government must be able to stand behind it. We have not come to a realization that we have a government that we elected to govern and its job is to govern until we have another election. That government must do that otherwise there is no point in us paying them if they are not doing their job. Yes, sometimes there is confusion about who is actually governing.[39]

The emphasis the former Director-General puts on government's role to govern, which he contrasts with stakeholders' contribution to the policy processes, highlights the different roles and functions policy actors have in the process. While the stakeholders could exercise their democratic right in making an input, government had also to exercise its responsibility of governing, and that entailed making decisions. This approach informed the operation of different Task Teams, Commissions and Technical Committees that were established to advise or make recommendations to the DOE. While consultation was widespread, these bodies had to make decisions that reflected their thinking on the best recommendations to make to government, drawing from stakeholder inputs as one source of information. Given that the policy process within the DOE and Parliament was led by newly appointed and elected people, the policy process also entailed a level of learning on the part of those involved. The learning process and the experience it entailed are captured by the former Director-General:

> You know everyone was learning. We just had to move in and start working. So both for government, for the different parts of government and the parliamentary system, [it] was a new system that we were using. The members of the Portfolio Committee were learning as they were doing their job, and they had to learn to relate to government officials. Nobody knew what the roles of the two structures were going to be, so we had to build together. In education we managed to develop a very sensible working relationship. But it was not there, it was created by the dynamic of what was going on. In a sense there was a lot of learning that took place for everybody.[40]

It appears that stakeholders were not aware of the kind of consultation which informed the NCHE's work, hence the clash of interests and expectations in terms of the outcome of the consultation process.

However, the Commission was something more than what the students wanted to reduce it to. It was a body established through a presidential proclamation, enjoying autonomy from government interference and was expected to produce expert advice for government on the transformation of the higher education system. Given the "immunity" the Commission had from government interference, it was unlikely that it would bow to stakeholder influence. Commissioners were accountable to government to produce the document without undue pressure from any source, including stakeholders. It was not a stakeholder body, it was an expert body.

The "after-consultation" approach seems to have been the prevalent one for policy development introduced by the NCHE. It allowed room for input and participation by stakeholders but left decision-making to experts (commissioners) and policy-makers in the DOE who justified their approach in decision-making with legitimacy. It is not clear at what stage the after-consultation approach was clarified and adopted by the Commission. There also seems to be some evidence that it evolved out of the process and experience of consultation with stakeholders. This is evident from Cloete's explanation that:

> The Commission was committed to a consultative process with the stakeholders. It encouraged stakeholders to make submissions. However, after

stakeholders made their submissions, there was nothing new that was submitted to the Commission which commissioners did not know. It was then realized that the report was to be written by the research group and not by stakeholders. The Commission started focusing its attention and resources on the research task groups.[41]

In focusing its attention on the research task groups, the Commission did not necessarily discard stakeholder participation but instead it brought stakeholders on board and used them as a sounding board for policy proposals. Cloete elaborated that: "They decided to use them to respond to policy proposals rather than have them develop policies. The Commission did this by inviting stakeholders to the consultative meetings, national conference and international conference."[42]

The perspectives shared by Cloete in terms of the change in strategy and how the consultative process was used, reveal the learning process the Commission itself had to undergo. It appears that the initial assumptions underpinning consultation were mainly to get new perspectives or policy proposals from stakeholders, but they seem to have failed to provide anything new which the commissioners did not know. However, it appears that for stakeholders what mattered was to have their views reflected and not necessarily to provide something new. A question that needs to be posed is, how does one account for the fact that stakeholders failed to provide new policy perspectives or proposals to the Commission? What does this say in terms of the quality of intellectual input stakeholders were able to make in relation to the expertise existing in the Commission? What does this imply in terms of the assumptions underlying consultation? If it was true that the Commission had received no new ideas from stakeholder input, then the following propositions are posed as emerging out of this situation: First, it might be a reflection of the value of having the Commission composed of people from diverse backgrounds that covered a range of stakeholders in the higher education sector. Therefore the views put forward to the Commission had already been heard by commissioners in their internal deliberations, drawing as they did from their experience. Second, credit might be due to the commissioners for their astuteness, expertise and knowledge of the higher education sector in South Africa. Third, the fact that it was from students that the Commissioners received the greatest challenge, and that the student voice was not represented on the Commission, could give validity to the first proposition.

The feedback received from stakeholders (national consultative conference) revealed differences within the Commission. There was no agreement from within on what they had heard from the consultative conference. It appears that the Commission had approached the consultative conference expecting a consensus view to emerge, but what some commissioners did not realize was that a conference does not emerge with consensus. Because of the different interests of stakeholders, policy tends to divide stakeholders, as they tend to write and respond to policy on the basis of their sectoral interests. The weekend following that of the consultative conference, the Commission had scheduled a special seminar to take the report to an international conference at Salzburg for comment from international experts. This was done because the new system was to be comparable to the best international practice and had to be in line with international trends. South Africa's new Constitution was written in the same way. It was based on best practices in the world. The seminar was attended by 60 delegates from 21 different countries, consisting of a mix of institutional leadership and policy analysts, and as it will be shown, represented the triumph of the global perspective in the Commission's report.[43]

The NCHE Discussion Document was well received by the seminar participants. Some of the accolades the NCHE's work received were from the head of higher education for UNESCO who noted that "the methodology which included the extensive consultative process, may well serve as a model for countries embarking on restructuring higher education systems."[44] A UK delegate wrote in *The Times Higher Education Supplement,* that "the way in which the Commission has conducted its work, the commitment to openness and exchange of views, the determination to redress historic inequities, and the direct linking of higher education to social justice offer salutary lessons for us."[45] The report was lauded by the seminar participants as providing not only a detailed review and critique of the South African higher education reform package, but also a unique insight into the process involved in such a complex undertaking. Bok, the president emeritus of Harvard University, noted that:

> The peer review of the NCHE reform proposals not only demonstrated a remarkable degree of maturity and confidence on the part of the South Africans, but also a rare opportunity to review a major reform process that is usually conducted outside of public scrutiny. With recent political and social transformation in various parts of the world, it is hoped that the South African reform process, of which this document is a part, can provide a useful model for understanding the dynamics of change in other countries" education system undergoing reform in times of transition. [46]

A member of the Commission related that after the good reception the Discussion Document had received from the international experts, the

Commission decided to go ahead with the core tenets of the Discussion Document and not allow itself to be impeded by the criticisms it received from the stakeholders' conference. Whilst the Discussion Document was given approval by international experts, it continued to come under harsh criticism locally. The following section will look at another forum where the document was discussed.

Simultaneous with the Salzburg seminar was a conference organized by a group of black professors to pull together opposition to the NCHE's Discussion Document[47] and to debate radical alternative perspectives on tertiary education transformation in South Africa.[48] According to a report in the *Higher Education Review,* the conference brought together some of the country's best African academics, intellectuals, scientists and administrators. It was supported by predominantly black national student organizations, namely the Pan-Africanist Students' Organisation (PASO) and SASCO, which sent delegates. Opening the Conference, Nkondo, one of the leading critics of the NCHE's Discussion Document, argued that "although the document was elegantly and cunningly written, it was however deeply flawed." He said that the Document failed to identify the following requirements for a framework for transformation:

- a coherent philosophy of education derived from the national aspiration for liberation and justice;
- an in-depth analysis of an appropriate curriculum based on the principles of liberation and justice, and sensitive to the imperatives of power and knowledge;
- an analysis of the potential forces and forms of resistance to transformation based on social provenance and orientation;
- an analysis of the kind of state being built and its potential role in the transformation of education for liberation as reflected in the texts of the liberation movement;
- description of the liberation process that should ensure extensive and rigorous consultation with all stakeholders, the empowerment of historically disempowered stakeholders, accurate representation of the views of each stakeholder, and a delicate weighing of the states of various submissions in terms of the historical orientation of each stakeholder.[49]

This input, in questioning the lack of a philosophy of education, and linking issues of curriculum change to liberation, brought back into focus a discourse and some of the tenets of the philosophy of People's Education that had informed the educational struggles in the 1980s. The slogan of "People's Education for People's Power" expressed a radical redefinition of both the content of, and the relationship between, the struggle for education and the national liberation struggle. As Wolpe points out, the historic significance of "People's Education for People's Power," lies in the fact that its conceptions not only challenged the previous conceptions of educational transformation in South Africa but, in so doing, placed on the agenda questions which constituted a necessary point of departure for formulating new policies and strategies under new conditions.

Seen from this perspective, the NCHE Discussion Document was fundamentally defective and out of tune with the rise of the new South Africa: the new reality that could not escape the need for a pedagogy of liberation. One philosophical assumption of the latter is that not only do human beings have the capacity and will to determine their own destiny but that the majority of South Africans have not overcome epistemological oppression. They cannot do so unless and until they become, together with the colonizers, co-creators of knowledge and the meaning of truth.[50] On this point, one delegate contended that it was ironic that those who should have been beneficiaries of the fruits of liberation were sidelined and silenced.

The critique of the NCHE's Discussion Document highlights the politically charged nature of the policy process but also shows that policymaking entails choice about what to include and what to exclude. The reasons why the role of education in relation to liberation has been ignored, and how to address the problem of the majority of South Africans having to overcome epistemological oppression, and the importance of the oppressed in becoming co-creators of knowledge and the meaning of truth, all need further research. This statement is based on the fact that the views expressed at this conference had been part and parcel of the anti-apartheid education struggle, but in the 1990s some of them had become marginalized, lonely and silenced.

REACTIONS, RESPONSES AND REVISIONS

The Commission's interaction with the external stakeholders shows that two main voices emerged that characterized contestation around its work. The first was the mainstream Commission's report at Salzburg, mainly a consensus document which aligned higher education in South Africa with global trends. The second was that of the voices at the conference of black professors in Venda, which related higher education to the values and principles that informed the liberation struggle in South Africa.

The triumph of the global perspective is perceived by analysts as part of a bigger and alien agenda aimed at protecting the interests of a white constituency and capital that would facilitate its participation in the global economy.[51] In education it has found expression through foreign agencies such as USAID and the Ford Foundation's involvement in the policy development initiatives as philanthropic organizations. These organizations are seen by these analysts as implementing the foreign policy of the United States by funding projects and ideas they want to see happening. The funding of these activities is an effective strategy for launching an attack on alternative ideas that may emerge counter to the policy agenda the foreign funders might be pursuing. In elaborating on how this strategy is implemented, Nevhutalo commented that:

> Not only do they fund policy development, they fund major policy conferences. So it is a disseminating strategy, they try and influence thinking by having it written, by having it distributed, by having it communicated, by having media in that communication, by inviting other people to try and legitimize it, because when you invite people to come and attend that conference, they are legitimizing that outcome of the work. Whether they have anything to say about the outcome of the conference, they are legitimizing it.[52]

Indeed, the Ford Foundation and USAID have been the major funders of policy work from the early days of UDUSA's involvement in policy work. They funded the Commission, and the Ford Foundation funded the Centre for Higher Education Transformation, which was one of the influential policy organizations in higher education outside of government.

This chapter supports the view of a bigger agenda being at work and sees the marginalization of certain voices within the policy debate in higher education as not accidental. The reasons behind this and the effect it has had on policy development and outcomes need thorough investigation. This section will focus only on the aspect that relates this phenomenon to the role of donors. Analysis of the effect of those silences needs to answer the following pertinent questions: why did the voices that were expressed in the past within different constellations of interests in the radical social and intellectual movements become lonely and individual? What does this shift mean in terms of its impact on the policy process? Silences have historically been linked to the nature of the state, the principles and the guidelines the state promotes. However, in South Africa there was a state with democratic principles and values and which guaranteed freedom of speech, yet there were some silences. Nevhutalo explains the existence of silences in relation to the global agenda that finances certain voices. In the context of South Africa, the effect of the donor funding in the policy process might be that it undermined activists' behavior within society by legitimizing certain viewpoints that were in line with the global agenda. For example, the USAID and Ford Foundation funded UDUSA's policy work. Even though UDUSA was established to cater for both the union interests of its members and the advance of the cultural boycott struggle, in the post-1990 period it focused on policy work that received more funding at the expense of the union work. The union interests of the membership were mainly expressed by the HBUs that also advocated that equality and redress policies be given priority. The policy work done by UDUSA made its way into the Commission with key members of the UDUSA policy forum playing a critical role in the work of the Commission. The funders of UDUSA policy work also came to fund other Commission and post-Commission institutions, such as the Centre for Higher Education Transformation (CHET). An analysis of the funding patterns by the Ford Foundation and USAID of the policy starting with UDUSA and moving with some policy experts from UDUSA into the Commission, the DOE and CHET, supports the view that it was not accidental that certain views in the policy work in higher education prevailed.

It further needs to be asked what the relationship was between the views being legitimized by donor organizations and state policy. An analysis of the shifts within the macro-economic strategy, and the quest to relate South Africa's policies to international trends, shows that at the time of the work of the Commission, state policies were not clearly defined but still in the making. Thus, a neo-liberal agenda which emptied higher education policy transformation agenda of its radical content, and thus undermined the activist dimension within civil society organizations and the liberation movement, legitimized some voices and the approach to change that was adopted by the state.

The Commission returned from Salzburg with a vote of confidence passed on the Discussion Document, unlike the mixed reactions and criticisms it had received locally. The challenge faced was to complete the final draft and hand it to the Minister by the new deadline of August 1996. The original timeframe the Commission had been given was two years, but the Minister of Education reduced this and the Commission was instructed to report within 18 months. Officials in the DOE pointed out that the Minister was under political pressure to deal with the challenges and pressure facing higher education institutions and could not delay any further.[53] Further, there was pressure on government to be seen to be doing something about transforming the historically inequitable, racist and undemocratic system of higher education. On the other hand, he could not confidently act before the Commission reported since there was a perception that it would produce policy recommendations that would assist in dealing with the challenges of transforming the higher education system.

The shortening of timeframes of the NCHE illustrates the impact political pressures can have on the development of policies. It also highlights the significance of time in the policy process, i.e., that policy development is time-bound. With the shortening of timeframes, a more proactive role and hands-on approach was expected on the part of government. On the other hand, Mosala, Head of Higher Education at the time of the Commission, laments the cutting of the timeframes of the Commission as he thinks it contributed to the difficulty of dealing with some implementation issues. He expressed his regret as follows:

> I somehow regret now looking back at it, because I think those kinds of Commissions should be allowed to do a thorough work and finish it. Some of the delays we are now having in implementing things have to do with the fact that some of the work was not completed and we now have to set up new task teams to do the work that the Commission could have done had we not put pressure on them.[54]

Some of the issues that the NCHE should have made recommendations on but did not, owing to time pressures, were the shape and size of higher education and the funding formula. According to Badsha, there is a public perception that the Commission failed to address the issues of shape and size (number of institutions required) of the system because of their contentiousness at the time. She commented that:

> If I can take the one example, size and shape of the system, in particular the shape, some people have argued that we ducked the issues there because we did not talk specifically in terms of the number of institutions of different types. We didn't tackle that hard issue. What we chose rather to do is to start the debate of what the criteria would be for ultimately determining the shape of the system. Every time around me I hear "the Commission ducked the issue of how many institutions we actually need, of what type," we ducked the issue of the future of HDIs. I think that if the Commission had interpreted it in that very specific way it would have got locked into a whole set of political battles which would have possibly undermined its other work. It decided instead to go the route of looking at broad principles and broad criteria. It is not that they couldn't be resolved, but the Commission felt it would be too contentious to even begin at that stage to address number of institutions, and shape and size in that amount of detail.[55]

The effect of the failure of the Commission to address the issues of shape and size was that in the year 2000 a task team was appointed to make a recommendation on it. Were there a number of contentious issues in the work of the Commission, and why did it not choose to address them from the early days of NEPI? Did consensus within the GNU mean avoiding contentious issues? Maybe some lessons need to be drawn from SASCO's perspective of consensus in relation to the constitution-making process. In its response to the NCHE Discussion Document, failure to reflect the inputs of stakeholders, which gave the impression that the views expressed in the NCHE discussion document represented consensus views amongst stakeholders, SASCO pointed out that:

> True consensus, as the constitution-making and parliamentary processes show, evolves out of a public disclosure of differences and head-on confrontation of areas of disagreements, not sweeping them aside. This often leads to an unsustainable false consensus which can only serve to postpone rather than resolve conflict.[56]

In addition to students, representatives of some institutions complained that the Commission was not listening to them. In explaining how the Commission received their submission when they made their presentation, a team member of the University of the Witwatersrand commented:

> They all said you have done such a lot of work, isn't that wonderful, isn't it interesting?—Really neutral. I got a sense that we almost knew more about higher education than some of the commissioners. Some of the commissioners didn't really know very much. They haven't even bothered to read our report. Only two or three had actually read it. You got the sense that the others didn't really care what was said; they knew what they already had in store. We had taken the trouble to go there and spend hours and at the end the questions they asked seem to suggest that they really didn't know much. The kind of questions they really asked seem to be fitting into the kinds of things they want to do. They were only interested in little bits and pieces which fitted with what they already thought.[57]

This comment suggests that the Commission was only interested in making decisions, without due regard to the input of stakeholders. However, the frustration of the official concerned should be understood in the light of the shift the Commission had made with regard to consultation, where it was now using stakeholders to bounce ideas and not to formulate policy. There appears also to have been a misunderstanding of what expectations were in participating in the process or being consulted. The view within stakeholders seem to have been, "If you consult me then you have to reflect my views in the report." However, as explained above, the prevailing view used by the Commission was an after-consultation. However, there was little or no evidence of this being explained to stakeholders, which left some of them dissatisfied with the process. Another example of this can be read from an assessment of the process by a member of the University of the Witwatersrand Task Team who made a presentation to the Commission. In answer to the question: "In the light of your experience in the task team and your interaction with the Commission, what does the process of policy development entail?" she said:

> I would give the answer that government set up commissions of inquiry to fool the people into thinking that they are listening. They then go ahead and do exactly what they like. I think commissions of inquiry are particularly that crucial. I don't think there is any quality policy that comes from them.[58]

While there were such strong statements made to express dissatisfaction with the process, on the other hand the students responded by issuing a joint statement on behalf of seven national student organizations withdrawing support from the NCHE. This also indicated a perception that the Commission was not listening to them. Some of the arguments presented were that the NCHE was not a legislative body, and students were going to lobby members of the Portfolio Committee to have their views, which had not been considered by the Commission, find their way into legislation.[59] In this case, the role of coalitions, networks and lobbying strategies would become useful. Furthermore, the Principals of Historically Disadvantaged Institutions constituted themselves into a Forum and requested a special meeting with the Commission to present their case. With so much criticism coming about the work and process of the Commission, its work might seem to have run the risk of being discredited. However, it got support from the Minister in his speech to the Consultative meeting of stakeholders on the transformation of higher education in July 1996. At that meeting he pointed out that:

> We appointed the Commission and tasked it with the responsibility to investigate and report to us. The Commission is now poised to submit its report. In order to do away with the confusion that seems to be generally prevalent with regard to its status, let me emphasize that this report will not constitute the government's positions on the matters raised in it. These remain recommendations for consideration by government. But government is obliged to consider all the recommendations carefully. We cannot allow a situation where we can appoint a Commission,

using taxpayers" money, and then ignore it completely and come with our own proposals. Our policy positions will therefore take seriously the recommendations of the Commission, even if we do not adopt those recommendations in the end.[60]

The intervention of the Minister and the emphasis he put on the importance of considering the recommendations of the NCHE, highlights the crisis of legitimacy which the NCHE's report was facing.

CONCLUDING REMARKS

This chapter has discussed the work of the NCHE as an agent for change and its role in policy process in higher education during the transition period. In outlining the process of policy development undertaken by the NCHE, this chapter has shown, amongst other things, continuity in the use of the Commissions during apartheid and in the new South African context and its reconceptualization to fit the new policy milieu in line with the framework of the GNU. It has explained how the process of the establishment of the Commission, its composition and mode of operation, took on board the principles of participation, consultation, inclusivity and consensus which were all part of the nation-building project of the GNU. Despite the consultative and participatory manner in which the work of the NCHE was undertaken, it became a contested domain among the commissioners. They held different perspectives and there was contestation between commissioners and stakeholders. In particular, the contestation emanated from the kind of expectations different stakeholders had of participation. The policy-making process itself was informed by differing approaches to consultation that both the commissioners and stakeholders operated on. As a result, the work of the Commission ran the risk of being discredited by some local stakeholders as they charged that the process of policy-making by the Commission was flawed. This provides an important lesson that an explanation should have been provided at the start of processes such as these, to avoid misunderstandings.

On the other hand, commissioners seem to have been ahead of the stakeholders in their knowledge of the higher education system, as reflected in the claim that there was nothing new to come from the latter's submissions. If this was the case, it could be a credit to the diverse and inclusive composition of the Commission. Also of interest was how, on the basis of the approval of the report by international experts, particularly at the Salzburg Seminar, the Commission went ahead with the finalization of its report. This was despite the negative response it had received from local stakeholders. Does it then mean that the voices of international experts were more important than the concerns of local stakeholders, especially with regard to some of the content and process issues of the report? It could be argued that the apparent privileging of the international voice in terms of the status of the NCHE's Discussion Document is related to the quest in the policy-making process to align higher education policy to global and international trends. It appears that the endorsement of the Discussion Document at Salzburg not only provided legitimacy to the work and outcome of the Commission, but also elevated the report to the status of a model for societies undergoing transition and handling reform. This is related to other initiatives where South Africa is held as a model, such as its new Constitution, policies or gender equality which are purported as representing the best in the world.

Turning to some of the problems emanating from the Commission's work, what stood out was the heterogeneity of voices that emerged and how some seem to have been legitimized at the expense of others. The role of donor agencies has been explained but there were also questions related to the issues that the Commission failed to address, such as the shape, size and funding formula of the higher education system. This has been partially explained as resulting from the political sensitivity of recommending the number of institutions for higher education at a time when the country was still trying to find its feet as a democracy. The political consequences for not addressing such issues far outweighed the price to be paid for making such recommendations. This could also be based on the fact that at the time the Commission reported, most of the Historically Black Universities (HBUs) were experiencing problems of increasing debt and crises related to non-payment of fees. They would thus be the logical targets in the event of recommendation for the reduction in the number of universities. Such a recommendation would not go down well with the new government which was still trying to negotiate itself in the various positions of power and entrench its hegemony within the state. The consequence of this was that the Commission set itself to produce a framework report that established parameters for addressing transformation issues by government at a later stage. Thus, the Commission's report became more of a consensus document than one that advocated a radical transformation of the system.

The process of the Commission further revealed less emphasis on drawing lessons from the African continent. Despite a mention of trips made to African countries to learn from their experiences, there is no real impact of this venture on the policy process. The only evidence of a lesson from the African continent relates to the dangers of a state-control model of policy development, which is used as a warning for South Africa not to follow. There should obviously be positive lessons that could be drawn from the African continent, such as curricula that emphasize postcolonial discourse which affirms the identity of the former oppressed, and the celebration of Makerere University in Uganda and Eduardo Mondlane University in Mozambique which became the centers of critique and producers of African intelligentsia.

Despite some of the problems associated with the work of the Commission, it served an important role of bridging the gap between the past and the new dispensation. It provided an opportunity for the public to participate in analyzing and critiquing apartheid's higher education system and by providing alternative visions to lay it to rest. The participation of the public in this process further provided learning opportunities for stakeholders as different capacities were built to prepare for interaction with the subsequent processes of policy development. This further prepared them for the implementation of policy as different institutions were already sensitized to the ongoing policy debates from the staff members who participated in the work of the Commission as commissioners or researchers.

The appointment of the Commission and its work served an important historical purpose during the transition period in terms of dealing with the history of apartheid education and proposing a new vision for higher education. It brought about a turning point in the history of policy development within the MDM structures where commissioners and policy-makers were not accountable to their constituencies in making their proposals, but rather to the Minister and Parliament. This had a bearing on how they dealt with stakeholder input and participation in the process, with challenges of formulating policy proposals. Assessing the significance of the consultative process during this period in the aftermath of the birth of the new democracy highlights that, while it was important to consult, those entrusted with the responsibility of making policies had to rise above party-political interests and consider the system as a whole. Within this framework, there was a growing view that consultation was mere symbolism, since the Commission was seen as not having taken the inputs of stakeholders into consideration. The process also revealed the multi-dimensional levels of consultation that the process was expected to assume. That is, while students had access to the Commission, they also expected their own institutions to consult them and to incorporate their input in the submissions they made.

Whether or not the process was really symbolic is another matter. Did non-inclusion of one's input in the policy document mean that one was not listened to? The Commission argued that it did consider the inputs of all stakeholders and the synthesis of these enabled the Commission to formulate its proposals. A lesson from this experience is that while a process of consultation is important, consultation does not guarantee incorporation of all those inputs in the final report. Furthermore, consultation is not open-ended. There comes a time when decisions have to be made, and in that case those who have been entrusted with the responsibility to do so should carry out that responsibility. The crucial thing, however, is to carry out that responsibility in such a way that those who were consulted are not marginalized and means should be devised to make them part of the final outcome.

The policy process undertaken by the Commission demonstrated the significance of dialogue, but also exposed some inherent contradictions. While staff associations such as UDUSA played a prominent role in the policy process leading to the 1994 election, they were less active during the period of the Commission as most of the policy experts were no longer active in the union but had left to take up government positions. Instead, students proved to be important social actors, keeping the Commission alert. The submission by SASCO was regarded within the Commission as ranking among the top three or four received. The final report recommends a framework of transformation that is not much different from the key proposals contained in the Discussion Document.

With regard to its terms of reference, especially in relation to the line of argument pursued in this chapter that the Commission was supposed to be a change agent, the Commission partially delivered on its mandate. For reasons explained in this chapter, the Commission deliberately avoided addressing hard issues such as the size of the system, as these were found to be contentious given the fragility of the transition at the time. Maybe there is some realism that needs to go with what commissions can do. Commissions are not and cannot be change agents, they can only make recommendations for change, which could either be accepted or rejected by government. Commissions' work is also shaped by the context in which they operate. They could therefore be regarded as reflecting the temperature of the nation.

Chapter Seven

The State Assumes Control

INTRODUCTION

For a period of over 18 months since the new government came into power, policy-making processes in higher education was outsourced to an external agency in the form of the NCHE. Following the release of the NCHE report, the government started getting involved by responding to the report in the form of a Green Paper, followed by the White Paper, the Bill and *Higher Education Act*. This chapter shows that although the process of policy-making leading to the adoption of the Act was conducted in a participatory, consultative and open way quite unprecedented in the country, it also saw the technocritization of the policy-making process where concerns were more about meeting parliamentary timeframes for submission of White Papers and Bills. As a result, the process followed an after-consultation model where participation and consultation processes informed policy-makers rather than stakeholders. This made the policy goals of the ruling party (governing elite) prevail rather than those of the opposition or stakeholders. It further represents the beginning of a move away from the open and accessible polity that characterized the work of the Commission, towards more closure as the ruling party started gaining control over important organs of state power.

CHANGING POLICY CONTEXT

In line with the principle of sufficient consensus that underpinned decision-making in the GNU, policy development was conceptualized as participatory, consultative and representative. Within higher education, consultation and participation initially found expression in the work of the NCHE. As some commentators observed, this was a preferable route to mobilize the higher education sector behind policy.[1] At Cabinet level, before policies were approved, the Minister of Education had to demonstrate that he had consulted sufficiently and that the public was behind the policy being tabled before Cabinet. The development of higher education legislation, which started with the writing and release of the Green Paper on Higher Education in December 1996, took place in a changed political context, far different from that of the development of the White Paper 1[2] and the period of the work of the NCHE. The following are some of the important developments: (a) By the time the Green Paper was written in December 1996, and the draft White Paper and Bill on Higher Education in April 1997, the ANC had been in office for more than two years. (b) The former apartheid departments were no longer in the picture and the new national Department of Education had been established with its own staff. (c) The new Higher Education Branch, though still very understaffed, was established. (d) The policy framework generated by the White Paper 1 on Education was now the basis for education thinking in the country. There was thus a valid policy framework which was authentic and which had won very wide approval. (e) The Interim Constitution was no longer there and the 1996 Constitution was in force. (f) The process of writing legislation had the advantage of the NCHE process and its report from which it worked.(g) The National Party had pulled out of the GNU in May 1996 so it had no Deputy Minister representing the National Party by the time the White Paper was being finalized.[3]

Coombe explains that the political dynamics within the Ministry of Education were different because of the factors highlighted above. Furthermore, the manner in which lobbies formally associated with the National Party interacted on education matters was very different for all of those reasons. As he points out:

> They [the NP] had receded in visibility and direct impact on the policy formulation process. They were making representation as stakeholders, like other stakeholders who were making submissions, even though they still had recourse in participating in the parliamentary process. But then the decline of the NP as a force within the new political structure was very evident to us.[4]

On the other hand, the ANC as a ruling party had gained some experience of being in government and this informed its approach to policy-making in higher education. The ANC as a ruling party was no longer talking about alternative structures of power, but about democratizing the structures of power through legislation. The ANC personnel who were deployed in government had begun to think about the fact that "since the democratic movement had taken power, we want structures of government that work for us."[5] In achieving this goal, there was a close working relationship between the Department of Education and the Portfolio Committee.

One of the structures which became influential within the ruling party in the development of higher education legislation was the ANC study group or caucus on education. The role the ANC education study group played in legislation was not always smooth. Mathieson points out that the challenge had been to strike a balance between a critical distance—which ensured that the legislature could intervene in the legislative and policy process with an independent voice—and the need for the ANC to work in a coordinated and united manner across the legislature and the executive. She asserts that during the first term of office, the ANC education study group asserted its right in the Education Portfolio Committee to intervene to change the legislation and policy that did not sufficiently reflect that of the ANC, or where sufficient consensus had been built by the Minister and the DOE within the education alliance.[6] The study group played an important role in establishing political linkages between the ANC inside and outside the state in the education sphere. In this way it encouraged the development of a coherent process for ANC education policy development, and helped prevent splintering between the ANC in government and its allies outside. According to Mseleku, the study group ensured that whatever legislation was adopted incorporated some kind of understanding of the constituencies, including the ANC itself. From whatever legislation on education, the locus of coordination, control, and decision-making rested with the ANC study group.[7] The Portfolio Committee, on the other hand, became a platform for contestation, and provided a sense of where the opposition was positioned and what issues it would be concerned with in relation to the legislation at hand.

After the NCHE report was handed over to the Minister of Education, a Green Paper was produced. In a letter that accompanied the release of the Green Paper, the Minister of Education stated that:

> The Green Paper represents a further stage of development in the process of public consultation with as broad a spectrum of interests and stakeholders concerned with higher education. It will be revised to reflect the feedback obtained from the release and from the process of consultation that is being organized with interest groups and stakeholders. The Green Paper signals the policy intentions of my government in regard to the reconstruction and development of higher education in South Africa. The Ministry urges stakeholders, institutions and individuals to study and assess the Report in order to gain fuller sense of the thinking behind the Green Paper.[8]

This statement clarifies the purposes of a Green Paper, namely that it is a discussion document from the Ministry aimed at inviting comments from the public in the process of policy formulation. The importance of the consultative process at this stage was emphasized by Mosala, head of higher education in the DOE at the time of the writing of the Green Paper and White Paper:

> Not everybody in the higher education sector had been in the Commission and not everybody's views had been incorporated by the Commission. The Commission eventually took its own position and wrote what it wrote. We used the Commission's work to draft a Green Paper which we sent back to the same stakeholders, and views were able to come in and be heard by us. [Some of these views] could have been previously heard by the Commission and might have been excluded and we would have never known that they were aired. We allowed the expression of views and perspectives that might have been excluded. The other real benefit was to buy in [people]; we were able to get people to own the product because they had to form it. [9]

While buying in people was possible, it is not clear how the DOE would have ensured that all voices were included. The parameters of inclusion and exclusion are always read differently depending on the ways in which people are made to be part of the process of policy-making. According to the views expressed by Mosala, the consultative process allowed stakeholders to be heard again by the Department and also to have ownership of the product. Though there was value in the consultative process, it is not clear whether stakeholders owned both the process and the product. This is because of the dissatisfaction of stakeholders with the way their submissions were dealt with both by the Commission and by the DOE. As explained in the case of the Commission, the concerns raised by stakeholders were based on an "in-consultation" approach to policy development.

Stakeholders such as students, staff associations, and management in the form of the CTP and CUP, had a tradition of policy-making which reflected their sectoral interests. Their policies would mainly be sectoral and seldom had to be formulated to accommodate opposing views from other sectors. For example, historically the CUP's policy formulation process was characterized by collating views from different institutions. [10] In relating how the CUP used to perform its advisory function, Gourley described it as a kind of "post box" function. She added that "they would ask everyone what they thought, collect all the answers and send them in." [11] The process by which policy development was undertaken as described by the CUP suggests that it used an "in-consultation" approach to policy development.

Following the consultative meetings and the feedback based on written submissions that were received on the Green Paper, the draft White Paper was released in April 1997. A peculiar situation occurred whereby the draft White Paper and the Bill on Higher Education were released at the same time for public comment. This situation is said to have been caused by the pressure to have legislation on higher education finalized during that particular parliamentary year. Coombe, who was overseeing the drafting of these two documents, attributed this development to time considerations:

> Minister Bengu had become very anxious about the length of time the NCHE was taking to deliver its final report. The NCHE said that it needed full two years to complete that task and he [the Minister] directed the chairperson to deliver the report earlier than that, after 18 months. He was feeling particularly anxious that the first term of the government was marching on and the higher education sector was extremely volatile. There were important matters of government that needed to be attended to. There were powers in respect to education institutions that were extremely limited in terms of the existing legislation. So there were many strong reasons why Minister Bengu wanted the process to be accelerated. To have waited until cabinet approved the White Paper and made that public before beginning the process of developing the Bill, would have meant losing possibly an entire parliamentary year. The parliamentary calendar is extremely important and needs to be taken into account when considering the timing of legislation.[12]

The simultaneous development of the White Paper and the Bill on Higher Education highlights the impact of time and parliamentary timeframes on the policy process. Rather than waiting for the White Paper to be completed and then translated into law, the DOE developed the White Paper and the Bill simultaneously. While the White Paper was written by officials of the DOE with the help of consultants, the process of writing the Bill was led by the state law advisers. Since it is common practice for a White Paper to be a basis for developing a Bill, the simultaneous release of these documents meant that writing of the Bill did not benefit from an officially approved White Paper. The process should have been taxing on the part of the policymakers in terms of ensuring that the writing processes of the two documents did not contradict each other. It further required multi-level skills on the part of stakeholders to be able to respond to the two documents simultaneously while maintaining coherence and consistency in their responses.

The problem the Commission experienced in its consultative process was also experienced by the Department in its consultative process in the writing of the Green Paper and White Papers. For example, according to Essop, the Chief Director in the Higher Education Branch and a member of the Task Team that drafted the White Paper, there were some people who were not happy with the White Paper because they thought that it had shifted away from the Green Paper because the latter had an entire chapter devoted to the legacy of apartheid[13] to the White Paper's one page. In reflecting on misunderstanding caused by this difference, Mr Essop said:

> The fact that people think that we have a White Paper meant for them that in each point you have to refer to certain things that have previously been raised (sic). The White Paper is a response to the Green Paper, it makes certain assumptions, and we didn't want to repeat every argument that was in the Green Paper. As soon as people read that, because of the nature of the section, they thought that we had shifted from the Green Paper. I don't think there were substantive differences.[14]

However, concerns about the departure of the White Paper from the Green Paper were supported by the challenges that characterized the writing of the former. A Green Paper is normally followed by a White Paper, but in the case of higher education, the Minister of Education was dissatisfied with the initial White Paper, seeing it as missing critical elements for effective transformation, as well as omitting formal commitments made by government to stakeholders for redress, equality, and increased access for black students. He concluded that, in spite of time constraints, the document did not meet expectations and could not be released as the final policy paper, but should be regarded as a draft White Paper. The "Draft White Paper" on Higher Education was released on 18 April 1997. This was an anomaly for the White Paper to be released in a draft because it was preceded by a Green Paper which served the same purpose as the draft. In the history of the policy process during the first five years of the new government, it was only in higher education that a White Paper was released in two drafts.

According to Moja and Hayward, the Draft White Paper differed significantly from some of the proposals contained in the Green Paper and the NCHE report. It focused primarily on the role of higher education in national development, but devoted little attention to many of the values and goals central to the recommendations of the NCHE report and the Green Paper.[15] They add that there was a general feeling that this document downplayed key values and principles about justice, equality, redress and transformation of higher education. In particular the Draft White Paper's primary focus was on recommendations that would create conditions necessary for economic development in South Africa and neglected what its predecessor documents saw as preconditions for development in South Africa—especially the recommendations for additional funding for redress for the HDIs. Another deficiency in the Draft White Paper was a lack of clarity on how transformation was to take place. According to Moja and Hayward, there was confusion about the locus of power and the responsibility for transformation between the Ministry of Education, the Council on Higher Education (CHE) and the stakeholders. While the Green Paper had clearly spelt out the functions of the CHE, the Draft White Paper seemed ambiguous about its power and authority, leaving too much room for contestation. It created the impression that the CHE was now defined as an arm of the Department of Education.

The two factors raised about the deficiencies in the Draft White Paper, i.e., its focus on development priorities at the expense of redress and equity and the lack of clarity concerning the role and functions of the CHE, reveal the contested nature of policy-making, even within the Ministry of Education. The imperatives for redress and equity and the need for transformation had clearly been spelt out by both the NCHE and the Green Paper. What led to these being given less prominence in the Draft White Paper is unclear. It might be considered as having to do with the authorship of policy, since the Department used consultants in the writing of the Draft White Paper. In this case, the prioritization of development at the expense of redress could be in line with neo-liberal thought, which was gaining currency in the battle for the soul of South African economic and educational policies. Either way it further substantiates the point made above regarding the legitimization of certain voices related to global capital and the global economy, and the marginalization of voices that had traditionally advocated social and redistributive justice.

PUBLIC HEARINGS AND THE POLICY PROCESS

This section focuses on the use of public hearings by the parliamentary Portfolio Committee on Education as a form of democratization and opening access of the policy process to the public. It analyzes how it was used by legislators to be informed on policies they were developing. Public hearings are sessions where key stakeholders are invited to make their inputs on policy or legislation being considered by Parliament. They are intended to provide an opportunity to key stakeholders to make their inputs, and the Portfolio Committee would then engage the stakeholders in questions on the basis of the case they were making. According to Pandor:

> Public hearings come from our own democratic tradition in South Africa and particularly from the experience of what were called "people's forums" in the period leading up to the [1994] elections. Then it was felt that "we don't want to have in South Africa a situation where

the writing of legislation becomes the sole property of people who are elected into government." The notion of public hearings seeks to incorporate public participation in policy-making—it is enshrined in the Constitution that parliament would have a participatory public [policy-making] process.[16]

The public hearings were not only oral, since stakeholders could also make written submissions and talk through these. The Portfolio Committee would analyze all the written submissions in relation to different sections or clauses of the White Paper or draft Bill. The exercise included internal debates between different parties on some of the issues being discussed.[17] The process of public hearings served the purpose of enlightening members of the Portfolio Committee about the thinking of the public concerning the policy or legislation being considered by Parliament. The former chairperson of the Portfolio Committee, Dr Nzimande, describes the significance of the public hearings held on the higher education policy:

> This is like the country talking on higher education. For instance, you would get a group that deals with disabilities—they come with very interesting approaches that you might not have thought about [them] at all, which were never written anywhere. Remember also that we were constructing new legislation; it is not like we were amending—we were breaking with the past and trying to construct something new that expresses the interest of the democratic South Africa—the overwhelming majority of it.[18]

The public hearings held by the Portfolio Committee provided the public with another opportunity to influence policy and legislation, and the Portfolio Committee members with an opportunity to hear what the public, the electorate and their constituencies had to say about policy or legislation being considered by parliament. This helped to bridge the gap between legislators and the electorate. Since the Portfolio Committee had the final say in the content of the policy documents before they were passed by Parliament, the input of stakeholders, if accepted, stood a chance of making its way into final policy or legislation.

Public hearings should also be seen in the light of the opening up of the parliamentary processes in the building of democracy in South Africa. First, they allowed the public to see and understand what was going on in parliament, which had been closed to the public during the apartheid era, or at least limited to a very small minority. According to Omar, the opening of Parliament is not just about public hearings; it is also about getting broadcast live on television. In addition, there is a public gallery that is open to all, not just to the minority as in the past. Even though there are still limitations to accessing these parliamentary proceedings based on access to resources, these are economic limitations rather than the political ones of before.[19] The public hearings were not without their own problems. In acknowledging the weaknesses of the consultative process, the former chairperson of the Portfolio Committee commented that:

> [Through the public hearings] we want people who are not necessarily experts to come and speak to us. This is not an easy thing because the thing that concerns us the most is the voice of the overwhelming majority of the poor people—how do you ensure that that voice becomes heard? They have no tickets to fly to Cape Town [the legislative seat of government]. The budget of the Portfolio Committee was minimal but sometimes we would allow students [to have a say] by flying them because they don't have money. The danger that faces us is that it is people with money and resources—highly educated—who are able to impact more on the process. So we were very conscious to try and strike the balance. One thing that I regret that we did not really do, but which I feel can still be done in my style, was to take the Portfolio Committee to a rural area to sit there for two weeks to listen to rural people talk about what their views are on higher education, on what their key aspirations are.[20]

This underscores the fact that the development and consultative process in policy-making privileges those with resources and who are educated. The fact that there are people in the rural areas who might not be literate does not mean that they do not have views about higher education. Some of the "illiterate" parents in those areas have children in higher education institutions and could have views based on the experience of their interaction with their children. Some concerns could be about finance and the uncertainty this creates of their children not completing their studies because of lack of resources. By taking the Portfolio Committee to these communities and allowing parents to express their views in their own languages, the marginal but important voices which constitute the voices of the majority of the country, could be heard. The question to be asked is what weight the voice of less educated rural constituencies would carry against those of organized and powerful higher education stakeholders such as the CUP, CTP, and business.

One criticism of the consultative process used by the Portfolio Committee relates to the capacity and expertise committee members have in using public hearings and inputs received in formulating policy and legislation. An official of the CTP argued that most of the members of the Portfolio Committee did not have the experience in running higher education institutions and therefore were not qualified to make decisions regarding policy and legislation affecting higher education. So entrusting such people with the authority of having a final say in the formulation of policy is something he sees as questionable. He made an observation during the public hearings that "the more persuasive you were during your presentation, the more likely you would be listened to by the Portfolio Committee and your points considered."[21] This view has been challenged from some quarters which see members of the Portfolio Committee as having the capacity and expertise to develop policy given their backgrounds in the schools, universities or organizations they were part of.[22] The question this contrasting view poses is: what kind of preparation or experience would sufficiently prepare legislators to make policies? This becomes relevant given the fact that most of the legislators were people who had previously never been involved in policy-making at this level. Whether this background has sufficiently prepared them to deal with the challenges at this level is something that needs further exploration. Omar, who believes in the capacity and expertise of the members of the Portfolio Committee, also questions the assumption that bureaucrats of the higher education institutions are equipped in all aspects of higher education. She rightly argues that it is not necessarily the case that a vice-chancellor is well conversant with curriculum or even management issues. So the deficiencies that the Portfolio Committee might have are not peculiar to this institution, given the way it has been structured.

There are ways in which the Portfolio Committee tried to address its lack of capacity in certain areas. The first is through these public hearings where different stakeholders make inputs and all involved apply their minds to the issues being raised. Secondly, there is a close interaction between the Portfolio Committee, the bureaucracy and the state legal drafters in the process of policy-making. These help to close the gaps in terms of capacity and expertise that might exist in the Portfolio Committee. Another aspect is that in the first five years of the new government, everybody was learning the art and politics of policy-making in the context of a new Constitution. So none could claim monopoly of expertise in this regard. This problem of experience of legislators was also a temporary measure that was peculiar to the transition phase in South Africa, and with experience now gained, would never be a problem in the future. The most positive element of the consultative process is that it raised awareness of policy among higher education stakeholders. Something worth noting about the policy development process were the many documents produced in the process, namely, the NCHE report, the Green Paper, the White Papers, and the Bill on Higher Education with the accompanying consultations and public hearings starting in

February 1995 and ending in December 1997 with adoption of the Act. Were all these documents necessary? Was there no shorter and more efficient way of achieving the same objectives and outcomes? In responding to the need for these documents and processes, Nzimande commented that:

> They were very necessary because there were some problems that were still there that we know about in higher education. A broad consensus has been forged on how we should structure higher education. It was important in a transition to take as many people as possible along, and to allow them to have their views heard. I know that the media sometimes will criticize them and say it is over-consulting. Yes, we were aware it takes time—this consultation delays certain necessary actions—but you have to strike a balance. It was necessary to go through these because this thing is laying foundations for the next hundred years. It does not mean it is not going to change, but it is laying a foundation, the basics, and the framework of the new system.[23]

Though there was commitment to consultation, it was however not an open-ended process. The development of these documents had to fit into the calendar of Parliament for the Act to be passed during that session of Parliament.

THE NEW GOVERNANCE STRUCTURES

Thus far this book has concentrated on the policy process and the extent to which it incorporated the principles of participation, consultation and representivity. While the thrust is on process issues, a need has been identified to ground the discussion of the process in terms of outcomes and the kind of framework emerging from it. The policy process from the NCHE to the adoption of the White Paper dealt with a general policy framework, without providing specific policy details. On the other hand, the translation of policy into law through the Higher Education Bill and Act dealt with establishment of the formal structures and policy instruments related to the governance of the system that would give effect to the development of policy details and implementation issues. The provision of policy details related to the governance is in line with the argument made in this book that the policy process was also informed and driven by constitutional concerns around power and control aimed at affirming the new state. The governance proposals provided for the establishment of enabling structures and bestowed the necessary power on the state to spearhead the transformation of higher education.

This section concentrates on the evolution of the governance policy from the NCHE through to the passing of the Act, showing that governance is the only policy area where specific details have been provided. Despite stakeholder participation in the process, which was trying to free higher education governance from the state domination of the apartheid period, the development and outcome of this policy saw a shift from cooperative governance with accessible polity, towards more closure and impenetrable polity, with more powers given to the Minister, the Higher Education Branch and institutional councils. The outcome of this policy saw structures with more stakeholder participation and representation given an advisory rather than executive role. In particular, the perceived elements of state control in the cooperative governance model adopted by the Department of Education should be understood in the light of the nature of a state undergoing transition and its struggle to gain control over the higher education system. Cooperative governance, which is a compromise between state control and state regulation, envisaged a partnership between the state and higher education stakeholders in the governance of higher education.

The NCHE proposed a governance model it regarded as a variant of South Africa's existing one, which it called "cooperative governance." This model could be broadly located within the framework of state supervision. However, the choice was not for or against a simple model, rather there are variants of state supervision within which the government could have a more or less directive role. The Commission characterized the past higher education system in South Africa as having certain conditions that distinguish it from countries where state supervision was dominant. These include the facts that: (a) In most state supervision situations the higher education systems were well established and supervision was required to modify and ensure greater effectiveness. In contrast, an integrated higher education system still had to be created in South Africa. (b) In South Africa there were no planning, regulative and administrative structures or capacity in place to coordinate and steer the system. (c) The historical antagonisms between the state and institutions, and between sectors and among institutions, meant that South Africa did not as in 1996 have the minimum conditions of trust, mutual understanding and a preparedness to take common responsibility required for a modern state. (d) The demands for equity after half a century of apartheid made it difficult for organized constituencies to develop self-binding behavior (to prioritize common interest over their own interest) for the larger common good.[24]

It was on the basis of the above factors that the Commission realized that conditions in South Africa did not favor a conventional state supervision model, and therefore proposed that a cooperative governance model would be ideal. This model could be regarded as a South African variant, with several distinguishing features of a state supervision approach. The

Commission argued that this new approach to governance shifted from a narrow concern with government to a wide range of governance mechanisms concerned with the growing role of associations, different agencies and partnerships, and that it reflected the dynamic and interactive nature of coordination. The government was not to become the single agent, but would have a range of roles and obligations in a variety of coordination arrangements. As a main role player, it would be expected to exercise its role and powers over the higher education system in a transparent, equitable and accountable manner and in discernible pursuit of the public good. [25]

For the managers of institutions, responsibility implies adoption of cooperative practices and the willingness to interact and establish relationships with a wide range of partners. For the staff, responsibility will, among other things, mean dedication to the values of higher education and a readiness to serve the values of academic integrity, in a spirit of independent and critical thinking. Students, as stakeholders, also have legitimate expectations and demands which should be met, while recognizing that the potential benefits of higher education carry their own responsibilities. External stakeholders will also have an impact on the successful transformation of higher education. Organized civil society has not only a rightful claim to its products and services but also a duty to support and assist it through its contributions, cooperation and critical but constructive engagement.[26] The Commission summarized the key tenets of cooperative governance as implying among others that: (a) all available capacity be mobilized for restructuring and greater effectiveness; (b) the "over-politicization" of the administration of issues needing sustained long-term development must be decreased; (c) different partners' responsibilities should be defined and clarified; and (d) new structures should be established where cooperative behavior could be fostered.

The Commission saw cooperative governance as offering a strong steering model with a strong planning and coordination role, providing for increased and firmer government and stakeholder participation, as well as for expert input from the higher education sector. For the operation of this cooperative governance, the commission proposed the following national structures: (a) the establishment of a Higher Education Branch in the DOE which would support the development of policy and be responsible for administering it as determined at different levels within the system; (b) the establishment of a Higher Education Forum (HEF), which would allow greater representation and participation of the organized constituency, as a new statutory advisory body to be consulted by the Minister on key policy issues that affected higher education; (c) the establishment of a Higher

Education Council (HEC), which would provide expertise not directly representative of sectoral or institutional interests. This body would have allocative and planning functions, as well as management responsibility for a variety of agency functions;[27] and (d) institutional Councils should remain the highest decision-making bodies in institutions. Institutional forums should be established in individual higher education institutions as advisory bodies for restructuring and innovation where representatives of all stakeholders could meet, mediate interests and advise relevant structures, such as the SRC, senate and council.

The government responded to the NCHE's policy recommendations in general and governance proposals in particular through the Green Paper, accepting certain recommendations and rejecting others. The government's response also signaled the state's intention to allocate more powers to the Minister and structures which the state would have direct access to as agents to lead transformation. It prefaced its response by pointing out that while the Ministry endorsed the NCHE's concept of cooperative governance, it believed that this model needed to be grounded in the context of autonomous institutions working cooperatively with a proactive government and a range of partnerships. It based its responses and proposals on a number of assumptions that created space for the Ministry to take a leading role in the transformation of higher education. These included the beliefs that no single actor or agency could claim responsible authority for determining the policies and priorities of the higher education system, and within the context of national goals the government would play a steering and coordination role with the participation of higher education stakeholders.[28]

The Department of Education rejected the proposals for the establishment of two statutory advisory bodies with different functions, arguing that these posed several problems: (a) Such an arrangement would in practice significantly constrain the powers of the Minister and the DOE, placing both in a position of weakness in relation to the two statutory authorities. Such an outcome would not reflect an appropriate balance of power between the elected and non-elected representatives in the context of parliamentary democracy. (b) The NCHE argued that the absence of certain preconditions during this phase of transition made the conventional model of state regulation (with a single buffer body) untenable. The Ministry argued however that it would be unwise to establish permanent statutory structures to deal with temporary, transitional difficulties. There were also concerns about the costs of establishing and operating the proposed new bodies, and about the new potential for duplication of the HEF, HEC and the Department. Given the existing capacity constraints, the Green Paper argued that it would be prudent to concentrate rather than disperse the available expertise.[29] The Green Paper proposed that a single advisory body in the form of a Council on Higher Education (CHE) be established by statute to provide independent, strategic advice to the Minister of Education on matters relating to the development of higher education.[30] Although it guaranteed the independence of the CHE through the provisions of the Act, it pointed out that this independence would be balanced by giving the Minister two particular powers under legislation: (a) the power to seek and receive formal advice on matters which were a priority for Government; and (b) the power to ask the CHE to take the Government's broader policy and budget framework into consideration when formulating advice.

The proposal for the establishment of the CHE also had far-reaching implications in the governance structures of higher education in South Africa in that it abolished the statutory status enjoyed by the Advisory Council on Universities and Technikons (AUT), the CUP and the CTP. This raised some initial resistance and concerns from the CUP and the CTP but the concerns were quietly diminished. The Green Paper proposed that the membership of the CHE reflect a balance of stakeholder interest and expertise on the basis of knowledge and understanding of higher education issues. It proposed that the CHE was to have a full-time chair and eighteen part-time members. These would include nine stakeholder representatives from the college, technikon and university sectors, with three students, three academic staff members and three institutional managers. The other ten members would be drawn from stakeholders outside higher education, such as business, industry, labor and community bodies. These would be chosen on the basis of their expertise, experience and knowledge of higher education.[31] The Green Paper gave powers to the Minister to appoint CHE members from nominees of representative groups. The Green Paper endorsed the NCHE's proposal for the establishment of the Higher Education Branch. The Green Paper held that relations between the Higher Education Branch of the DOE and the CHE should exemplify the imperatives of cooperation and partnership within governance at system level.

Cooperative governance was presented in the Green Paper as having implications for the relations between the state and higher education institutions. It stated that it was not in the interest of higher education for government to micro-manage institutions, nor desirable for the Department of Education to be too prescriptive in the regulatory frameworks. Support was given to the measures proposed by the NCHE for transforming institutional governance structures and procedures. These included improving the balance of representation on Councils, restructuring Senates and Academic Boards and the formation of Student Services Councils. In particular the DOE favored the establishment of Broad Transformation Forums (BTFs) for institutional stakeholders as interim advisory bodies for restructuring and innovation, for identifying problems, for mediating interests and for advising structures such as councils, senates and student representative councils.[32] While the Green Paper gave the BTFs advisory functions, it accorded institutional councils the status of the highest decision-making bodies in public higher education institutions. They would be responsible for institutional mission, financial position, performance, quality and reputation.[33]

The government's response to the governance proposals indicates the assertive position it was adopting in ensuring that it needed the necessary powers to enable it to drive the transformation of higher education or to intervene whenever a need arose. Thus the writing of the Green Paper was the first opportunity the DOE had to formalize and regulate the powers it needed in order to spearhead transformation; hence the clarity and assertiveness in those areas relating to the powers the Minister and the DOE would need in fulfilling their responsibilities to provide leadership in higher education.

THE STAKEHOLDERS' RESPONSES

In addition to individual responses which stakeholders made to the Green Paper on Higher Education, the Green Paper was also subjected to scrutiny at a conference organized by the Centre for Education and Policy Development (CEPD) in February 1997, at the request of the ANC's study group and supported by the Ministry of Education. The conference noted with concern the fact that the delicate balance of authority of the NCHE report had disappeared in the Green Paper.

Stakeholders appealed for a pragmatic approach whereby the White Paper (which would follow the Green Paper) would unequivocally state the extent of the powers vested in the Minister and those in institutions. In particular, the Green Paper's rejection of the HEF and HEC received criticism from several stakeholders, in particular Bunting, who charged that this represented a departure from the cooperative governance model proposed by the NCHE. In his critique he highlighted elements of the governance proposals in the Green Paper which were consistent with the NCHE and where they clashed. He observed that in the final analysis the proposals were not consistent with a state supervision model. They breached the principles of democratic participation and transparency, and consequently slid back into a version of the pragmatic autonomy of the previous government, negating the principle of cooperative governance. He argued that these problems were highlighted in the

Green Paper's rejection of the NCHE's proposal for the HEF and the HEC, asserting that if it had accepted the NCHE's cooperative governance proposals (as it claimed it had), then questions of "complicated and potentially ambiguous" relations between the Minister, the Department, the HEF and HEC would not arise. The NCHE treated these relations as those of a partnership in which each member had clearly specified functions.[34]

Bunting argued that there must therefore be some other, unstated, reason why the Green Paper rejected, in his view, the NCHE's proposals. He suggested the probable reasons for the Green Paper's rejection of the NCHE's proposals concerning the HEF and HEC:

> An unstated assumption in the Green Paper is that South Africa's social, political and economic transformation has to be driven by a "strong state." In the case of higher education the underlying assumption was that the transformative processes must be driven by the Minister of Education who must have total power and control over the system. The transformation agenda, the assumption seems to be, would fail if the Minister "surrendered" any of these powers to other bodies. The exercise by the Minister of the "total power" in the higher education system would be legitimate because he/she is answerable to a democratically elected parliament.[35]

He supported his own view that the Green Paper was employing a "strong state" with reference to specific sections, particularly the governance and funding chapters. The following examples are quoted here:

- *The Council on Higher Education (CHE):* The Green Paper proposed that the HEC and HEF be collapsed into a single body. The CHE would be an advisory body only. It would consist of stakeholder representatives and experts who would have no allocative or management functions delegated to them.[36]
- *Steering the system:* The government, presumably through the Ministry and DOE, would steer the higher education system. The CHE would not be involved.[37]
- *Institutional plans:* Institutional plans would be subjected to negotiations between institutions and the Ministry of Education. The proposed CHE would not be involved.[38]
- *Allocation of redress funds:* These would be allocated by the Department on its assessment of relative institutional needs.[39]
- *Institutional management:* The Minister would have the legal right to have independent assessments made of the management of an institution when he/she considered it necessary.[40]

These examples appear in themselves to be relatively trivial, but to the critics of the Green Paper they signaled a fundamental shift away from the cooperative governance model of the NCHE. According to Bunting, there was in the passages in which these examples fall, no sense of a group of partners involved in planning the system. The Green Paper could not, in other words, claim that it had proposed a cooperative governance model and at the same time give "total power" to the Minister.

With all policy formulation, approval and implementation powers vested in the Minister of Education and in the Department, the proposals were in effect seen as constituting a version of a state control model of higher education governance. Bunting then concluded his critique by asserting that, if the argument that the Green Paper slipped back into the state control model was correct, the implication would be that whatever autonomy institutions had would not in fact be by right. Institutions would have a degree of "pragmatic autonomy"—autonomy granted to them by the Minister on pragmatic, administrative grounds, which, he argued, could be revoked at any time.[41] This point has characterized debates on the nature of the state that should lead transformation in higher education. The popular view has been that the nature of the challenges during transition required a strong state that should have constitutional and legislative powers to drive the transformation process.

Not all stakeholders were as critical of the Green Paper. The Committee of Technikon Principals responded to the governance proposals by strongly supporting the one for central coordination rather than central control of the system of higher education, based on the belief that the autonomy of technikons would be lost under the latter. The CTP also supported the establishment of the CHE as an advisory body and not the two bodies proposed by the NCHE. Despite the criticisms presented above, in particular of the powers vested in the Minister, the government proceeded to formalize adoption of the Green Paper's proposal for cooperative governance in the White Paper on Higher Education and the Higher Education Bill. The only difficulty was with the way the Draft White Paper dealt with the powers of the CHE which implied that it was an extension of the DOE.

The responses to the governance sections in the White Paper and Bill will be treated interchangeably as the two documents were released at the same time. Despite both documents adopting the governance proposals as reflected in the Green Paper, some changes were however effected as a result of the input received. For example, in response to the concerns raised by the CTP and CUP in relation to the under-representation of heads of higher education institutions on the CHE, the Bill proposed that four principals of universities and four principals of technikons should be appointed to serve on it. However, both the White Paper and the Bill gave the powers to appoint these members to the Minister, based on the nominations by the principals of these institutions. In its adoption of the governance proposal, the White Paper on Higher Education Bill explains governance at systematic level as follows:

> To give effect to the transformation of higher education in the spirit of cooperative governance, the Ministry will enhance the capacity of the Higher Education Branch of the Department of Education, establish a Council on Higher Education (CHE) and enable reform of governing structures of higher education institutions. These measures will provide opportunities for organized constituencies to express and negotiate their concerns, and will permit the government and the representative structures of the higher education sector to plan and transact the transformation and development of the system in an orderly way.[42]

The governance model adopted by government saw more powers passed on to the Minister of Education, raising concerns on the part of the parliamentary opposition. There was concern among some higher education stakeholders about the powers conferred upon the Minister. For example, the CUP in its response to the White Paper and Higher Education Bill, argued that those powers could potentially lend themselves to unintended abuse in the future. Citing an incident in 1988 when universities successfully went to court to prevent the then apartheid Minister of Education from using financial muscle to impose his will, the CUP argued that this would be possible under the proposed legislation. The CUP raised the concern that though the [present] Minister of Education and the Director-General were well acquainted with higher education,[43] there was no guarantee that such would always be the case, hence a possible abuse of power in the future. The CUP urged that there be checks and balances on the power vested in an individual post, even at ministerial level.[44]

On the other hand, the CTP raised concerns about the fact that the members of the CHE would be nominated by the body concerned and appointed by the Minister. The CTP argued that this implied that the Minister had the right to veto a nomination of the body or association concerned and refer it back for further nomination. According to the CTP:

> This provision goes against democratic principles and it is therefore suggested that bodies and associations concerned should have the final say in who their representatives on the CHE should be. Should this principle strictly be applied, it could cause problems in the composition of the

CHE and it is therefore suggested that provision should be made that the nominations of bodies or associations are automatically the official representatives of such bodies and associations in the CHE. [45]

The powers given to the Minister to appoint CHE members were formally adopted in the Higher Education Act, despite such advice to the contrary.[46] The Higher Education Bill gave powers to the Minister of Education to determine policy on higher education after-consultation with the CHE.[47] This included the authority to establish higher education institutions, approve or withdraw provision of programmes and close down an institution, enforce mergers or withhold money to enforce compliance with provisions laid down.[48] In introducing this Bill in Parliament, the Minister argued that such authority was required as government needed to take a lead in establishing an efficient, effective and affordable higher education system, something, he said, that had been neglected to the detriment of the country. He pointed out that this authority would be exercised within the framework of the proposed national plan for higher education after-consultation with the CHE.[49]

The powers conferred on the Minister also became a point of contention in the debate on the Bill in Parliament. It centered around two issues, firstly, the powers of the Minister over academic freedom and autonomy of higher education institutions, and secondly, the powers given to the Minister to determine the language policy for these institutions. In objecting to the Bill, Adv. D M Bakker of the National Party pointed out that while the National Party was in favor of transformation, they also believed that effective and viable transformation could take place only within the framework of academic freedom and a fair degree of autonomy of institutions of higher education. He argued that:

> Although academic freedom and autonomy are mentioned in the preamble to this Bill, it is clear from the excessive powers given to the Minister, that such autonomy is conditional upon compliance with the policy of the Minister. Concern is thereby raised that the Ministry wants to use transformation and cooperative governance to centralize power, instead of supporting and encouraging institutional self-regulation.[50]

Even though it is open to speculation how transformation could be used to centralize power, and one of the widely held views within the ANC had been that for transformation to be effected there was a need to give sufficient power to the Minister to lead, it is however not clear how cooperative governance could be used to centralize power. The way in which cooperative governance has been used shows that there were different perspectives on it among the policy-makers. There were also objections made over the way in which the CHE had to provide its advice to the Minister, the powers the Bill gave to the Minister to establish public higher education institutions, to compel any education institution such as a university, college or technikon, to merge, and to close public higher education institutions. The National Party raised concerns that the Bill allowed the Minister to make such decisions without even consulting the council of the relevant university. It argued that:

> These excessive powers of the Minister can easily lead to the abuse of power and create the impression that higher education institutions will have to do what the Minister prescribes, or run the risk of confrontation and the possibility of being penalized financially. This absolutely undermines the principle of academic freedom and autonomy. The NP argued in the Portfolio Committee for a better balancing of the Minister's powers, for example by extending the power of the Council on Higher Education and compelling the Minister at least to make decisions in-consultation with the CHE instead of after-consultation.[51]

It appears from the NP's objections that it subscribed to an in-consultation rather than an after-consultation approach to policy formulation. This position was supported by the Democratic Party and the African Christian Democratic Party.[52] On the other hand, the ANC argued against the in-consultation approach in its rejection of the NCHE's proposal for the establishment of two statutory bodies, namely the HEF and HEC, and the powers they were to assume. It argued that such an outcome would not reflect an appropriate balance of power between elected and non-elected representatives in the context of parliamentary democracy.[53] Drawing from the arguments advanced by the representatives of the parties in Parliament, it could be argued that an after-consultation approach is related to the centralization of power, whereas an in-consultation approach is related to the decentralization and balancing of power.

There were two further objections raised to the Bill's proposal concerning ministerial powers namely, (a) the powers given to the Minister to determine the language policy of higher education institutions, and (b) the manner in which this policy made its way into the Bill. With respect to the latter, in the first draft Bill, clause 27(2) had left the power to determine language policy in the hands of the council and senates of institutions. According to Bakker, during the public hearings there was a general consensus on this provision and all role players seemed satisfied with the position. He points out, however, that at the last moment:

[t]he Portfolio Committee was confronted with substantial and far-reaching amendments which were introduced by the Department which significantly changed the determination of language policy of public higher education institutions which make a total mockery of public hearings and the consultation process. This amendment places the final decision regarding language policy in the hands of the Minister only. If the Minister and the Department do not intend to misuse the power given to them by this surprise amendment, why did they want this provision included in the Bill? The tactics used to include the amendment most definitely indicate a hidden agenda.[54]

The NP's submission to the Portfolio Committee was that language policy should be determined by the council of a higher education institution in consultation with the Council on Higher Education. The concerns raised by the NP with regard to the way in which the amendment to the language policy was carried out raise some important questions regarding the purposes of consultation and public hearings that were conducted. It appears that as with stakeholders during the NCHE process, there were certain expectations made out of consultation, that certain positions would be written or retained in the policy document as per agreement during the consultation process. On the other hand, it appears that the ANC and the DOE reserved the right to formulate policy as they deemed fit in pursuit of the transformation agenda in higher education. In doing this, they applied an after-consultation approach to policy-making. The significance of such an approach in this case would have been that if it was made explicit to participating parties in government, the opposition parties would have had no grounds to complain about the ANC having shifted from the position that was presented or agreed upon during the public hearings.

The seriousness with which the Opposition viewed the powers given to the Minister was demonstrated by disruptions to the parliamentary proceedings by Afrikaner youth linked to the Freedom Front Party during the second reading of the Bill in Parliament. Proceedings had to be suspended for 42 minutes as order was restored.[55] In their analysis of the way Parliament responded to the disruptions by these youth, Moja and Hayward paid tribute to the maturity with which parliament responded to disruptions and ascribed this to commitment to democratic values in the post-1994 period. They asserted that:

The tact and the thoughtfulness with which this serious and potentially violent disruption was handled by Parliamentary leadership is a tribute to commitment to democratic values and patience even in the face of extreme opposition. The response was a testament to accommodating differences while ensuring that the business of Parliament is carried out in a proper and dignified manner. It was a telling example of the new openness and tolerance of the post-1994 election period. In an earlier era, the disruption—especially if it had been by black students—would have been met with force.[56]

The leader of the Freedom Front, General Constand Viljoen, objected to the Bill on the grounds that the powers given to the Minister were to the detriment of the "Afrikaner and Afrikaans students as it deprived them of their right to receive tertiary education in their own language."[57] Viljoen could have been referring to the youth who had earlier disrupted Parliamentary proceedings in protest against the Bill as it did not cater for the retention of Afrikaans as medium of instruction in higher education institutions. In his response to language policy being left in the hands of the Minister, Mike Ellis of the Democratic Party warned that:

> The language issue is potentially one of the most explosive facing South Africa, if mishandled by Government. It can be equally explosive if mishandled by institutions, as we saw with the Potgietersrus school issue.[58] But institutional transgressions will always be sorted out and should never be used as an excuse by the State to introduce black-type legislation which places power in the hands of the Minister, as this Bill now does. The language of institutions should be left to individual institutions to resolve and should never be left to an ideological and dogmatic central Government approach.[59]

The defense offered by the ANC for supporting the Bill was based on the view that the Minister would never abuse his power or use it to the detriment of institutions. It argued that the autonomy of the institutions would only be interfered with if autonomy was used for unconstitutional ends, i.e., using language as an exclusionary mechanism.[60]

The ways in which debates on the Higher Education Bill were conducted, the objections to certain policy positions and the triumph of the ruling party's policy positions, call for interrogation of the notion of democracy in policy-making. Some stakeholders and the opposition felt that policymakers (the Department and the ruling party) did not handle the process of policy formulation and adoption in a democratic way in line with the principles of consultation and participation which underpinned the process. In their view, democratic practice would have meant adoption of policy positions as agreed during the consultative process. Taking the example of the language policy as presented by the National Party, since in the public hearings the prevailing opinion was that institutional councils should determine language policy, these positions should never have been changed.

There are some loopholes in a policy that leaves language policy in the hands of the institutional councils with their potential for obstructing transformation. Even though this position might have been popular at the time, it does not necessarily mean that it was a correct one to adopt in pursuit of a transformation agenda. For example, given the practice of apartheid in education, race and ethnicity determined the type of institutions people would attend; therefore students, staff, governing bodies and alumni of institutions reflected the racial and ethnic groups they served. As a result the councils of most historically white institutions remained predominantly white and English or Afrikaans. They would be the ones to determine whether or not they wanted to change. Given the history of resistance to change and to embrace the agenda of the new government by some institutions, to leave decision-making concerning such a sensitive issue as language to these structures would risk delaying their change. If the councils of some of them would adopt the language policy that denied access to some students, the government or Minister would have no power to intervene, as that would have been interfering with the autonomy of institutions. To allow such a situation to prevail would also have been defeating the goals of transformation and democratization.

It was on the basis of these considerations that the position adopted by the DOE and the Portfolio Committee, to give the Minister the power to determine the language policy of higher education institutions, was in line with democratic principles. This is based on the fact that parliament was elected on the basis of universal suffrage and therefore the Minister would represent the majority of the electorate. The position adopted by the ANC should also be understood in the light of the experience they had gained of being in power and a growing view that it should not be afraid to govern.

At institutional level, the Bill legislated institutional councils by giving them executive roles to serve as highest decision-making bodies, and institutional forums became advisory bodies. This was contrary to popular views in the pre-1994 period where campaigns were waged by students and staff organizations to have broad transformation forums as higher decision-making bodies. The shift came with and was informed by the wisdom gained from being in government. The kinds of questions said to have been posed within the ANC and its alliance structures indicate a shift from populist ideas of the past when such slogans as "the people shall govern," would be used to campaign for access to governance structures of these higher education institutions. The ANC wanted to maintain the status quo of using governance structures that had been discredited in the past by democratizing them and using them to advance its transformation agenda.

In this context, the question was raised whether it was helpful to de-mocratize the structures of government on the one hand and take away their power to govern on the other? It became a serious debate within the ANC and its allies both in government and outside. Mseleku illustrates the shift in the emphasis which the ANC as government had to put on the location of power within the governance structures:

> Whereas before we were not debating the powers of government but were debating how to take power away from them, not transforming them into BTFs, now we are saying what type of government do we put in place for an alternative South Africa? We are no longer talking about taking power away from them [councils], we are saying how do we de-mocratize them? Once we have democratized them then the debate was, should these BTFs have more power than the power of government? And that's where the divergence began with members who were in gov-ernment and members of the Portfolio Committee putting strongly the fact that if we are democratizing those structures and we are getting par-ticipation from all those players in the structure of government, then dual power is a problem where you have a powerful BTF. So some of the debates came with the experience of being in government which was no longer talking about alternative structures of power, but talking about democratizing the structures of power through legislation.[61]

This shifted emphasis on the way in which the issues of legislation of BTFs and the role and powers to be conferred on them was handled by govern-ment. The net effect of this debate was that there was an attempt within the ANC government to locate more powers within the institutional councils, which were seen as organs of government, rather than in institutional fo-rums. Thus the Higher Education Act gave powers to institutional councils to govern the public higher education institutions and made them the high-est decision-making bodies,[62] and the institutional forums were to advise the council on issues affecting the institution. There seems to be a relationship between how the CHE would relate to the Minister on the one hand, and how the institutional forums would relate to the institutional councils. The Higher Education Bill and the Act reduced the roles of both the CHE and the institutional forums to an advisory one by giving more powers to the Minister and the institutional COUNCILS respectively.

This proposal seems to have maintained the status quo, for while the Act provided for more representation of stakeholder bodies on the council and senate, the majority of people participating in these structures were still drawn from traditional white male groups. Skills and qualifications still resided within this group and they continued to constitute the majority of the senior academic and administrative positions in higher education. Furthermore, Council would also have ministerial appointees, as was the case in the past. Students were not happy with the way institutional forums came to be legislated and the powers they were given. As Mseleku admitted, "up to today when you have a discussion with the students they would say we are not satisfied with what became of the legislation around the Broad Transformation Forum."[63]

CONCLUDING REMARKS

This chapter has discussed government's takeover of the policy process from the NCHE, and demonstrated how it has through formal policy and legislation, ensured that sufficient power is vested within government and structures which it could influence in leading the transformation of the higher education sector. This was in some way compensation for a period of vacuum during 1995–1996, when policy development was outsourced to the NCHE. It has further discussed the value of the consultation process as finding expression through the public hearings in terms of opening up the policy process and the parliamentary proceedings to the public. This new practice, a departure from the apartheid days, served the purpose of mobilizing the higher education sector behind policy. They kept the higher education community informed of government thinking concerning higher education policy and legislation but also helped legislators to keep abreast with public opinion regarding legislation or policy being considered.

The way in which the ANC responded to the proposals of the NCHE concerning cooperative governance is characteristic of the nature of states in their quest for power. In a young democracy which was faced with enormous challenges for transformation, to give concurrent powers to elected leaders and appointed representatives would have hamstrung the powers of the government to lead or to intervene in situations that needed government intervention. Maybe it is naïve to assume that a new government born out of a history of conflict, which had to negotiate itself into power, would be amenable to proposals that would weaken its effectiveness to act. A hybrid of state supervision in the form of cooperative governance as legislated by government was seen by government as meeting the kind of challenges it faced. Subsequent to the passing of this legislation, there have been amendments to the Act that gave the Minister more powers. These include, among the others, the power to provide for the appointment of and functions of an independent assessor, to appoint an administrator to an institution which is being investigated for misadministration. Critics of government might argue that the system has moved more towards state control.

The development of the governance policy framework represents a terrain of struggle for the state to gain and maintain control over the higher education sector. This played itself out in the ways in which the state responded to the NCHE's proposal for cooperative governance and its rejection and acceptance of some of the details of the proposals. The chapter has demonstrated how on the basis of its experience in government, the ANC shifted from the MDM policy of making forums and structures with stakeholder participation as the locus of power, to making them advisory bodies, located in the executive, and placing decision-making powers in the hands of the Minister, the Higher Education Branch and councils of institutions. The distinction made between "democratization of governance" by taking power away from government and democratization which empowered government to rule, was a tactical move that later justified the ANC's decision to centralize power in institutional councils which the state could easily access through ministerial appointments. It was also part of the sobering process which came with experience of being in government and realization that governments are there to govern, and they should be given the powers to perform that role. The sooner the stakeholders and the public come to this realization, the more they will come to terms with the fact that their input and participation in the policy process do not mean that they are equal partners with government in decision-making. Government consults and solicits participation from stakeholders, but decision-making lies with government, in line with an after-consultation approach to policy-making. This confirms Weiss's view that in policy-making knowledge is not power, "but power is power."[64]

Chapter Eight

Policy Literacy and Organizational Learning

INTRODUCTION

This chapter reflects on the lessons arising out of the policy process discussed in this book. It argues that in addition to some of the factors which constrained the new government during the transition period, namely, the effects of the pact, the neo-liberal macroeconomic policies and global pressures, the inheritance of the bureaucracies and associated institutional cultures, the nature of the process of policy development used in higher education in South Africa also required a certain level of policy literacy on the part of all policy actors in order for them to participate meaningfully in this process. Policy literacy refers to the knowledge and skills, existence of intellectual resources, and an understanding of the complexity of the context of policy process required to develop appropriate policies for the new dispensation. There was, however, another reality that made South Africa's transition to democracy and the development of policies more daunting, namely the changing global context that was influenced by the globalization phenomenon. The latter was not only unique to South Africa but many countries of the world were also affected as they gradually became influenced by the ascendancy of neo-liberal agenda in influencing the world economic system. This was partly shaped by the collapse of communism in Eastern Europe which left capitalism without challenges and alternatives to it.

The dawn of the new dispensation that came with the installation of the new government necessitated a new way of doing things, one which would be based on the vision, principles and values as espoused in the Interim Constitution, and the subsequent new Constitution that was adopted as the supreme law of the country. As a result the development of policies under these conditions became a learning process for all those who were involved. With respect to policy development, the new political dispensation had left a dearth of relevant policies and policy experts. This called for skills, knowledge of the Constitution and its implications for policy, and knowledge of the different phases through which policy had to pass. Knowledge was required of the different actors involved in the process and the power they had, as well as an understanding of the different policy documents produced in the process and the varied significance and meanings attached to them. Understanding of the complexity of the context was necessary, as well as timely repositioning and striking of alliances between the strategic policy actors in order to make an impact on the policy process and its outcome. This entailed knowledge of the context in which the process unfolded, the interrogation of that context, a situational analysis of resources (human and material) and the financial resources required to make an impact. Knowledge of all these is referred to as "policy literacy."

POLICY LITERACY AND POLICY FATIGUE

One aspect of policy literacy is related to the knowledge of the differences between various policy documents, the format of these documents and the purposes they serve. For example, the NCHE was tasked with the responsibility of making policy recommendations to government concerning issues of transformation of higher education. Thus the policy recommendations contained in the report were subject to acceptance or rejection by government. The Green Paper, as a discussion document and a response to the NCHE report, contained details, debates and arguments aimed at helping the public grasp the orientation of the Department with regard to policy being considered. Some of the details were dropped in the White Paper when the Department outlined its policy position following consultations on the Green Paper. The dropping does not necessarily mean that they were insignificant, but they could have been covered in the formulation of policies being considered. The same applies to the comments received from the public. These could have been embedded in some of the policy statements in the White Paper. However, the White Paper still contained details that elaborated, substantiated and justified the policy positions the Department had adopted.

The Green and White Papers were different from the Bill and the Act which represented the legislation phase of the policy process. These concentrated on the formal structures, powers, functions, goals and values that were required to regulate policy. They were formulated in a way that did not require justification. Legislation has to be clear, and if there is to be an investigation or dispute, people normally refer to the law as their starting or reference point. Legislation becomes the written law that governs the conduct of different parties. So some of the rationale that exists in the policy ought to be in the law to guide its interpretation and application, especially when there is dispute. White Papers indicate government's commitments, while legislation is supposed to provide specific mechanisms and structures through which the policy is going to be expressed. This does not mean there is no rationale in legislation, only that the legislation indicates binding commitment from the government and this must be made on the basis of what the policy says.[1] All these factors had implications for how stakeholders interacted with these documents in terms of understandings, interpretations and responses.

The development and writing of these documents also requires certain technical skills that serve the purposes of these documents. For example, whereas the NCHE report and the Green and White Papers can be written by researchers, the Bill and the Act are written by the legal division of the Department. In explaining the relevance of writing skills in the writing of policy, Cloete explains that:

> There is a technical writing of policy which is different from participation and consultation. This is what many stakeholders lacked. The Commission wanted ideas and not figures. Whereas Wits (University), for example, provided the Commission with figures and statistics, which the Commission did not need as they could access them from the Department of Education and the World Bank, the University of Cape Town (UCT) provided the Commission with ideas, and this was useful. For example, the World Bank was able to supply the Commission with a top consultant on Student Financing; the Centre for Higher Education Policy Studies (CHEPS) in Holland was able to supply the Commission with material on quality.[2]

Whereas Cloete seems to be overstating his point as evidence, his point is inseparable from evidence at the research phase. Ideas are generated from data which can include statistics. On the other hand, there is also a taken-for-granted assumption that policy skills provided by the World Bank are applied in a value-free manner. There is always a need not to take for granted services provided by philanthropic multinational organizations which are often looking for markets for their policies. Despite the unproblematic approach of the services provided by the multinational cooperatives assumed by Cloete, and the dichotomy he makes between ideas and statistics, the point sheds light on some of the aspects of policy making. That is, for one to make an impact on it and its outcomes, the kind of data required and how it should be presented is important. This seems to make the distinction between the usefulness of the University of the Witwatersrand and UCT's contributions to the work of the Commission. Furthermore, it was important for stakeholders to know the kinds of expertise and information available to the Commission so that they could avoid making submissions that would not be of use to the Commission.

The state legal advisers also check whether the style conforms to the conventions of the writing of legislation, but at the time still based them on the apartheid style of writing of legislation, with its legal jargon which was inaccessible to ordinary policy-makers. There is evidence that this scenario may be changing, with legislation being written in plain English without reference to Latin. This domain was the preserve of the white members of Parliament in line with the apartheid policies, and the new incumbents in government had to learn these conventions. Both the old and new officials had distinctive but complementary skills that served the purpose of policy-making. The need for various skills that draw on the expertise of both researchers and legal experts could sometimes lead to conflicts in the policy process as the two groups will read the policy, law and the context in different ways. For example, one of the policies passed by the DOE in relation to the Further Education and Training sector was the recognition of prior learning, including that acquired through non-formal means in NGOs. At the same time, legislation was passed that required registration of providers and made it an offence for someone to provide some form of learning without being registered. The latter was meant to protect the public from bogus or "fly-by-night" providers; however this ruling later proved to be restrictive, especially for non-formal education provided by NGOs and other providers who were not registered. This created a dilemma for the DOE and stark differences emerged between the legal team that insisted on the registration of providers and could not see the tension between policy and legislation and members of the Further Education Task Team. A member of the Further Education Task Team explained the differences between the two sets of policy-makers:

> The deputy Directors-General, the officials and the Portfolio Committee understood the dilemma we were in, so they had to find a legal formulation that had to resolve the dilemma for them. But the lawyers were not prepared to listen, they did not even notice that there was [a] dilemma and were not even prepared to apply their minds to it. That is because their conception of education is formal. In other words, they had not taken on board the thrust of the policy, which is to recognize

education across the formal, non-formal and informal divides. That is why we were recognizing this as a dilemma.[3]

Policy literacy also entails having some experience of the area being dealt with, keeping an open mind and being receptive to new ideas. It requires a level of maturity that enables participants in the policy process to engage in dialogue with other policy actors, dealing with conflicting views, resolving conflicts and developing consensus. In Hall's terms "it requires an intimate knowledge of government vision and ideological position to be able to make a meaningful contribution that can impact on policy outcomes."[4] Hall's comment could imply that if a contribution is made that falls outside the vision and ideology of government; the likelihood is that it might not impact on policy. His comment is based on his personal experience of attempting to fight for teacher education to continue to be offered in some colleges of education that had a history of producing good teachers. However, he laments the fact that this plea was not heeded, and in his view the decision was based on ideological grounds to close colleges and no amount of persuasion could change the views of Commissioners or officials of the DOE. The counter argument was that the decision to close colleges was made because most of them were under-enrolled, making them expensive to run, hence the decision to relocate teacher education to universities. This latter perspective was based on the research report of the National Teacher Education Audit conducted in 1995. The counter arguments, for and against the offering of teacher education in colleges, present some of the dilemmas of using research as a basis for decision-making in policy-making. They highlight the fact that sometimes ideological or political considerations influence policy decisions and sometimes research data is used as a basis.

For the public to be able to participate in a meaningful way in the policy process, understanding of these processes is crucial, otherwise they may focus on issues which have little impact on the outcomes of policy. This also entails understanding the purposes of some steps in the process, such as public hearings and invitations for written submissions to the documents. There should be an understanding among stakeholders of what purposes these processes have and what each stakeholder should expect from them. With proper policy literacy among stakeholders, they will be able to understand that the format in which policy is being presented could be such that it gives an impression that their views have not been accommodated, which might not be the case. Nevertheless, the question of content could be used to assess the extent to which the views of stakeholders concerned have been incorporated. This can serve the purpose of preventing misunderstanding among participants concerning the outcomes of policy processes. Policy literacy also entails an understanding of the approach to policy development and the assumptions that underpin the policy process, especially the participation of stakeholders. As explained above, there were approaches assumed in the unfolding of the policy process, namely the in-consultation and the after-consultation. Each assumes a particular way in which stakeholder input in the policy process should be treated. Some of the misunderstandings between stakeholders and policy-makers, especially NCHE commissioners, arose as a result of lack of understanding of the difference between these approaches and their application to the policy process.

The question that needs to be posed is: given the apparent significance of policy literacy in the policy process, how could policy actors acquire it? Many of the participating stakeholders were not sufficiently equipped to continue to the end. Most exhausted their resources and energies in the work of the Commission, not aware that there would still be significant stages of the policy process to come, such as the Green Paper, the White Paper and the Higher Education Bill. The White Paper and the Bill stages were more important than the NCHE stage as they represented the formal adoption of policy and legislation. By the time the process reached the White Paper and Bill stages, some stakeholders, such as students, had experienced *policy fatigue*. That means they had run out of ideas and resources to sustain their participation in the process. This was particularly the case with mass-based civil society organizations. It could be argued that this might have defeated some of the goals of participation and therefore the democratization of the policy-making process.

By the time the process reached the legislation stage, it was dominated by policy actors who were endowed with resources and skills: political organisations and statutory bodies such as the CUP and the CTP who had the privilege of access to human and material resources from their affiliate institutions to sustain their participation in the policy process. For example, the CUP had formal standing committees that debated numerous issues requiring its response. These committees were academic planning, finance, interlibrary cooperation, executive, educational, staff matters, sports council, legal and press.[5] In commenting on the preparation of its submission to the NCHE, the CUP stated in the preamble to its document that it "was debated by several sub-committees of the CUP as well as at a special gathering of the CUP members itself."[6] The CTP drew on the institutional resources it had at its disposal to respond to the need for input into different policy initiatives by government. This was mainly through the Committee for Tutorial Matters (CTM), which dealt mainly with academic matters, and the Finance

Committee, which gave advice and input to the CTP on its funding issues. There was also a legal committee, labor committee, staff relations sub-committee and the committee for student affairs.[7] Both the CUP and the CTP had the additional advantage of continuity of membership and leadership, which helped them maintain consistency and coherence in their participation and input throughout the process. On the other hand, the participation of student stakeholders was weakened by a lack of resources and the turnover in student leadership (which was as a result of the short period— three to six years) they had to complete their studies. This resulted in the loss of important human resources and skills that could have been developed during the process as some student leaders left the system upon completion of their studies.

ORGANIZATIONAL LEARNING AND OUTSOURCING

Having ascribed importance to policy literacy in this context, the question that needs to be posed is how this policy literacy could have been acquired. Two possibilities are explored. One was through contracting an agency or individuals with expertise to help build capacity among stakeholders; the other was to learn by doing. The problem with the first option was that there were few if any agencies equipped to carry out this task. The context of transition in which the policy process took place was new to everybody involved, and the complexity of the challenges had not been anticipated by anybody. With regard to contracting individuals to help build capacity, the available expertise was thinly spread to meet the arising needs. In fact, where it existed, it was mainly used in government agencies such as the Commissions or Task Teams appointed to provide policy advice to government. The other problem which stakeholders such as the students faced when buying expertise for capacity building was with finding of sufficient resources to pay for those services.

There are differing opinions from within the Commission, in terms of whether there was sufficient expertise in the country to build capacity among stakeholders to participate effectively in the policy process. Cloete believes that expertise was available and that the problem experienced was not with expertise but with resources. He points out that resources from the international community and local donors were all made available to the Commission, but were less accessible to stakeholders. For example, after the conference of black professors at the University of Venda decided to write an alternative policy to that of the Commission, they went to the World Bank and USAID to raise funds. The response of these bodies was that they had made resources available to the Commission and should therefore work with it.[8] If such voices or initiatives were provided with resources, they would have added interesting dimensions to the work of the Commission. Since students did not have resources, there was a feeling within the Commission that it should have taken some of the issues they raised and commissioned someone to conduct research and write a report. If this option had been pursued, it would have strengthened the student capacity that was already being built through the students' own initiative.

While Hall agrees with Cloete on lack of resources among stakeholders for capacity-building, he is skeptical about whether the expertise existed for it. In his response to a question of building capacity for policy literacy, Hall, a former member of the teacher education Task Group of the NCHE, responded:

> The question that I am grappling with is who would have done it? If you say it is an external agency, or an NGO, then it would have to be independent of government. I don't know the mechanisms because the time lines were relatively short. We're talking about three years. The stakeholders themselves ought perhaps to have acquainted themselves with the process. The question that then needs answering is, how [could they have acquainted themselves with the process in such tight time frames]? They may have been able to commission somebody at the time that was well informed to do it. But those people are few and far between. You know you can count literally on ten fingers the number of people in this country that have the skills to take Green Papers to White Papers to Acts; probably on one hand.[9]

Thus, according to Hall, the problem was not only with the lack of expertise but also with constraints of time to build capacity, given the timeframes available for government to deliver on policy. Reddy, in agreeing with Hall, also emphasizes the problem of time constraints and lack of expertise to build capacity. He argues that when the process started in 1995 with the appointment of the NCHE, there was what might be termed a vacuum of policy literacy. This was because prior to 1995 there had been a preoccupation with the "struggle politics" dating back to the pre-1990 era.[10] Given the socio-political context of the time, and the fact that policies were based on a new government vision which had never before been developed, there was (in Reddy's view) no institution or agency sufficiently well equipped to meet the new demands of capacity-building in policy literacy. This was made even more difficult by the tight timeframes in which policy had to be developed.[11] Higher education as a policy discipline is well established in the United States and in Europe, but it was not possible to transplant that expertise for use in the South African policy process. Reddy suggests that the only solution was to learn by doing and from experience:

> Given our particular historical context, the lack of policy literacy in 1995 was an inevitable consequence of our history and we had no other way of developing policy literacy than by doing and learning. The policy development process and experience of the past five years later produced policy think-tanks. There are policy developing institutes and now South Africans can develop policy in a much more systemic, much more rigorous, much more scholarly way than was the case before.[12]

The point of the learning process which policy actors had to go through has also been raised and emphasized by the former Director-General of education in reflecting on the experience of the DOE in the first five years in office. In responding to what he refers to as "the almost shrill voices that one picks up in the media about education, about the popular sense of miracles in education that members of the press and the public in some cases think are possible," he points to the fact that some journalists don't understand that the questions they are raising have to do with a level of complexity of a kind that nobody anticipated or even had the time to try to anticipate.[13] As he puts it:

> Both for government, for the different parts of government and the parliamentary system, it was a new system that we were using. The members of the Portfolio Committee were learning as they were doing their job. They had to learn to relate to government officials, nobody knew what the roles of the two structures were going to be so we had to build together. But it had to be—it was not there, it was created by the dynamic of what was going on. In a sense there was a lot of learning that took place for everybody.[14]

The points highlighted above concerning how policy literacy could have been acquired show the importance of the availability of skills, time, and resources in building policy literacy. These were particularly acute given the new political and ideological context in which the policy process was unfolding. The impact of organizational learning that came with the experience of being in government helped the new government in terms of its approach to policies that were developed after this experience had been acquired. It helped government to reflect on and avoid the mistakes of the past in order to develop policies that would enhance its effectiveness.

One way in which the policy literacy vacuum was dealt with was to use external consultants in the development of policy. Consultants were used in the policy process in the work of the NCHE and the development of the

Green and White Papers, but not the legislation which became a domain and preserve of legislators. According to Reddy, the use of consultants in the work of the Commission was a guarded and monitored process to ensure that they were never allowed to run alone with any particular sector of their work. For example, consultants were deployed in the various task teams and technical committees of the Commission to work with local policy researchers and commissioners. Two or three consultants would work with a team of seven or eight local "experts" in a task team. Reddy adds that it was not a consultant dominated process, but an interactive process whereby "we were learning from them and they were learning about our context."[15]

There are different perspectives on the usefulness of consultants in the local policy context, especially in the task teams of the Commission. Hall, reflecting on his experience of working with them in the Teacher Education Task Team, argued that he had not found them to be effective. While acknowledging the skills of the overseas consultant he worked with, he was concerned that the consultant used an overseas frame of reference rather than a local one. He gave an example: "I gave the consultants the funding figures on teacher training, they looked at them, and they seemed not to make sense to them. But they really didn't understand the scene because their teacher training and funding overseas were so different."[16] Questioning the usefulness of overseas consultants, as in the example cited above, raises the issue of which kinds of consultants were brought to help, the kinds of skills they brought and how those were used. It further highlights the fact that consultants are not needed in every aspect of the policy domain. That being said, the value of comparative work in informing the local policy process is not dismissed.

The other problem related to the use of overseas consultants is in regard to the amount of skills they were to transfer. While Reddy argues that there had been a mutual learning process, Hall states that in his experience little transfer of skills had taken place. He points out that:

> I am very critical in general about overseas consultants because I don't believe that the transfer of skills is as great as they would like to make out. They tend to come in, do their work, then they withdraw, and the result is that there is very little skilling of local people. I can give you numerous examples of USAID and British Aid coming in my field and leaving the country having done nothing. They write a fancy report which sometimes just sits on the shelf and gathers dust. [17]

This contradicts the version provided by Reddy about the way in which overseas consultants worked within the Commission. While they might have worked in the way suggested by Reddy within the Commission, this was not necessarily the case in other areas. Thus, discussion of the use of consultants has to consider the purpose for which their services were sought and the context in which they operated. This determined the way in which they worked and the kind of product they delivered.

The chairperson of the Commission alluded to another method of consultation that was unique, in the form of the Salzburg seminar where the NCHE Discussion Document was discussed. There, the Commission had access to the expertise of consultants whom it engaged over the document— "not them telling us what to do."[18] The approach used at Salzburg is summarized in the Seminar report in the following paragraph:

> Bringing together a group of more than fifty senior experts from around the world with members of the Commission, the session included presentations by the NCHE representatives on key issues affecting Higher Education such as governance, finance and curriculum reform and relevance. Following Salzburg Seminar tradition, mornings were devoted to a series of plenary lectures during which the Commission members presented specific aspects of their findings and recommendations, followed by questions, comments and general discussion. In the afternoons, the NCHE members met with four or five smaller groups of experts to discuss specific issues. Throughout the sessions the opportunity for informal discussion was readily available.[19]

The value of the use of consultants in South Africa was that they helped in the policy literacy process because of their expertise and by so doing filled what could be referred to as a "policy vacuum." The process described above highlights the fact that policy is not just text; it calls on people, skills, procedures, conventions and formats of writing, participation and consultation, and above all, the involvement of different policy actors who all bring different orientations and expertise to the process. Not only were consultants used by the Commission, but they were also used by government in the writing of the Green and White Papers on higher education. Their use within the Commission and the DOE was varied. While the Commission used them for general advice on policy and the building of capacity, and not in the writing of policy, the DOE used them in the writing of policy.[20] However, their involvement in the writing of these documents was also closely monitored and controlled by the DOE, as the former Director-General put it:

> The White Paper is a government document and ultimately the government must be able to stand behind it and enact it. Our approach in the Department of Education has always been that ultimately the document

must reflect the policy of government and so, although various members of the Department and sometimes outsiders will be involved in drafting, the documents were subjected to very intense internal scrutiny. There were always senior departmental workshops for most or all the documents which will end up either as White Papers or legislation. So the work might be done at different levels under the supervision of one or more senior departmental officials, [and] the writing in some cases might be done by an outside expert but under the direct working relationships with the senior officials of the Department. But ultimately it all boils down to a situation in which the entire senior force of the Department will be involved in the grounding and restructuring of the document or even rewriting sections.[21]

Apart from helping to fill the policy vacuum, the role of consultants in the higher education policy development process should also be understood in the light of the need to align South Africa's policies with global trends. As Coombe commented:

In the specific process of the White Paper, in the policy framework formulation, we were likewise conscious of the need to engage internationally, to test ideas against global trends. We undertook a study, including a limited number of studies, and we felt very confident that by the time the policy framework had been prepared, that we were working within the grain of an international, a progressive international view of how education should be run. It was very explicit to higher education.[22]

The NCHE's work had a very clear international focus, and its engagement with experts at Salzburg is cited as an example of how the South African policy process incorporated an international component and input. This was an important consideration as it "positioned our new policy framework and laws in a way that would win international recognition and validation."[23] Government accessed international expertise to be used in a form of a reference group in the writing of the Green and White Papers, which included two consultants from India, one from Australia and other specialists from elsewhere in Africa. One of the Indian consultants had worked for the World Bank; the other was the chair of the University Grants Commission of India. The Australian consultant was a senior official from the Ministry of Education who advised particularly on the new funding system for higher education.[24] In highlighting the significance of the role of the reference group, Coombe commented that:

The specific advice we were receiving with respect to the Green Paper and White Paper process was not random advice or generalized advice. It was advice relating particularly to the policy direction which had already been foreshadowed in the NCHE report, which had been refined in the Green Paper process. Matters such as program-based funding, and a process of transforming the institutional landscape of higher education in order to improve cost effectiveness, [as well as] the use of resources in a more effective manner, the reshaping of institutional identity and missions in relation to a broader view of the system as a whole. These matters had become prioritized by the ANC. So the kinds of expertise that was needed to advise on the specific formulation in the policy documents was much clearer.[25]

The involvement of consultants in the policy process in higher education was not without problems. Whereas the NCHE might have been in control of the participation of consultants in its work, that sense of control seemed to have slipped when the policy process entered the Green and White Paper processes, which were under the control of the DOE. For example, it is reported that there was a problem with the first draft White Paper on Higher Education, produced by the DOE.[26] It did not bear much resemblance to, nor draw from the Green Paper and the consultation that accompanied the process. This draft, which was never made public, is said to have been written by one of the consultants that was used by the DOE. The problems with this draft were so serious that the ANC study group on Education had to intervene and make recommendations for its rewriting. This led the Minister of Education to appoint a task team that would exercise damage control measures to rectify the problems. Other problems with the paper were that (a) the entire conception of curriculum qualification was not consistent with the National Qualifications Framework (NQF); (b) the funding sections were market-based; and (c) there was nothing about institutional transformation or mechanisms at institutional level, or government structures and other kinds of structures to deal with transformation issues. The task team produced a draft White Paper which was also subjected to further consultation.

The above view shows the extent to which consultants sometimes had free rein in their activities. The problem could be attributed to various factors. It might have had to do with capacity, in the sense that some people were overloaded and overwhelmed by the volume of work and the size and scale of the tasks that they had to perform indirectly. This does not, however, suggest they did not have the intellectual capacity. The work overload led to a situation where tasks were handed over to consultants and there was no close supervision or policy management of their work. The problem of contract management is not only experienced in young democracies such as South Africa, but has been experienced in stable countries such as the United Kingdom and Australia. The other problem with management of the role and work of consultants might have to do with South Africa's transition, resulting in what Omar refers to as "political overload." This is explained as what some have seen as the triple transition South Africa went through. Transition in South Africa was not just a take-over from apartheid followed by replacement with the same structures and systems. Firstly, new structures had to be established. Secondly, not only were new structures established, but existing apartheid ones also had to be integrated. There was a new set of government arrangements, a hybrid federal Constitution that required a reconfiguration of what used to be apartheid national structures. This represented a second layer of restructuring during transition. Thirdly, there was a change of the economic model from a state to a market led one, although it was not clear at that time that it was going to be market led.[27] These factors resulted in a situation where there were no established procedures, systems, institutional culture or norms to draw on. Providing leadership in this state of instability and flux was not something that came easily. It required a certain level of expertise, political leadership and vision that would constitute policy literacy.

Jansen summarizes the challenges of capacity experienced during the first five years in relation to the four key players involved, who all had some expertise, but not all that was required. These include the new bureaucracy who had a problem with inexperience and capacity. The problem of the old bureaucracy was sometimes a problem of attitude and of orientation. As he puts it:

> You have a problem on both sides in that you have willing, visionary and committed new bureaucrats who don't have a clue about systems and how they work and how they can be changed. On the other hand you have a group of people who have the skills but those are skills developed within a particular paradigm. It was a very narrow set of skills that could easily be applied to a particular context and paradigm system, and skills that could be honed on the basis of an equal system of education which had been set. So I would not at all valorize the kinds of the leftover expertise, the expertise of the apartheid bureaucrats, because in many ways that was a sort that could keep the system going, but on the other hand it could have undermined the kind of progressive ideas for education.[28]

Jansen suggests that one way in which government tried to resolve its problem with the old bureaucrats was to rely on two other groups, namely international consultants and the strategic management teams (SMTs). He argues that the international consultants played a very prominent role in kick-starting several policies. However, they also had their own problems. As he put it:

> There also you have a dilemma in that you have well-meaning people
> with money, and with expertise and with a repertoire of policy options
> and experiences, but people who do not necessarily understand the con-
> text. People who are not in it for the long haul, particularly people who
> are highly paid for six weeks to do a piece of work.[29]

Thus the use of international consultants was also not necessarily a solution
to the challenges faced by the DOE in the formulation of policies. The SMTs
are the other component which government also used in addressing the problem of capacity. According to Jansen, all those strategic management teams
were very often high-level national experts. But the problem with those
SMTs was that they were not necessarily composed of people with educational expertise. The members had enormous political expertise and skills,
they brought credibility to the policy-making process, but they were not necessarily education specialists from whom you could draw expertise. Even
though some of the SMT members are perceived as having had political skills
rather than education skills, this shortcoming may have been compensated
for by other education people drawn into the SMT who had extensive experience in the education field. The challenge faced by the involvement of these
SMTS in the policy process during transition was to find a balance for the
strengths and weaknesses in these groups. Jansen asserts that:

> Somewhere in that mix you had government trying to formulate policies
> that took those four groups together and what they enabled government
> to do was to decide on policies but without any understanding. None of
> those had the skills, had the understanding of how do we move towards
> implementation without being critical where there are such gross dispar-
> ities. That is, I think, in summary, one of the greatest deficiencies with
> the policy-making process of the past six years. We did not have a group
> that could take us from an analysis of the problem to implementation of
> our strategic policies.[30]

While that capacity and expertise to develop policies in a self-critical way
which related policy formulation to policy implementation did not exist during that period, this has now been developed through the process of learning by doing and learning from mistakes. As Reddy puts it, "South Africa is
now in a better position to develop policy in a more confident way than it
was six years ago."[31] This missing link has been established through experience of being in government. It is part of the literacy that has been acquired
through learning by doing.

The passing of the *Higher Education Act* and the establishment of new
governance structures proposed by the Act provided the new government

with useful legislative and policy tools to spearhead transformation. With an experience of being in government, and the demise of the government of national unity arrangement, the ANC government became more assertive in taking actions it deemed necessary to effect change.

CONCLUDING REMARKS

This chapter has reviewed the policy process in higher education in South Africa and has highlighted some of the lessons drawn from it. It has argued that in addition to the constraints of the pact, global pressures and neo-liberal policies and the inheritance of the bureaucracy, there was need for policy literacy for both government officials and stakeholders to be able to efficiently manage the policy making process than it was the case. This has been justified on the basis of the different stages the process had to go through. In the absence of policy literacy, the process of policy development became a learning experience for all involved. Contrasting views were presented concerning how policy literacy could be addressed. These range between those who saw the problem as lying not with expertise but with resources, to those who saw it as being about expertise and timeframes.

The chapter has further explored the contribution of the old and the new bureaucracy, the consultants and the SMTs, in the building of capacity. All had strengths and weaknesses which impacted on the policies being developed. In particular, the use of consultants also served the purpose of helping to align South Africa's higher education policies with international trends and developments. However, the use of consultants was not without problems, and these have been highlighted. In the absence of sufficient expertise to build capacity, learning by doing became the way local stakeholders, including government, dealt with the challenges. In this process organizational learning among most agencies took place and capacity was built. This became useful in the later processes of policy development where government became more assertive about the policy goals and outcomes to be achieved.

There have been two competing arguments put forth to explain the challenges associated with effective participation by stakeholders and the use of experts in this transformation process. One was the discourse of resources (financial) which few stakeholders had access to, as well as the enabling structures. The other is the discourse of timeframes, which some believe impinged on the policy process, especially in relation to the work of the NCHE and the parliamentary calendar for tabling and adoption of policy and legislation. There is, however, another third element which constitutes the third argument, namely, the discourse of leadership in and for policy. As much as the repositioning and reorganization of the Department of Education and the effective utilization of the old and new bureaucracy depended on leadership, so did the policy process. Leadership in policy refers to knowledge of intricacies of the policies been considered, and leadership for policy refers to provision of vision, strategies and defending policies being considered. All these are constituent elements of policy literacy argued in this chapter.

Chapter Nine
Conclusion

The first ten years of democracy in South Africa have seen monumental changes which were aimed at redressing over four decades of racial oppression and economic exploitation of black people. Apartheid had during these years managed to establish a material and cultural face that came to be associated with South African society. This posed challenges for the new government when it came into power in 1994. This book reflected on what some of these challenges entailed, by focusing on policy process and restructuring of higher education during the period 1994 to 1997. The research question posed in this study was, why was it the case that despite democratic aspirations that informed the struggle against apartheid and subsequently informed the policy-making process in education, the outcomes thereof were different from the intended goals? Furthermore, what was the impact of the application of the principles of participation, consultation and representation on the policy process and its outcome? This has been explained in terms of the effects of the negotiation and constitutional pact, the global pressures and ensuing neo-liberal policies, the complicated twist of bureaucratic re-organization and associated institutional cultures and policy literacy dimensions.

This book has demonstrated that even though the policy process was conceptualized around democratic principles, values and framing devices, the context in which it unfolded was complex and entailed factors which were more important than concerns about the application of these principles. Thus the outcome of the process reflected concerns about nation building, state formation, aligning policy with global trends and building capacity and consensus around policy. In addition there was a quest for the state to assert control over levers of state power and decision-making structures that would enable it to lead the transformation of higher education.

Overall, this book has demonstrated the complementary contributions of research, politics, lobbying and networks, availability of resources and macro-economic policies in the outcomes of policy. As nation building and state formation became the preoccupation of the new government of national unity during transition, these priorities entailed the adoption of values and principles that would inform the project. The development of macro-economic and political frameworks was essential to the nation-building project, with the establishment of institutional structures helping to give effect to government's policy. It was in this context that the development of higher education policy took place. Contrary to the experiences of some developing countries, especially where some post-colonial governments have had to start from nothing in the development of policies, the new South African government inherited a rich legacy of policy development. This legacy was characterized by the engagement between researchers (stakeholders) and the liberation movement that led to the production of policy proposals and principles to be used by the new government when it came into power. The partnership between stakeholders and the liberation movement in the development of future education policies made it difficult for the new state led by the ANC to ignore the role of stakeholders. There are different perspectives to explain the state-stakeholder partnership. Some attribute it to the weakness of the state in terms of lack of capacity to develop new policies, others to the fact that stakeholders had made themselves indispensable as the new state had to rely on them, along with some civil society organizations, in the recruitment of the new bureaucracy.

The book also indicates that owing to the complexity of state formation and governance, there was no direct relationship between policy research developed in the run-up to the 1994 elections and the policies adopted by the new government. Formal policies that were developed can be explained in terms of the governmentalization of policy whereby party political interests had to be transformed into government policies. This process entailed shifts and compromises, with toning down of the radical content in some of them. The mediation took the form of establishment by the state of new institutions, structures, institutional practices and a new bureaucracy. It occurred in the context of the new Interim Constitution that was the supreme law of the country, and the macro-economic policies (RDP and GEAR) that informed the government policies at different times. These conditions of governance were new to everyone and no individual or organization had anticipated them. There was thus a policy vacuum that required the mobilization of available expertise to meet the new challenges. As a result the period under which the new higher education policy was developed was one of learning for all those who were involved. This included commissioners, stakeholders and the new bureaucracy and legislators who had to learn new ways of developing and interpreting policy on the basis of the new Constitution, making sure they adapted to the changing macro-economic policy framework of government. The filling of this policy vacuum entailed reliance on combined strengths of the old and new bureaucracy, international consultants and the strategic management teams (SMTs).

Contrary to the new Constitution, which was clear in providing guidelines for governance at macro-level, the macro-economic framework of the new government went through a process of change from the RDP to GEAR within the first three years of the new government's coming to power. This posed a dilemma for policy development, as policies developed under the RDP framework had to be renegotiated to be in line with the neoliberal GEAR policy framework. This process did not just involve changing policy content; it also entailed a new way of thinking about policy, and a reorientation of the values and principles that should inform policy-making. Given the robust way in which the GEAR policy was introduced, in that it was not subjected to the consultative process that had characterized the development of the RDP and the new Constitution, but rather was introduced in top-down fashion and as non-negotiable, it became difficult for policy-makers and stakeholders to interact with it. As a result, policies developed within this framework became a source of contestation between stakeholder organizations and the government as the former continued to make policy inputs on the basis of the RDP and government made its policies on the basis of the GEAR policy.

This shift in the macro-economic policy of government had an impact on the transformation agenda that had informed higher education policy development in the run-up to the 1994 elections. The policy framework of the RDP assumed extra resources would be made available to address transformation and redress needs in the higher education system. Given the gross inequalities within the system, the RDP framework had further assumed a leading role would be played by the state, and, in the context of education, that the Minister of Education would be a key agent in leading transformation. However, with the GEAR policy coming into the picture, the new macro-economic framework introduced a cut in state expenditure, making no extra resources available for the state. This was accompanied by the introduction of the Medium Term Expenditure Framework which gave the Ministry of Finance a key role in determining which kind of policies could be passed by government departments. Unlike the 1990–1994 period, where policy positions which were adopted within the mass democratic movement were subjected to intense negotiation, the new milieu saw a less flexible system in negotiating policy options introduced by the Ministry of Finance. It sat in policy development forums of different government departments and issued directives to the effect that no policies that assumed availability of new resources should be approved. The net effect of this approach was that in higher education the transformation needs that were identified in the period 1990–1994 and the NCHE were sacrificed at the altar of the neo-liberal GEAR policy. The higher education institutions, through the cutting of government subsidies and contribution to the National Student Financial Aid Scheme (NSFAS), felt the immediate effect of this policy. This contributed to a situation where transition to democracy took place under severe constraints of lack of resources, and where economic power was removed from line ministries and was centralized under the Ministry of Finance. While the Minister of Education was sympathetic to the plight of higher education institutions, he was also constrained by the policies of his own government.

The new state tried to overcome some of its weaknesses by conferring more powers to the Minister of Education, the Higher Education Branch and the Institutional Councils in the Higher Education Act to act as agents of transformation. However, these measures, noble as they might have been for the proponents of a strong state, were ineffective since the powers of the Minister of Education to address imperatives of redress in higher education were constrained by his lack of decision-making power over the amount of resources that would be made available for education in general and higher education in particular. These powers also had the potential of causing the Minister of Education to interfere with the autonomy of institutions. This possibility has caused tension in the debates of governance of higher education in terms of how to empower the state to spearhead transformation of higher education without interfering with the autonomy of institutions.

This book has further reviewed South Africa's transition to democracy and has highlighted its similarities and differences with transitions elsewhere. It has dismissed the argument of the uniqueness of South Africa's experience while highlighting those features which were indeed distinctive. The relevance of these constraints to education was also explored in this study, notably (a) the constraints put on the new government in terms of appointing new people in line with the "sunset clause"; and (b) the continued existence of old departments, the secured positions of the old bureaucracy, the continued use of the laws until they were repealed and replaced by new laws. These conditions laid the seeds for resistance against and possible undermining of the new government's transformation agenda. (c) The abandonment of the

Macro-economic Research Group (MERG) and the RDP policy frameworks, which accorded the new state a central role in the reconstruction and development of the country, and the adoption of the neo-liberal policy of GEAR, accorded a central role for the market in economic development and reconstruction of the country.

This book has not only been about the impact of macro-economic policies and the new Constitution on the development of policies; it has also been about analyzing the processes that accompanied the development of higher education policy in terms of approaches used, operational principles informing the process, actors involved, and types of documents produced and their meaning and significance. It has shown that despite the process being conceptualized as participatory, consultative, and representative of stakeholder inputs, this framework led to some confusion between stakeholders and policy makers. The confusion arose out of a lack of clarity in the approaches that informed participation and consultation with stakeholders. While policy-makers operated on the basis of "after-consultation," stakeholders operated on the basis of "in-consultation." These un-clarified concepts led the policy process to be characterized by contestations, protests, and threats of withdrawal from participation by stakeholders in the various stages of the process. Based on the way it unfolded, it could be concluded that the after-consultation approach used by policy makers was in line with government's move towards centralization of power as it gradually took control of the key organs of the state. On the other hand, the "in-consultation" approach assumed by stakeholders is in line with what could be regarded as a populist approach to policy-making, where the voices of constituencies and decision-makers carry the same weight.

However, as the ANC gained experience in government, it started redefining the notions of governance, transformation and locus of power. No longer were structures and institutions that had been perceived as targets for take-over by the people (pro-democracy forces) seen that way, but since there was a legitimate government in place, these were to be used as instruments of governance by the new state. They were no longer to be alienated from the state, but were to be democratized through policy-making and legislation to serve the goals of the democratic government. This experience and the maturity which the new government gained from being in office, was in tandem with the experiences of stakeholders who saw government action as moving away from the mandate and goals that had informed the struggle against apartheid education. This perception was reinforced by the failure of government to address such basic needs within higher education as redress funds and transformation projects.

Policy-making in government is not only about these principles; there are features of government that outweigh their significance and application. As a result, their application was not as had been expected and perceived by stakeholders, but assumed the form of informing government, which had decision-making authority. The effect was that some stakeholders felt that government was not taking their participation and consultation seriously, leading to some disillusionment. This was compounded by policies that came to be adopted by government and which represented a departure from those policies that had been developed in the run-up to the 1994 elections. The non-statutory status of the institutional forums (former BTFs), the discontinuation of the availability of a redress fund, the rejection of the Higher Education Forum, are all illustrative of this fact.

The government was also faced with other challenges of nation building and a struggle for hegemony both locally and internationally, which, this study argues, had an impact on and characterized the policy-making process. This has been demonstrated by three key documents that came to frame its approach to higher education, namely: The Interim Constitution, which became supreme law under the GNU, the macro-economic framework of government as finding expression through GEAR and the NCHE's Framework for Transformation report. Despite some local dissent with regard to these documents, they have been internationally acclaimed.

The struggle for policy-making and hegemony in higher education has been characterized by tensions in the allocation of power between state organs and statutory and advisory bodies created under "co-operative governance." While line departments had lost some of their decision-making power in relation to policy-making to the Ministry of Finance, some of them, such as Education, tried to redeem themselves by centralizing power in the hands of the Minister and official organs of state power, such as the Department of Education's Higher Education Branch and Institutional Councils. Thus the Department of Finance, the Minister of Education, the Department of Education and Institutional Councils in higher education are the ones in command. Other statutory bodies such as the Council on Higher Education and Institutional Forums are relegated to an advisory role. In terms of its distinctiveness regarding the process of policy development, South Africa stands out in terms of having mobilized stakeholder participation and making policies an area for public scrutiny. However, the outcome of the process is the same as in some other developing countries. It has legitimized the traditional role of governments and nation-states, which is to govern. As with the experiences of other developing countries, the power of the new South African government to rule is strong in relation to internal and local stakeholders, but weak relative to global and market forces, as demonstrated by the macro-economic policies of government. The initial open and accessible polity that characterized policy-making in the run-up to the 1994 elections, and in the early days of the new government, has been replaced by features of impenetrable polity which have emanated from the struggle for hegemony and the experience the new government gained from being in office.

The ANC government has further become more assertive in providing leadership and spearheading transformation in higher education. While the policy and legislative process of the period 1994–1997 produced frameworks and policy structures for transformation, there was more need to provide details. Thus, the second term of government, 1999–2004, has been characterized by the development of policy details. One of the immediate actions taken by the new Minister of Education in 1999 was to request the CHE, a statutory body established by the Act, to advise him how to transform the institutional landscape of higher education. The CHE established a task team which carried out the work. The composition of the task team showed depth, maturity and growth in policy expertise and experience of South Africa in the new context. Unlike the earlier processes where wider consultations were held before the held task teams were appointed, this one became the prerogative of the CHE.

The second major initiative was the appointment of the National Working Group (NWG) following problems with the CHE report and adoption of the National Plan for Higher Education. The NWG was established to advise the Minister of Education on how to reconfigure the higher education system including the reduction of a number of higher education institutions. Again, the composition of the NWG showed the experience, capacity and sophistication that had been developed within government. Unlike in the past where government relied on outside consultants and experts outside of government, the NWG was composed of top senior government officials drawn from the Ministries of Finance, Education, the Presidency, and from business and labor. This team represented a phase where government relied less on external agencies but on knowledge of macro-economic realities, availability of resources and the role higher education was to play in development. As democracy became consolidated, the ANC is now in control of levers of power, and could rightly claim, "The people are governing."

Notes

NOTES TO CHAPTER ONE

1 Mandela, N. (1994). *Long walk to freedom: the autobiography of Nelson Mandela*. London: Little Brown, p. 747.
2 Adler, G. & Webster, E. (1995). Challenging transition theory: the labor movement, radical reform, and transition to democracy in South Africa. *Politics and Society*, vol. 23, no. 1, pp. 75-106, March.

NOTES TO CHAPTER TWO

1. The term Black will be used to refer to all the racial groups that were oppressed under apartheid, namely, Indian, Colored and African.
2. Ashley, M.J. (1989). *Ideologies and schooling in South Africa*. Rondebosch: South African Teachers' Association, p. 7.
3. Ibid.
4. Ibid.
5. Enslin, P. (1984). The role of fundamental pedagogics in the formulation of policy in South Africa. In Kallaway, P. (ed.). *Apartheid and education: the education of black South Africans*. Braamfontein: Ravan Press in association with the Education Policy Unit and Centre for African Studies, University of Cape Town, p. 140.
6. Eiselen, W.M.M. (1951). *Report of the commission on native education*. Pretoria: Government Printer, p. 181.
7. Verwoerd, H.F. Speech to Senate, 7 June 1954, in Kallaway, P. (ed.). *Apartheid and education: the education of black South Africans*. Braamfontein: Ravan Press in association with the Education Policy Unit and Centre for African Studies, University of Cape Town, p. 173. 175.
8. Mandela, N. (1994). *Long walk to freedom: the autobiography of Nelson Mandela*. London: Little, Brown, p. 195.
9. Eiselen, op. cit.
10. Eiselen Report, quoted from Christie, P. & Collins, C. (1984). *Bantu education: apartheid ideology and labour reproduction*. In Kallaway, P. (ed.). p. 175
11. Badat, S. (2002). *Black student politics: higher education and apartheid from SASO to SANSCO, 1968–1990*. London: RoutledgeFalmer, p. 193.

12. Christie & Collins, op. cit., p. 173.
13. Nkomo, M.O. (1984). *Student culture and activism in black South African universities: the roots of resistance.* Westport, CN: Greenwood Press, p. 59.
14. Quoted from Bhana, S. (1977). The racial factor in Indian university education. In Van der Merwe, H. & Welsh, D. (eds). *The future of the university in Southern Africa.* Cape Town: David Philip, p. 217.
15. South Africa. Parliament. House of Assembly. (1910-). *Debates of the House of Assembly (Hansard).* vol. 97, p. 2066, pp. 2075–2076, 1958; vol. 99, pp.1535–1540, 1959; vol. 100, pp. 3169–3173, p. 3186, pp. 3503–3514.
16. Bhana, op. cit., p. 217.
17. Nkomo, op. cit., p. 57.
18. Quoted in Nkomo, op. cit., p. 56.
19. SAIRR Survey, 1960, quoted in Nkomo, op. cit., p. 69.
20. Meyer, L.E. Oppression or opportunity? Inside the black universities of South Africa. *Journal of Negro Education,* vol. 45, no. 4, pp. 365–382, Fall.
21. Kgware, W.M. (1977). The role of black universities in South Africa. In Van der Merwe, H.W. & Welsh, D. (eds). *The future of the university in Southern Africa.* Cape Town: David Philip, p. 227.
22. Nkomo, op. cit., p. 66.
23. Ashley, op. cit., p. 15.
24. National Commission on Higher Education (South Africa). (1996). *National Commission on Higher Education report: a framework for transformation.* Pretoria: NCHE, p. 42.
25. Ibid.
26. Ibid.
27. Gottschalk, K. (1971). Race and economics in South Africa. *Ufahamu: Journal of the African Activists Association,* vol. 1, no. 2, pp. 6–12.
28. Nkomo, op. cit., p. 4.
29. Ibid., p. 75.
30. Cloete et. al. (1994) *Commissions: A brief overview,* Higher Education Task Team, Centre for Education and Policy Development, Braamfontein, p. 2.
31. Ashforth, A. (1990). *The politics of official discourse in twentieth-century South Africa.* Oxford: Clarendon Press, pp. 2–3.
32. Nkomo, op. cit., p. 90.
33. Ibid., p. 94.
34. Badat, op. cit., p. 86.
35. Nkondo, G.M. (ed.). (1976). *Turfloop testimony: the dilemma of a black university in South Africa.* Johannesburg: Ravan Press [for the Black Academic Staff Association of the University of the North], pp. 5–6.
36. Badat, op. cit., p.175.
37. Ibid., p. 180.
38. Cloete, et. al. (eds), (2002), *Transformation in higher education: global pressures and local relations in South Africa,* Lansdowne, Juta. pp. 93–94
39. Kallaway, P. (ed.). (1984). *Apartheid and education: the education of black South Africans.* Johannesburg: Ravan Press in association with the Education Policy Unit and Centre for African Studies, University of Cape Town, p. 3.

40. Friedman, S. (1995). *Every navigator needs a map: the case for independent policy research in South Africa.* Johannesburg: Centre for Policy Studies, p. 3.
41. Ibid., p. 4.
42. Essop, A. (ed.). (1992). *Back to learning: the National Education Conference 1992. Conclusions from the National Education Conference, held in Broederstroom, 6–8 March 1992.* Johannesburg: Ravan Press, p. 7.
43. For more information see: Muller, J. (1987). People's Education and the National Education Crisis Committee. *South African Review,* 4, Johannesburg: Ravan Press ; Mashamba, G. (1990) *People's Education for People's Power,* Johannesburg, Education Policy Unit, University of the Witwatersrand, Johannesburg. 7;
44. Wolpe, H. (1991). Some theses on people's education. In *Perspectives in Education,* vol. 12, no.2, p. 77.
45. Ibid., pp. 79–80.

NOTES TO CHAPTER THREE

1. African National Congress. (1985). Selected writings on the Freedom Charter, 1955-1985: a SECHABA commemorative publication. London: ANC.
2. Badat, S. (1995). Educational politics in the transition period. Comparative Education, vol. 3, no. 2, p. 151.
3. Ibid.
4. National Education Policy Investigation (Research Group). (1993). The framework report and final report summaries: a project of the National Education Coordinating Committee/the National Education Policy Investigation. NEPI, a project of the NECC. Cape Town: Oxford University Press: NECC, p. 3.
5. Ibid.
6. Singh, M. (1992). Transformation Time! Transformation: Critical Perspectives on Southern Africa, no. 17, pp. 56-57.
7. Ibid.
8. Chisholm, L. (1992). Policy and critique in South African educational research. Transformation: Critical Perspectives on Southern Africa, nos 18/19, p. 156.
9. Ibid., p. 157.
10. Chetty, D. R. (1993). Educational policy proposals in the interregnum. Johannesburg: Educational Policy Unit, University of the Witwatersrand, p. 6.
11. Ibid., pp. 5-6.
12. National Education Policy Investigation (Research Group), op. cit., p. 10.
13. Nzimande, B. (1992). The national education policy initiative. Transformation: Critical Perspectives on Southern Africa, nos 18/19, pp. 161-163.
14. Singh, M. (1992). Intellectuals and the politics of policy research. Transformation: Critical Perspectives on Southern Africa, nos 18/19, p. 69.

15. Badat, S. (1991). Democratising education policy research and social transformation. In Unterhalter, E., Wolpe, H. & Botha, T. (eds). Education in a future South Africa: policy issues for transformation. London: Heinemann.

16. Nzimande, op. cit., p. 162.

17. Interview with Dr N. Cloete, former general secretary of UDUSA and former research director of the NCHE, 23 February 2000, Pretoria.

18. Interview with Professor M. Singh, former president of UDUSA, 3 March 2000, Pretoria.

19. See Appendix 2, National Education Policy Investigation (Research Group), op. cit., p. 60.

20. Appendix 1, Minutes of UDUSA National PSE Policy Forum, in Bunting, I. (ed.). (1994). Reconstructing higher education in South Africa: selected papers. Braamfontein: Union of Democratic University Staff Associations.

21. Interview with Dr N. Cloete, 20 October 1998, Pretoria.

22. Interview with Mr David Makhura, former President of SASCO, 22 July 1998, Johannesburg.

23. Interview with Ms Stephanie Allais, former SASCO policy coordinator, 27 August 1998, Johannesburg.

24. Jansen, J.D. (2000). Framing education policy after apartheid: on the politics of non-reform in South Africa education, 1990-2000, Johannesburg, Centre for Development and Enterprise. Unpublished paper, p. 10.

25. Jansen J.D. (2001). The race for educational policy after apartheid. In Jansen, J.D. & Sayed, Y. Implementing educational policies: the South African experience. Cape Town: University of Cape Town Press, p. 12.

26. Ibid., p. 11.

27. Jansen J.D. (2000), op. cit., pp. 9-10.

28. South Africa. Department of National Education. (1992). Education renewal strategy: management solutions for education in South Africa. Pretoria: Department of National Education, pp. 16-17.

29. University and Technikons Advisory Council (South Africa), (1984/5). Committee of Technikon Principals. (1994). Chairman's report, Pretoria p. 4.

30. Interview with Professor B. Figaji, former NCHE Commissioner and current member of the CTP, 8 September 2000, Johannesburg.

31. Interview with Professor B. Gourley, Vice-Chancellor of the University of Natal, 11 July 2000, Durban.

32. Interview with Dr N.C. Manganyi, former Director General of the Department of Education and former Vice-Chancellor of the University of the North, 6 September 2000, Pretoria.

33. Interview with Professor J. Reddy, former Vice-Chancellor of the University of Durban-Westville, 13 November 2000, Johannesburg.

34. Forum of Historically Disadvantaged Tertiary Institutions (September 1995) Submission to the NCHE, Pretoria, p. 1.

35. Greenstein, R. (1995). Education policy discourse and the new South Africa. Perspectives in Education, vol. 16, no.1, p. 202.

36. Chisholm, op. cit., p. 157.

37. Morris, M. (1993). Methodological problems in tackling micro and macro socio-economic issues in the transition to democracy in South Africa. Paper

prepared for Conference on Methodological Challenges in and for the Human Sciences, Slovak Academy of Sciences, Bratislava, Slovakia, April, p. 13.

38. Chetty, op.cit., p. 6.
39. For details see National Education Policy Investigation (Research Group), op. cit., pp. 10-11; African National Congress. (1994). A policy framework for education and training. Braamfontein: ANC, pp. 3-4; South Africa. (1995). Education and training in a democratic South Africa: first steps to develop a new system. Pretoria: Ministry of Education, pp. 21-22.
40. National Education Policy Investigation (Research Group), op. cit., p. 124.
41. Interview with Professor M. Singh, op. cit.
42. National Education Policy Investigation (Research Group), op. cit., pp. 6-7.
43. It should be noted that NEPI used the nomenclature Post-Secondary Education (PSE) for higher education. The nomenclature higher education is used for the NEPI section that deals with PSE for consistency purposes in this document.
44. National Education Policy Investigation (Research Group), op. cit., pp. 208-209.
45. Interview with Professor M. Singh, op. cit.
46. Ibid.
47. National Education Policy Investigation (Research Group), op. cit., p. 216.
48. Ibid., p. 112.
49. Ibid., p. 113.
50. Ibid.
51. National Education Policy Investigation (Research Group), op. cit., p. 58.
52. Wolpe, H. & Sehoole, T. (1995). Higher education financing within the context of restructuring of higher education. Paper presented at the Higher Education Funding Conference, Eskom Centre, Midrand, p. 7.
53. See Jansen, J.D. (2001), op. cit., p. 18.
54. For details, see Manganyi, N.C. (2001). Public policy and the transformation of education in South Africa. In Jansen, J.D. & Sayed, Y. Implementing educational policies: the South African experience. Cape Town: University of Cape Town Press, p. 33.

NOTES TO CHAPTER FOUR

1. Saul, J.S. (1997). Liberal democracy vs. popular democracy in Southern Africa. *Review of African Political Economy,* vol. 24, no. 72, p. 219, June.
2. Ibid.
3. Shivji, I. quoted in Saul, ibid., p. 229.
4. Barber, B. quoted in Saul, ibid., pp. 230–231.
5. Saul, op. cit., p.231.
6. Adler, G. & Webster, E. (1995). Challenging transition theory: the labor movement, radical reform, and transition to democracy in South Africa. *Politics and Society,* vol. 23, no 1, p. 84, March.
7. Przeworski, A. (1991). *Democracy and the market: political and economic reforms in Eastern Europe and Latin America.* Cambridge: Cambridge University Press, pp. 66–67.

8. Ibid., p. 68.
9. Ibid., p. 85.
10. Adler & Webster, op. cit., p. 85.
11. Ibid., p. 85.
12. Ibid., p. 98.
13. Ginsburg, D., Webster, E., *et al.* (1995). *Taking democracy seriously: worker expectation and parliamentary democracy in South Africa.* Durban: Indicator Press, p. 3.
14. Ibid., p. 76.
15. See South Africa. (1993). *Constitution of the Republic of South Africa, Act 200 of 1993: as amended by Acts 2, 3, 13, 14, 24 and 29 of 1994.* Cape Town: Government Printer, p. 24.
16. Freund, B. & Padayachee, V. (1998). Post-apartheid South Africa: the key patterns emerge. *Economic and Political Weekly,* vol. 33, no. 20, p. 1174, May 16.
17. Adler & Webster, op. cit., p. 92.
18. See South Africa, op. cit., p. 106.
19. Freud & Padayachee, op. cit., pp. 1173–1174.
20. Interview with Professor N. C. Manganyi, 6 September 2000, Pretoria.
21. Habib, A. (1995). The transition to democracy in South Africa: developing a dynamic model. *Transformation: Critical Perspectives on Southern Africa,* no. 27, p. 51.
22. Ibid., pp. 52–53.
23. Interview with Mr. T. Mseleku, Director-General of Education, 30 June 2000, Pretoria.
24. South Africa, op. cit., p. 150.
25. Interview with Dr N.C. Manganyi, 6 September 2000, Pretoria.
26. Ibid.
27. South Africa, op. cit., p. 162.
28. Ibid.
29. Comment by Joel Samoff in which he drew some parallels between South Africa's transition and that of Zimbabwe during my paper presentation at the Annual Conference of the Comparative and International Education Society, Washington, DC, March 2001.
30. Interview with Ms Mary Metcalfe, former Member of Executive Council for Education in the Gauteng Province, 14 November 2000, Johannesburg.
31. South Africa, op. cit., p.166.
32. National Education Policy Investigation (Research Group). (1992). *Post-secondary education: report of the NEPI post-secondary education research group.* Cape Town: Oxford University Press: NECC, p. 31.
33. South Africa, op. cit., section 47.
34. Castells, M. (2001). The new global economy. In Muller, J., Cloete, N. & Badat, S. (eds). *Challenges of globalisation: South African debates with Manuel Castells.* Cape Town: Maskew Miller Longman, p. 1.
35. Ibid., pp. 1–2.
36. Friedman, T. (1999). *The lexus and the olive tree.* London: HarperCollins, p. 151.

37. Adelzadeh, A. (1996). From the RDP to GEAR: the gradual embracing of neo-liberalism in economic policy. *Transformation: Critical Perspectives on Southern* Africa, no. 31, pp. 66–95.

38. Marais, H. (1998). *South Africa: limits to change.* Cape Town: University of Cape Town Press, p. 147.

39. Freund & Padayachee, op. cit., pp. 1174–1175.

40. University of the Western Cape. Macroeconomic Research Group. (1993). *Making democracy work: a framework for macroeconomic policy in South Africa: a report to members of the Democratic Movement of the Western Cape.* Bellville: Centre For Development Studies, p. 265.

41. Marais, op. cit., p. 159.

42. University of the Western Cape. Macroeconomic Research Group, op. cit., p.163.

43. Ibid., p. 281.

44. Marais, op. cit., p. 160.

45. Rapoo, T. (1996). *Making the means justify the ends? The theory and practice of the RDP.* Johannesburg: Centre for Policy Studies.

46. African National Congress. (1994). *The reconstruction and development programme: a policy framework.* Johannesburg: ANC: Umanyano Publications, p. 7.

47. Adelzadeh, A. & Padayachee, V. (1994). The RDP White Paper: reconstruction of a development vision. *Transformation: Critical Perspectives on Southern Africa,* no. 25, p.1.

48. Freund & Padayachee, op. cit., p. 1175.

49. Ibid.

50. Ibid.

51. Marais, op. cit., p.158.

52. Adelzadeh, op. cit., pp. 72–73.

53. Interviews with Dr T. Coombe, former Deputy Director-General in the Department of Education, 15 and 16 May 2000, Pretoria.

54. Ibid.

55. Interview with Dr P. Pillay, former Director of Development Planning in the President"s Office, 6 November 2000, Randburg.

56. Marais, op. cit., p. 178.

57. Carnoy, M. (2001). The role of the state in the new global economy. In Muller, J., Cloete, N. & Badat, S. (eds). *Challenges to globalisation: South African debates with Manuel Cassells.* Cape Town: Maskew Miller Longman, p. 26.

58. Block, F. (1986). The political choice and the multiple "logics" of capital. *Theory and Society,* vol. 15, nos 1/2, pp. 175–192.

59. McMichael, P. (1996). Globalization: myths and realities. *Rural Sociology,* vol. 61, no. 1, pp. 25–55.

60. Atasoy, Y. & Carroll, W.K. (2003) Global shaping and its alternatives. Bloomfield, CN: Kumarian Press, p. 5.

61. Ibid., p. 28.

62. See National Commission on Higher Education (South Africa). (1996). *National Commission on Higher Education report: a framework for trans-*

formation. Pretoria: NCHE, p. 1; South Africa. Department of Education. (1997). *Education White Paper 3: a programme for the transformation of higher education*. Pretoria: Department of Education, p. 9. See also Kraak, A. (2000). *Changing modes: new knowledge production and its implications for higher education in South Africa*. Pretoria: HSRC.

63. Interview with Dr P. Nevhutalo, former UDUSA general secretary and present director at the National Research Foundation, 17 November 2000, Pretoria.
64. South Africa. Department of Education, op. cit., pp. 19–20.
65. Ibid., p.19.
66. See Committee of University Principals' memorandum, of a meeting with the Minister of Education scheduled for 28 January 1997, Pretoria, pp. 1–2.
67. Ibid., p. 2.
68. See Committee of University Principals' facsimile to the Deputy President with respect to the cabinet meeting scheduled for 5 February 1997, Pretoria.
69. Interview with Professor I. Mosala, former Head of Higher Education, Department of Education, 1 September 2000, Johannesburg.
70. National Commission on Higher Education (South Africa), op. cit., p.241.
71. Interview with Mr T. Mseleku, op. cit.
72. Ibid.
73. Ibid.
74. Samoff J. & Carrol, B. (2004). Conditions, coalitions, and influence: the World Bank and higher education in Africa. Paper presented at the Annual Conference of the Comparative and International Education Society, Salt Lake City, 8–12 March, pp. 51–52.
75. Ibid.
76. Interview with Mr T. Mseleku, op. cit.

NOTES TO CHAPTER FIVE

1. See South Africa. (1993). *Constitution of the Republic of South Africa, Act 200 of 1993: as amended by Acts 2, 3, 13, 14, 24 and 29 of 1994*. Cape Town: Government Printer. Schedule 6, p. 220.
2. Interview with Mr R. du Preez, 21 April 2000, Pretoria.
3. Archer, M.S. (1979). *Social origins of educational systems*. London: Sage, p. 238.
4. Weber, M. (1947). *The theory of social and economic organization*, translated by A.M. Henderson and Talcott Parsons; edited with an introduction by Talcott Parsons. Glencoe, IL: Free Press.
5. For an elaboration of this see South Africa. Department of Education. (1953). *The Bantu Education Act, Act 47 of 1953, as amended by the Bantu education amendment acts*. Pretoria: Government Printer: Department of Bantu Education. Also, South Africa. (1964). *Bantu Special Education Act 24 of 1964*. Cape Town: Government Printer.
6. See South Africa, op.cit., p. 102.
7. Interview with Mr R. du Preez, op. cit.

8. Manganyi, N.C. (2001). Public policy and the transformation of education in South Africa. In Jansen, J.D. & Sayed, Y. (2001). *Implementing educational policies: the South African experience.* Cape Town: University of Cape Town Press, p.33.

9. Interview with Mr R. du Preez, op. cit.

10. Burns, T. & Stalker, G.M. (1961). *The management of innovation.* London: Tavistock.

11. Interview with Ms M. Metcalfe, 14 November 2000, Johannesburg.

12. Interview with Professor I. Mosala, 1 September 2000, Johannesburg.

13. Ibid.

14. Interviews with Dr T. Coombe, 15 and 16 May 2000, Pretoria.

15. Ibid.

16. For details of the form of resistance, see Moja, T. & Hayward, F. (2000). Higher education policy development in contemporary South Africa. *Higher Education Policy,* vol. 13, no. 4, pp. 335–359.

17. Interview with Mr T. Mseleku, 2 August 2000, Pretoria.

18. Ibid.

19. Interview with Dr. I. Rensburg, Deputy Director-General in the Department of Education, 9 March 2000, Pretoria.

20. Interviews with Dr T. Coombe, op. cit.

21. Interview with Mr T. Mseleku, op.cit.

22. Interview with Professor M. Morris, 10 July 2001, Durban.

23. Interview with Professor I. Mosala, op. cit.

24. Interview with Professor N. Badsha, 26 July 2000, Pretoria.

25. Interview with Ms M. Metcalfe, op. cit.

26. Interview with Mr T. Mseleku, op. cit.

27. Ibid.

28. Interview with Professor I. Mosala, op. cit.

29. Interview with Mr T. Mseleku, op.cit.

30. Ibid.

31. Interview with Mr H. Davies, former chief education specialist in the DNE and now consultant to the Department of Education, 17 November 2000, Pretoria.

32. Interview with Professor I. Mosala, op. cit.

33. Ibid.

34. Interview with Mr T. Mseleku, op. cit.

35. Blau, P. (1956). *Bureaucracy in modern society.* New York: Random House.

NOTES TO CHAPTER SIX

1. African National Congress. (1994). *A framework for education and training.* Braamfontein: ANC, p. 2.

2. Interview with Dr B. Nzimande, 10 March 2000, Johannesburg.

3. Interview with Professor N.C. Manganyi, 13 October 1999, Pretoria.

4. Interim Strategic Management Teams were teams formed around new Ministries to provide capacity and advise the new Ministers immediately after the new government took office, while waiting for new positions to be

advertised and filled by new incumbents according to the public service commission regulations.

5. South Africa. (1994). Draft White Paper on education and training. *Government Gazette,* vol. 351, no.15974, p. 19.

6. The Van Wyk de Vries Commission focused on universities only.

7. South Africa, op. cit., p. 19.

8. Interview with Dr D. van Rensburg, former member of the nominees committee and present principal of Technikon Pretoria, 6 June 2000, Pretoria. Following the mergers that were announced in 2003 Technikon Pretoria is now Tshwane University of Technology, and Prof. R.L. Ngcobo is Principal and Vice-Chancellor.

9. See Terms of Reference of the President of the Republic of South Africa to the National Commission on Higher Education. (1995). *Government Gazette,* vol. 356, no. 5640, 3 February.

10. Ibid., p. 1.

11. Interview with Professor N. Badsha, 13 November 1998, Pretoria.

12. Interview with Dr T. Moja, former executive director of the NCHE, and advisor to the Minister of Education, 25 November 1998, Pretoria.

13. Interview with Dr D.van Rensburg, op. cit.

14. See letter of signatories in the final NCHE report. National Commission on Higher Education (South Africa). (1996). *National Commission on Higher Education report: a framework for transformation.* Pretoria: NCHE, p. i.

15. Interviews with Dr T. Coombe, 15 and 16 May 2000, Pretoria.

16. Centre for Education Policy Development. (1994). *Higher education implementation plan report.* Braamfontein: CEPD, p 5.

17. Interview with Dr T. Moja, op.cit.

18. See Dr T. Moja's interview with Pat Callan, the Director of the California Higher Education Policy Center in Washington, in Cloete, N. *et al.* (1994). *Commissions: a brief overview.* Higher Education Task Team, Centre for Education and Policy Development, Braamfontein, p. 23.

19. See African National Congress, op. cit., p. 112.

20. This category includes Africans, Coloureds and Indians.

21. See National Commission on Higher Education (South Africa), op.cit., pp. 405–414.

22. The Commissioner chooses to remain anonymous.

23. Interview with Professor B. Figaji, 8 September 2000, Johannesburg.

24. See Alternative views of commissioners, in National Commission on Higher Education, op. cit., pp. 317–318.

25. Interview with Ms R. Omar, 6 March 2000, Johannesburg.

26. Interview with Professor B. Figaji, op.cit.

27. Ibid.

28. Interview with Professor R. Ngcobo, former NCHE Commissioner, 2 August 2000, Pretoria.

29. Interview with Dr N. Cloete, 20 October 1998, Pretoria.

30. See National Commission on Higher Education, op. cit., p. 25.

31. Ibid.

32. Ibid. pp. 25–27.
33. Ibid., p. 3.
34. Ibid., p. 5.
35. Ibid., p.19.
36. Ibid., p. 20.
37. Interview with Dr R. Stumpf, former NCHE commissioner, 12 October 1999, Stellenbosch.
38. Ibid.
39. Interview with Professor N. C. Manganyi, 13 October 1999, Pretoria.
40. Ibid.
41. Interview with Dr N. Cloete, op. cit.
42. Ibid.
43. National Commission on Higher Education (South Africa). (1996). NCHE consultation and participation process. *National Commission on Higher Education Newsletter,* p.3.
44. Ibid., p. 4
45. *The Times Higher Education Supplement,* 24 May 1996.
46. Salzburg Seminar. (1996). *Educational reform in South Africa. Special report.* Middlebury, VT: Salzburg Seminar. A Salzburg Seminar special report on reform recommendations of the South African National Commission on Higher Education, p. 1
47. *Higher Education Review,* 10 May 1996.
48. Khosa, M.M. (1996). Searching for radical alternatives. *Higher Education Review,* p. 15, May 12. .
49. Seepe, S. (1998). *Black perspective(s) on tertiary institutional transformation.* Florida Hills: Vivlia, pp.26–27.
50. Seepe, S, (1998) op. cit., p. 34.
51. These views were expressed by Dr P. Nevhutalo and Professor G.M. Nkondo during the interviews.
52. Interview with Dr P. Nevhutalo, 17 November 2000, Pretoria.
53. These views were expressed during interviews with Dr I. Rensburg, Dr T. Moja and Professor I. Mosala.
54. Interview with Professor I. Mosala, 1 September 2000, Johannesburg.
55. Interview with Professor N. Badsha, op. cit.
56. SASCO (1996) False Concensus and a weak state—The twin evils of public evils policy-making and development governance: SASCO's critique of the NCHE's Discussion Document, paper prepared by SASCO for the NCHE's Consultative conference, 26–28 April 1996. p. 5.
57. Interview with Professor B. Bozzoli, chairperson of the task team that prepared the submission of the University of the Witwatersrand and also made a verbal presentation of the Report to Commission, 29 September 1998, Johannesburg.
58. Ibid.
59. Interview with Mr D. Makhura 22 July and 11 August 1998, Johannesburg.
60. Bengu, S. (1996) Address to the consultative meeting of stakeholders on the transformation of higher education, Pretoria.

NOTES TO CHAPTER SEVEN

1. Interview with Dr B. Nzimande, 10 March 2000, Johannesburg, and Professor N.C. Manganyi, 13 October 1999, Pretoria.
2. This was the first education policy document to be adopted by the new government in establishing a new framework for the transformation of apartheid education at all levels.
3. Interviews with Dr T. Coombe, 15 and 16 May 2000, Pretoria.
4. Ibid.
5. Interview with Mr T. Mseleku, 2 August 2000, Pretoria.
6. See Mathieson, S. (2001). The role of the ANC Education Study Group and the legislative and policy process. In Jansen, J.D. & Sayed, Y. (2001). *Implementing educational policies: the South African experience.* Cape Town: University of Cape Town Press, p. 50.
7. Interview with Mr T. Mseleku, op. cit.
8. See letter to stakeholders, the public and interested parties in South Africa. (1996). *Green Paper on higher education transformation.* Pretoria: Department of Education.
9. Interview with Professor I. Mosala, 1 September 2000, Johannesburg.
10. Interview with Professor B. Gourley, 11 July 2000, Durban.
11. Ibid.
12. Interviews with Dr T. Coombe, op. cit.
13. See South Africa. (1996), op.cit., Chapter Two.
14. Interview with Mr A. Essop, Chief Director in the Higher Education Branch and one of the authors of the Green Paper, 21 November 1998, Pretoria.
15. Moja, T. & Hayward, F.M. (2001). In Jansen, J.D. & Sayed, Y. *Implementing educational policies: the South African experience.* Cape Town: University of Cape Town Press, p. 118.
16. Interview with Ms N. Pandor, 19 November 1998, Johannesburg.
17. Interview with Dr B. Nzimande, op. cit.
18. Ibid.
19. Interview with Ms R. Omar, 13 October 2000, Johannesburg.
20. Interview with Dr B. Nzimande, op. cit.
21. Interview with Professor B. Figaji, 8 September 2000, Johannesburg.
22. Interview with Ms R. Omar, op. cit.
23. Interview with Dr B. Nzimande, op. cit.
24. National Commission on Higher Education (South Africa). (1996). *National Commission on Higher Education report: a framework for transformation.* Pretoria: NCHE, pp. 176–177.
25. Ibid., p. 177.
26. Ibid., p. 178.
27. Ibid., pp. 183–191.
28. South Africa. (1996), op. cit., pp. 37–38.
29. Ibid., p. 41.
30. Ibid.
31. Ibid.
32. Ibid., p. 45.

33. Ibid., p. 46.
34. Bunting, I. (1997). Higher education governance: proposal of the Green Paper on higher education transformation. Paper presented at the National Conference on the Higher Education Green Paper, Braamfontein, 14–16 February, p. 15.
35. Ibid., p. 16.
36. South Africa, op.cit., pp. 41–43.
37. Ibid., p. 50.
38. Ibid., p. 54.
39. Ibid., p. 56.
40. Ibid., pp. 39 and 46.
41. Bunting, op. cit., p. 17.
42. South Africa. Department of Education. (1997). *Education White Paper 3: a programme for the transformation of higher education.* Pretoria: Department of Education, p. 18.
43. Both the Minister of Education and the Director-General of Education were former principals of universities and former members of the Committee of University Principals (CUP).
44. Universities and Technikons Advisory Council (South Africa). Committee of University Principals. (Undated). Response to the draft White Paper on higher education, pp. 2–3.
45. Universities and Technikons Advisory Council (South Africa). Committee of Technikon Principals (1997). Comments on the draft White Paper on higher education, p. 9.
46. See South Africa. (1997). *Higher Education Act, 101 of 1997.* Cape Town: Government Printer, p. 14.
47. South Africa. (1997). *Higher Education Bill.* s.l.: s.n, p.10.
48. Ibid.
49. See South Africa. Parliament. National Assembly. (1997). First session, second parliament, 27–30 October 1997, *Debates of the National Assembly.* Cape Town: Government Printer, column 5562.
50. Ibid., column 5570.
51. Ibid., column 5571.
52. Ibid., columns 5585 and 5586.
53. See South Africa. (1996), op. cit., p. 41.
54. South Africa. Parliament. National Assembly, op. cit., column 5571.
55. Ibid., column 5549.
56. Moja, T. & Hayward, M. (2000). Higher education policy development in contemporary South Africa. *Higher Education Policy,* vol.13, no. 4, pp. 335–359.
57. South Africa. Parliament. National Assembly, op. cit., column 5576.
58. Potgietersrus school was ripped apart by racial tensions in 1997 when parents of white Afrikaans-speaking pupils forced black pupils out of the school and wanted to prevent them from attending. In this context language was used as a reason for excluding black pupils from this school.
59. South Africa. Parliament. National Assembly, op. cit., column 5584.
60. Ibid., column 5589.

61. Ibid.
62. See South Africa. (1997), op. cit., p. 24.
63. Interview with Mr T. Mseleku, op. cit.
64. Weiss, C. H. (1993). Exploring research utilization. Paper presented to the workshop organized by USAID for policy researchers in South Africa, Braamfontein, p. 37.

NOTES TO CHAPTER EIGHT

1. Interview with Ms R. Omar, 6 March 2000, Johannesburg.
2. Interview with Dr N. Cloete, 20 October1998, Pretoria.
3. The member preferred to remain anonymous.
4. Interview with Professor G. Hall, 14 November 2000, Johannesburg.
5. Interview with Professor J. Grobelaar, former chief director of CUP, 28 March, 2000, Auckland Park.
6. See University and Technikons Advisory Council (South Africa). Committee of University Principals. (Undated). Comment on the NCHE discussion document: a framework for transformation.
7. Interview with Mr B. Whyte, Registrar of the Committee of Technikon Principals, 23 August 2000, Pretoria.
8. Interview with Dr N. Cloete, op. cit.
9. Interview with Professor G. Hall, op. cit.
10. Interview with Professor. J. Reddy, 13 November 2000, Johannesburg.
11. Interview with Professor G. Hall, op. cit.
12. Interview with Professor J. Reddy, op. cit.
13. Interview with Professor N.C. Manganyi, 13 October 1999, Pretoria.
14. Ibid.
15. Interview with Professor J. Reddy, op. cit.
16. Interview with Professor G. Hall, op. cit.
17. Ibid.
18. Interview with Professor J. Reddy, op. cit.
19. Salzburg Seminar. (1996). *Educational reform in South Africa. Special report.* Middlebury, VT: Salzburg Seminar. A Salzburg Seminar special report on reform recommendations of the South African National Commission on Higher Education, p. 2.
20. Interview with Dr N. Cloete, op. cit.
21. Interview with Professor N. C. Manganyi, op. cit.
22. Interviews with Dr. T. Coombe, 15 and 16 May 2000, Pretoria.
23. Ibid.
24. Ibid.
25. Ibid.
26. Interview with Ms N. Mohamed, 9 December 1998, Johannesburg.
27. Interview with Ms R Omar, op. cit.
28. Interview with Professor J.D. Jansen, Dean of the Faculty of Education, University of Pretoria, 6 September 2000, Pretoria.
29. Ibid.
30. Ibid.
31. Interview with Professor J. Reddy, op. cit.

Bibliography

PRIMARY SOURCES

Government publications

South Africa. (1964). *Bantu Special Education Act, Act 24 of 1964. Act to provide for the establishment, control, management, maintenance and subsidization of special schools for the provision of special education for handicapped Bantu children.* . . . Cape Town: Government Printer.

———. (1993). *Constitution of the Republic of South Africa, Act 200 of 1993: as amended by Acts 2, 3, 13, 14, 24 and 29 of 1994.* Cape Town: Government Printer.

———. (1994). Draft White Paper on education and training. *Government Gazette,* vol. 351, no. 15974.

———. (1995). *Education and training in a democratic South Africa: first steps to develop a new system.* Pretoria: Ministry of Education.

———. (1996). *Constitution of the Republic of South Africa, Act 108 of 1996.* Pretoria: Government Printer.

———. (1996). *Green Paper on higher education transformation.* Pretoria: Department of Education.

———. (1997). *Higher Education Act, Act 101 of 1997.* Cape Town: Government Printer.

———. (1999). *Higher Education Amendment Act, Act 55 of 1999.* Cape Town: Government Printer.

———. (1997). *Higher Education Bill, 1997.* s.l.: s.n.

South Africa. Department of Bantu Education. (1953). *The Bantu Education Act, Act 47 of 1953 as amended by the Bantu education amendment acts.* Pretoria: Government Printer: Department of Bantu Education.

South Africa. Department of Education. (1997). *Education White Paper 3: a programme for the transformation of higher education.* Pretoria: Department of Education.

South Africa. Department of Education. Committee to Review the Organisation, Governance and Funding of Schools. (1995). *Report of the committee to review the organisation, governance and funding of schools.* Pretoria: Department of Education.

South Africa. Department of National Education. (1982). *Funding systems for universities.* Pretoria: Government Printer.
———. (1992). *Education renewal strategy: management solutions for education in South Africa.* Pretoria: Department of National Education.
South Africa. Parliament. House of Assembly. (1910-). *Debates of the House of Assembly (Hansard).* Cape Town: Government Printer.
South Africa. Parliament. National Assembly. (1996). Third session, first parliament, 8–10 October 1996. *Debates of the National Assembly.* Cape Town: Government Printer.
———. (1997). First session, second parliament, 17–19 June 1997. *Debates of the National Assembly.* Cape Town: Government Printer.
———. (1997). First session, second parliament, 27–30 October 1997. *Debates of the National Assembly.* Cape Town: Government Printer.
Terms of reference of the President of the Republic of South Africa to the National Commission on Higher Education. (1995). *Government Gazette,* vol. 356, no. 5640, 3 February.

Other reports and documents

African National Congress. (1994). *A policy framework for education and training.* Braamfontein: ANC.
———. (1994). *The reconstruction and development programme: a policy framework.* Johannesburg: ANC: Umanyano Publications.
Centre for Education Policy Development. (1994). *Higher education implementation plan report.* Braamfontein: CEPD.
Eiselen, W.M.M. (1951). *Report of the commission on native education.* Pretoria: Government Printer.
Howie, S.J. (2001). *The third international mathematics and science study: report. (TIMMS-R). Executive summary.* Pretoria: Human Sciences Research Council.
National Commission on Higher Education (South Africa). (1996). *National Commission on Higher Education report: a framework for transformation.* Pretoria: NCHE.
———. (1996). NCHE consultation and participation process. *National Commission on Higher Education Newsletter.*
National Education and Training Forum. (1993). *Founding agreement.* s.l.:s.n.
National Education Policy Investigation (Research Group). 1992. *Post-secondary education: report of the NEPI post-secondary education research group.* Cape Town: Oxford University Press: NECC.
———. (1993). *The framework report and final report summaries: a project of the National Education Coordinating Committee/the National Education Policy Investigation. NEPI, a project of the NECC.* Cape Town: Oxford University Press: NECC.
Proceedings of the workshop of the HETT, 16 April 1994. In Centre for Education Policy Development. (1994). *Higher education implementation plan report.* Braamfontein: CEPD.
Universities and Technikons Advisory Council (South Africa). Committee of Technikon Principals. (1984/1985). *Annual report.* Pretoria: s.n.

———. (1997). Comments on the draft White Paper on higher education. May.

———. (Undated). Comments on the Green Paper on higher education.

Universities and Technikons Advisory Council (South Africa). Committee of University Principals. (Undated). Comments on the NCHE discussion document: a framework for transformation.

———. (Undated). Response to the draft White Paper on higher education.

———. (Undated). Response to the Green Paper on higher education transformation.

University of the Western Cape. Macroeconomic Research Group. (1993). *Making democracy work: a framework for macroeconomic policy in South Africa: a report to members of the Democratic Movement of the Western Cape.* Bellville: Centre for Development Studies.

Venter-Hildebrand, M. (ed.). (1996). *A framework for transformation of higher education in South Africa, 28–29 April 1996: edited transcript of issues discussed at a two-day NCHE national stakeholders meeting, held at the Eskom Conference Centre, Midrand.* Pretoria: NCHE.

SECONDARY SOURCES

Journal articles

/Adelzadeh, A. (1996). From the RDP to GEAR: the gradual embracing of neo-liberalism in economic policy. *Transformation: Critical Perspectives on Southern Africa,* no. 31, pp. 66–95.

√Adelzadeh, A. & Padayachee, V. (1994). The RDP White Paper: reconstruction of a development vision. *Transformation: Critical Perspectives on Southern Africa,* no. 25, pp. 1–18.

√ Adler, G. & Webster, E. (1995). Challenging transition theory: the labor movement, radical reform and transition to democracy in South Africa. *Politics and Society,* vol. 23, no. 1, pp. 75–106, March.

/ Badat, S. (1995). Educational policies in the transition period. *Comparative Education,* vol. 31, no. 2, pp. 141–159, June.

√Block, F. (1986). The political choice and the multiple 'logics' of capital. *Theory and Society,* vol. 15, nos.1/2, pp. 175–192.

Chisholm, L. (1992). Policy and critique in South African educational research. *Transformation: Critical Perspectives on Southern Africa,* nos. 18/19, pp.149–160.

√Freund, B. & Padayachee, V. (1998). Post-apartheid South Africa: the key patterns emerge. *Economic and Political Weekly,* vol.33, no. 20, pp., May 16.

Ginsburg, D. (1996). The democratization of South Africa: transition theory tested. *Transformation: Critical Perspectives on Southern Africa,* no. 29, pp.74–102.

Gottschalk, K. (1971). Race and economics in South Africa. *Ufahamu: Journal of the African Activists Association,* vol.1, no. 2, pp.6–12.

Greenstein, R. (1995). Education policy discourse and the new South Africa. *Perspectives in Education,* vol.16, no.1, pp.193–204.

Habib, A. (1995). The transition to democracy in South Africa: developing a dynamic model. *Transformation: Critical Perspectives on Southern Africa,* no. 27, pp. 50–73.

McMichael, P. (1996). Globalization: myths and realities. *Rural Sociology*, vol. 61, no.1, pp. 25–55.

Meyer, L.E. (1976). Oppression or opportunity? Inside the black universities of South Africa. *Journal of Negro Education*, vol. 45, no. 4, pp. 365–382, Fall.

Moja, T. & Hayward, M. (2000). Higher education policy development in contemporary South Africa. *Higher Education Policy*, vol.13, no. 4, pp. 335–359.

Moja, T., Muller, J. & Cloete, N. (1996). Towards new forms of regulation in higher education: the case of South Africa. *Higher Education*, vol. 32, no. 2, pp. 129–155.

Nzimande, B. (1992). The national education policy initiative. *Transformation: Critical Perspectives on Southern Africa*, nos. 18/19, pp.161–165.

Saul, J.S. (1997). Liberal democracy vs. popular democracy in Southern Africa. *Review of African Political Economy*, vol. 24, no. 72, pp. 219–236, June.

Singh, M. (1992). Transformation time! *Transformation: Critical Perspectives on Southern Africa*, no. 17, pp. 48–60.

———. (1992). Intellectuals and the politics of policy research. *Transformation: Critical Perspectives on Southern Africa*, nos.18/19, pp. 66–71.

Wolpe, H. (1991). Some theses on people's education. *Perspectives in Education*, vol. 12, no. 2, pp. 77–83, Winter.

Theses and dissertations

Cross, M. (1994). Culture and identity in South African education: 1880–1990. Unpublished PhD dissertation, Faculty of Education, University of the Witwatersrand, Johannesburg.

Hofmeyr, J.M. (1991). Policy change in South African education: the role of the public and private sectors in in-service teacher education. Unpublished PhD dissertation, Faculty of Education, University of the Witwatersrand, Johannesburg.

Conference papers, workshops, discussion papers and others

Bunting, I. (1997). Higher education governance: proposal of the Green Paper on higher education transformation. Paper presented at the National Conference on the Higher Education Green Paper, Braamfontein, 14–16 February.

Charles, H.J. (1997). Contextualisation. In Marais, H.C., Grobbelaar, J.W. & Potgieter, K.M. (eds). *Critical issues in South African higher education reform: UNESCO/SAUVCA workshop*. Pretoria: SAUVCA.

Chetty, D.R. (1993). Education policy proposals in the interregnum. Johannesburg: Education Policy Unit, University of the Witwatersrand.

Chisholm, L. (2000). C2005 review and the policy process. Paper presented at the 27th Annual Conference of the Kenton Education Association, University of Port Elizabeth, 26–27 October.

Cloete, N. *et al.* (1994). *Commissions: a brief overview*. Higher Education Task Team Report, Centre for Education and Policy Development, Braamfontein.

Friedman, S. & Reitzes, M. (1995). Democratic selections? Civil society and development in South Africa's new democracy. Johannesburg: Development Bank of Southern Africa. Development Paper 75.

Jansen, J.D. (2000). Rethinking education policy: symbols of change, signals of conflict. Paper presented to the HSRC Roundtable: An Education Policy Retrospective, 1990–2000. Analysing the Process of Policy Implementation and Reform, HSRC, Pretoria, 24–25 October.
———. (2000).
Mohammed, N. & Cloete, N. (1996). Transformation forums as revolutionary councils, midwives to democracy or forums for reconstruction and innovation. Joint research project: Union of Democratic University Staff Associations and Education Policy Unit, University of the Western Cape.
Morris, M. (1993). Methodological problems in tackling micro and macro socio-economic issues in the transition to democracy in South Africa. Paper prepared for Conference on Methodological Challenges in and for the Human Sciences, Slovak Academy of Sciences, Bratislava, Slovakia, April.
Salzburg Seminar. (1996). *Educational reform in South Africa. Special report.* Middlebury, VT: Salzburg Seminar. A Salzburg Seminar special report on reform recommendations of the South African National Commission on Higher Education.
Samoff, J. & Carrol, B. (2004). Conditions, coalitions, and influence: the World Bank and higher education in Africa. Paper presented at the Annual Conference of the Comparative and International Education Society, Salt Lake City, 8–12 March.
Van Vught, F.A. (1993). Policy models and policy instruments in higher education: the effects of governmental policy-making on the innovative behavior of higher education institutions. Centre for Higher Education Policy Studies, University of Twente, Netherlands.
Weiss, C.H. (1993). Exploring research utilization. Paper presented to the workshop organized by USAID for policy researchers in South Africa, Braamfontein, March.
Wolpe, H. (1993). Context, principles and issues in policy formulation for post secondary education. *PSE Policy Workshop Proceedings,* Cape Town, 3 July-1 August 1993.
Wolpe, H. & Sehoole, T. (1995). Higher education financing within the context of restructuring of higher education. Paper presented at the Higher Education Funding Conference, Eskom Centre, Midrand, 31 July- 1 August.

Books and chapters in books

African National Congress. (1995). *Selected writings on the Freedom Charter, 1955–1985: a SECHABA commemorative publication.* London: ANC.
Archer, M.S. (1979). *Social origins of educational systems.* London: Sage.
Ashforth, A. (1990). *The politics of official discourse in twentieth-century South Africa.* Oxford: Claredon Press.
Ashley, M.J. (1989). *Ideologies and schooling in South Africa.* Rondebosch: South African Teachers' Association.
Atasoy, Y. & Carroll, W.K. (eds). (2003). *Global shaping and its alternatives.* Bloomfield, CT: Kumarian Press.

Badat, S. (1991). Democratising education policy research and social transformation. In Unterhalter, E., Wolpe, H. & Botha, T. (eds). *Education in a future South Africa: policy issues for transformation*. London: Heinemann.

———. (2002). *Black student politics: higher education and apartheid from SASO to SANSCO: 1968–1990*. New York: RoutledgeFalmer.

Ball, S. (1994). Researching inside the state: issues in the interpretation of elite interviews. In Halpin, D. & Troyna, B. (eds). *Researching education policy: ethical and methodological issues*. London: Falmer Press.

Barber, B.R. (1995). *Jihad vs. McWorld*. New York: Times Books.

Bhana, S. (1977). The racial factor in Indian university education. In Van der Merwe, H.W. & Welsh, D. (eds). *The future of the university in Southern Africa*. Cape Town: David Philip.

Blau, P.M. (1956). *Bureaucracy in modern society*. New York: Random House.

Bunting, I. (ed.). (1994). *Reconstructing higher education in South Africa: selected papers*. Braamfontein: Union of Democratic University Staff Associations.

Carnoy, M. (2001). The role of the state in the new global economy. In Muller, J., Cloete, N. & Badat, S. (eds). *Challenges of globalisation: South African debates with Manuel Castells*. Cape Town: Maskew Miller Longman.

Castells, M. 2001. The new global economy. In Muller, J., Cloete, N. & Badat, S. (eds). *Challenges of globalisation: South African debates with Manuel Castells*. Cape Town: Maskew Miller Longman.

Christie, P. & Collins, C. (1984). Bantu education: apartheid ideology and labour reproduction. In Kallaway, P. (ed.). *Apartheid and education: the education of black South Africans*. Johannesburg: Ravan Press in association with the Education Policy Unit and Centre for African Studies, University of Cape Town.

Cloete, N. & Bunting, I. (2000). *Higher education transformation: assessing performance in South Africa*. Cape Town: CHET.

Cloete, N, et. al. (eds) (2002), *Transformation in higher education: global pressures and local relations in South Africa,* Lansdowne, Juta.

Cross, M. (ed.). (1999). *No easy road: transforming higher education in South Africa*. Cape Town: Maskew Miller Longman.

Du Toit, A. (1992). South Africa as another case of transition from authoritarian rule. In Slabbert, F. Van Zyl. *The quest for democracy: South Africa in transition*. London: Penguin.

Enslin, P. (1984). The role of fundamental pedagogics in the formulation of policy in South Africa. In Kallaway, P. (ed.). *Apartheid and education: the education of black South Africans*. Johannesburg: Ravan Press in association with the Education Policy Unit and Centre for African Studies, University of Cape Town, pp. 139–147.

Essop, A. (ed.). (1992). *Back to learning: the National Education Conference 1992. Conclusions from the National Education Conference, held in Broederstroom, 6–8 March 1992*. Braamfontein: Ravan Press.

Friedman, S. (1995). *Every navigator needs a map: the case for independent policy research in South Africa*. Johannesburg: Centre for Policy Studies.

Friedman, T. (1999). *The lexus and the olive tree*. London: HarperCollins.

Ginsburg, D., Webster, E. *et al.* (1995). *Taking democracy seriously: worker expectations and parliamentary democracy in South Africa.* Durban: Indicator Press.

Jansen, J.D. (2001). The race for educational policy after apartheid. In Jansen, J.D. & Sayed (eds), Y. *Implementing educational policies: the South African experience.* Cape Town: University of Cape Town Press.

Jansen, J.D. & Sayed, Y. (2001). *Implementing educational policies: the South African experience.* Cape Town: University of Cape Town Press.

Johnson-Hill, J. (1998). *Seeds of transformation: discerning the ethics of a new generation.* Pietermaritzburg: Cluster Publications.

Kallaway, P. (ed.). (1984). *Apartheid and education: the education of black South Africans.* Johannesburg: Ravan Press in association with the Education Policy Unit and Centre for African Studies, University of Cape Town.

Kgware, W.M. (1977). The role of black universities in South Africa. In Van der Merwe, H.W. & Welsh, D. (eds). *The future of the university in Southern Africa.* Cape Town: David Philip.

Kraak, A. (2000). *Changing modes: new knowledge production and its implication for higher education in South Africa.* Pretoria: HSRC.

Mandela, N. (1994). *Long walk to freedom: the autobiography of Nelson Mandela.* London: Little Brown.

Manganyi, N.C. (2001). Public policy and the transformation of education in South Africa. In Jansen, J.D. & Sayed, Y. (2001). *Implementing educational policies: the South African experience.* Cape Town: University of Cape Town Press.

Marais, H. (1998). *South Africa: limits to change: the political economy of transition.* Cape Town: University of Cape Town Press.

Mathieson, S. (2001). The role of the ANC Education Study Group and the legislative and policy process. In Jansen, J.D. & Sayed, Y. (2001). *Implementing educational policies: the South African experience.* Cape Town: University of Cape Town Press.

Muller, J., Cloete, N. & Badat, S. (eds). (2001). *Challenges of globalisation: South African debates with Manuel Castells.* Cape Town: Maskew Miller Longman.

Nkomo, M.O. (1984). *Student culture and activism in black South African universities: the roots of resistance.* Westport, CN: Greenwood Press.

Nkondo, G.M. (ed.). (1976). *Turfloop testimony: the dilemma of a black university in South Africa.* Johannesburg: Ravan Press [for the Black Academic Staff Association of the University of the North].

Przeworski, A. (1991). *Democracy and the market: political and economic reform in Eastern Europe and Latin America.* Cambridge: Cambridge University Press.

Rapoo, T. (1996). *Making the means justify the ends? The theory and practice of the RDP.* Johannesburg: Centre for Policy Studies.

Reimers, F. & McGinn, N. (1997). *Informed dialogue: using research to shape education policy around the world.* Westport, CN: Praeger.

Rein, M. (1976). *Social science and public policy.* Harmondsworth: Penguin.

Seepe, S. (ed.). (1998). *Black perspective(s) on tertiary educational transformation.* Florida Hills: Vivlia.

Unterhalter, E., Wolpe, H. & Botha, T. (eds). (1991). *Education in a future South Africa: policy issues for transformation.* London: Heinemann.

Van der Merwe, H.W. & Welsh, D. (eds). (1977). *The future of the university in Southern Africa.* Cape Town: David Philip.

Weber, M. (1947). *The theory of social and economic organization,* translated by A.M. Henderson and Talcott Parsons; edited with an introduction by Talcott Parsons. Glencoe, IL: Free Press.

Newspaper reports

Higher Education Review, 10 May 1996.

Khosa, M.M. (1996). Searching for radical alternatives. *Higher Education Review,* p. 15, 12 May.

The Times Higher Education Supplement, 24 May 1996.

INTERVIEWS

National Commission on Higher Education (NCHE)

Professor Jairam Reddy (Chairperson), 13 November 2000, Johannesburg.

Dr Tebogo Moja (Executive Director), 25 November 1998, Pretoria.

Dr Nico Cloete (Director of Research), 25 November 1998 and 23 February 2000, Pretoria.

Professor Brian Figaji (Commissioner), 8 September 2000, Johannesburg.

Mr Reggie Ngcobo (Commissioner), 2 August 2000, Pretoria.

Ms Rachmat Omar (Commissioner), 6 March 2000 and 13 October 2000, Johannesburg.

Professor Nasima Badsha (Commissioner), 13 November 1998 and 26 July 2000, Pretoria.

Professor Rolf Stumpf (Commissioner), 12 October 1999, Stellenbosch.

NCHE Task Team Members

Professor Ian Bunting, 11 October 1999, Cape Town.

Professor Graham Hall, 14 November 2000, Johannesburg.

Professor Michael Cross, 14 October 1998, Johannesburg.

Professor Pam Christie, 20 August 1998, Johannesburg.

Officials of the Department of Education (National)

Dr Trevor Coombe (former Deputy Director-General), 15 and 16 May 2000, Pretoria.

Mr Rolf du Preez (former Director-General), 21 April 2000, Pretoria.

Dr Ihron Rensburg (Deputy Director-General), 9 and 29 March 2000, Pretoria.

Dr N. Chabani Manganyi (former Director-General), 13 October 1999 and 6 September 2000, Pretoria.

Mr Thami Mseleku (Director-General), 30 June and 2 August 2000, Pretoria.

Mr Ahmed Essop (Chief Director of Education), 21 November 1998, Pretoria.

Mr Hugh Davies (former chief education specialist), 17 November 2000, Pretoria.

Advocate Silas Nawa (Legal Division of the Department of Education), 3 March 2000, Pretoria.

Professor Itumeleng Mosala (former Head of Higher Education), 1 September 2000, Johannesburg.

Statutory Bodies

Committee of University Principals (South African University Vice Chancellor's Association)

Professor Gessler M Nkondo (Vice-Chancellor of the University of Venda), 21 August 1998, Thoyandou.

Professor Colin Bundy (Vice-Chancellor of the University of the Witwatersrand), 29 September 1999, Johannesburg.

Professor Brenda Gourley (Vice-Chancellor of the University of Natal), 11 July 2000, Durban.

Professor J van Zyl (Vice-Chancellor of the University of Pretoria), 20 September 2000, Pretoria.

Dr Piyushi Kotecha (Chief Executive Officer of the South African University Chancellors' Association), 11 September 2000, Pretoria.

Professor Jos Grobelaar (former Chief Director of the Committee of University Principals), 28 March 2000, Auckland Park.

Professor Ephraim Mokgokong (former Vice-Chancellor of the Medical University of Southern Africa, 11 September 2000 (Pretoria).

Committee of Technikon Principals

Professor Brian Figaji (Vice-Chancellor of Peninsula Technikon), 8 September 2000, Johannesburg.

Professor George Lenyai (Vice-Chancellor of Technikon Northern Gauteng), 18 May 2000, Soshanguve.

Mr Brian Whyte (Registrar of the Committee of Technikon Principals), 23 August 2000, Pretoria.

Professor Attie Buitendacht (Vice-Chancellor of Technikon Southern Africa), 8 September 2000, Roodepoort.

Professor Denis van Rensburg (Vice-Chancellor of Technikon Pretoria), 6 June 2000, Pretoria.

Professor Itumeleng Mosala (Vice-Chancellor of Technikon Pretoria), 1 September 2000.

Professor Reggie Ngcobo (Deputy Vice-Chancellor of Technikon Pretoria), 2 August 2000.

South African Student Congress (SASCO)

Mr David Makhura (former Chairperson), 22 July and 11 August 1998, Johannesburg.

Ms Stephanie Allais (former Policy Coordinator), 27 August 1998, Johannesburg.

Mr Makhukhu Mampuru (former Policy Coordinator), 18 June 1998, Johannesburg.

Mr Chemist Khumalo (former member of SASCO), 20 June 1998, Johannesburg.

Mr James Maseko (former General Secretary of SANSCO which later became SASCO), 7 October 1998, Johannesburg.

Portfolio Committee on Education

Dr Blade Nzimande (former Chairperson of the Portfolio Committee), 10 March 2000, Johannesburg.

Ms Naledi Pandor (member of the Portfolio Committee on Education), 19 November 1998, Johannesburg.

Ms Jean Benjamin (member of the Portfolio Committee on Education), 11 October 1999, Cape Town.

Professor Selby Ripinga (Chairperson of the Portfolio Committee), 11 October 1999, Cape Town.

Union of Democratic University Staff Association (UDUSA)

Dr Nico Cloete (former General Secretary), 20 October 1998 and 23 February 2000, Pretoria.

Professor Mala Singh (former President), 3 March 2000, Pretoria.

Professor Mike Morris (former General Secretary), 10 July 2001, Durban.

Dr Prince Nevhutalu (former General Secretary), 17 November 2000, Pretoria.

Mr Goolam Aboobaker (former Treasurer), 23 May 2000, Johannesburg.

Mr Derrick Young (former Treasurer), 3 October 2000, Johannesburg.

Professor Ian Bunting, 11 October 2000, Cape Town.

Dr Pundy Pillay, 6 November 2000, Randburg.

Professor Ahmed Bawa, 12 July 2000, Durban.

Dr Prem Naidoo, 9 March 2000, Pretoria.

University of the Witwatersrand

Task team members who prepared the submission to the NCHE

Professor Belinda Bozzoli (Chairperson of the task team), 29 September 1998, Johannesburg.

Professor P.L. Bonner (member of the task team), 14 March 2000, Johannesburg.

Professor N.J. Coville (member of the task team), 6 August 1998, Johannesburg.

Professor Michael Cross (member of the task team), 19 August 1998, Johannesburg.

Professor Pam Christie (member of the task team), 19 November 1998, Johannesburg.

Professor Jonathan Hyslop (member of the task team), 18 August 1999, Johannesburg.

Christine Williams (Secretary of the task team), 10 September 1998, Johannesburg.

Other Interviewees

Professor Linda Chisholm (policy analyst and former Director of Education Policy Unit, University of the Witwatersrand), 3 December 1999, Johannesburg.

Ms Nazeema Mohamed (former researcher with the American Council for Education), 9 December 1998, Johannesburg; 23 October 2000, Pretoria.

Professor Joel Samoff (international consultant and policy analyst), 14 July 1998, Cape Town.

Ms Mary Metcalfe (former MEC for Education, Gauteng Province), 14 November 2000, Johannesburg.

Professor Jonathan Jansen (Dean of the Faculty of Education, University of Pretoria), 6 September 2000, Pretoria.

Dr Dick Fehnel (former head of the Ford Foundation, South Africa), 4 March and 10 April 2000, Johannesburg.

Professor Peter Hunter (Chairperson Hunter Review Committee), 16 October 2000, Johannesburg.

Index

Printed in the United States
122105LV00002B/40/P

9 780415 974455